Grandissimo Pavarotti

GRANDISSIMO PAVAROTTI

Text by

Martin Mayer

Gerald Fitzgerald

Career Chronology, Recorded Repertory, Photo Editor, Captions

DOUBLEDAY & COMPANY, INC., GARDEN CITY, NEW YORK
1986

DESIGNED BY LAURENCE ALEXANDER
IN COLLABORATION WITH GERALD FITZGERALD

LIBRARY OF CONGRESS CATALOGING-IN-PUBLICATION DATA
MAYER, MARTIN, 1928–   . GRANDISSIMO PAVAROTTI
1. PAVAROTTI, LUCIANO. 2. PAVAROTTI, LUCIANO—PORTRAITS.
3. PAVAROTTI, LUCIANO—DISCOGRAPHY.
I. FITZGERALD, GERALD, 1932–   . II. TITLE.
ML420.P35M4   1986   782.1'092'4 [B] 86-2042
ISBN 0-385-23138-5

GREETINGS

*Anniversaries invariably stir memories, and as I collaborated with
the authors of this book, I realized perhaps for the first time just how
much there is to remember about my life—especially in the last twenty-five
years, since that exciting night I made my debut as Rodolfo in*
La Bohème. *A life spent in music, I believe, is a life spent in beauty,
and in this regard mine has been blessed, and then some.*

*I am reminded anew of the many people who have played important roles
in my life. The anniversary of my debut is most certainly a time for giving
thanks, and these words of gratitude come from the heart. First of all,
thank you, my family, for standing beside me, always encouraging me
onward, and coping fantastically with all the problems a career such as
mine entails. And thank you, my teachers—marvelous mentors who guided me
in developing the skills to realize my artistic dreams. And thank you,
my countless, wonderful musical colleagues, who have helped make our work
an inspiration and joy. And thank you, my other friends, some of whom
I have known since childhood, who have taken delight in my singing
and wished me well. And finally, thank you, my incredible public—
so true, so good, so generous. I consider myself a lucky man to have shared
these years with you.*

Luciano Pavarotti

Luciano Pavarotti

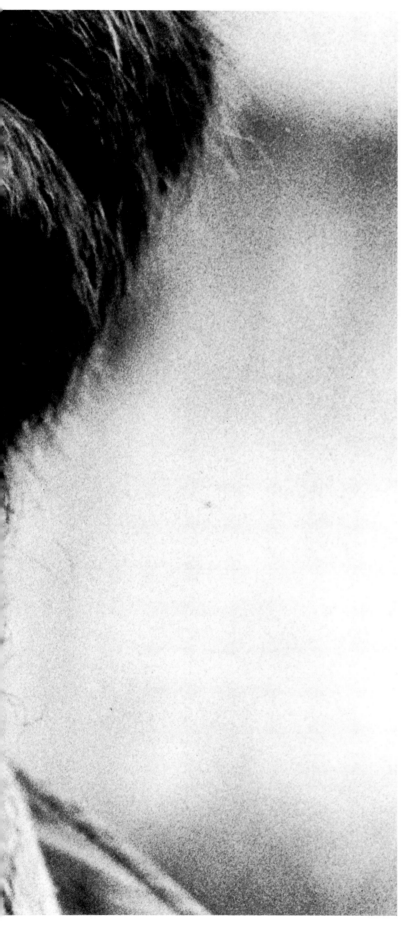

Contents

Herbert von Karajan, chief conductor and artistic director of the Berlin Philharmonic Orchestra

Foreword

Dear Luciano,

If I had not learned it from you personally, I would not have believed that you are already celebrating your twenty-fifth anniversary on the stage. That I have played a part in your career is my best reward.

I recall with pleasure that you sang La Bohème in your debut at La Scala under my direction. The performance of Verdi's Requiem there commemorating the tenth anniversary of Arturo Toscanini's death was also a memorable experience for us all. When we perform together, the result is a celebration for everyone involved—including myself.

Because I know how young you were when you began your international career, I am hopeful that you will be entertaining the people of the world with your voice for many years to come.

With genuine admiration and best wishes.

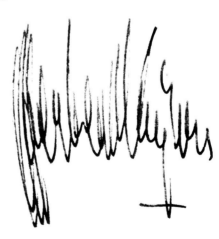

Herbert von Karajan

THE TENOR

Radames in Aïda *at the San Francisco Opera, 1981, when Pavarotti sang Verdi's Egyptian warrior for the first time*

T he tenor voice," said Luciano Pavarotti authoritatively, shifting his weight in the large chair behind his eighteenth-century desk in his studio at his home in Modena. "The tenor voice is not a natural voice. When people say 'natural voice,' what they mean to say is 'natural sound.' But even that is technique: you make the sound dark, or clear, or 'natural.' The tenor voice is more than one voice. It has nothing to do with speaking voice. Di Stefano has a growling voice, Del Monaco had a squeaking voice. A tenor cannot open his voice in the morning by singing in the shower. The tenor voice must be constructed, and you have to find it, build it, every day."

How long does it take to get the tenor voice seated in the body, every day?

"Oh, not long, if there is no trouble. Perhaps ten, fifteen minutes. And if it is not there, you must stop working, and come back to it, two, three hours later, for another ten or fifteen minutes. If you have to do this three, four times in a day, then you are in trouble. The natural voice of a man is the baritone voice, in singing as in speaking. On the other hand, the baritone must be much more the artist, much more the actor, because in the melodrama he always presents the double face, he is treacherous like Iago or the Count di Luna. It is easy to act the tenor roles, because the tenor is always the nice guy."

Almost always, maybe?

There is a moment's thought, and a querulous look. "The one opera where the tenor is a bad guy is *Rigoletto*," Pavarotti said. "But you don't condemn the Duke as you do Iago or the

Count di Luna. And certainly the Duke is fascinating."

In our time, tenors are fascinating, in part, I think, because tenor is not a natural voice, because the listener understands at some level that he—or she, of course—is a witness, at best a *target,* of a carefully accomplished and very physical outpouring. The dominance of the tenor is not a phenomenon that began at the beginning of opera and remained attached to the art form: it seems to have begun, indeed, only in the mid nineteenth century, when the community of theatergoers lost their memory of the castrati. (Whose obvious unnaturalness was, of course, part of their fascination: soprano or mezzo, they had a child's voice with a man's force. Its effect on both sexes was described by Stendhal as "transports of delirium and rapture," and its special appeal to women was legendary. This is by no means easy to explain after the cultural changes of three centuries, though something not entirely different seems to happen in other cultures, including our own, where forced nasal high male voices carry strong emotive content.) "The true art of the bel canto," Rossini said from his retirement, in 1855, "ended with the disappearance of castrati; one must agree to that, even if one cannot wish to have them back." In the eighteenth century, as Henry Pleasants notes in his book *The Great Singers,* "tenors did not count for much."

For the tenor voice, until the 1830s, was a light voice—in Pavarotti's terms, a natural voice, like baritone, a voice that a man could turn on stepping into the shower—and the art of the tenor was less in the production of a variety and beauty and penetration of tone than in the mastery of ornamentation, at first as the creativity of the singing artist, later as the skillful accomplishment of the composer's text. The florid passages that appear today in the tenor's role in the printed score of *The Barber of Seville* were probably devised by Manuel García, who created the role of Count Almaviva for Rossini and would teach the art of managing trills and skips and grace notes to Jenny Lind, to his famous daughters María Malibran and Pauline Viardot, and to his namesake son, who at the age of one hundred, in the twentieth century, was still teaching aspiring tenors in London. (A businessman as well as a teacher, a composer, and an artist—the stuff about empty-headed tenors had not yet begun to plague the public prints—García the elder as impresario introduced opera to New York, bringing Rossini's *Barber* and also Mozart's *Don Giovanni,* in which he sang the baritone title role, to the pleasure not only of the innocent New Yorkers but of Mozart's librettist Lorenzo da Ponte, then the occupant of a chair in Italian literature at the college that became Columbia University.)

Rossini, who had already been annoyed when the castrato Velluti twisted one of his melodies completely out of shape in the only opera he ever wrote for such a voice, was always of two minds about free ornamentation. There is a famous story of Adelina Patti singing "Una voce poco fà" from *Barber* with the old man himself at the piano at one of his Paris *soirées,* and Rossini at the end complimenting her and inquiring who had written that beautiful song. Rossini's successors wrote out any ornaments they wanted. (Rossini, too, it seems, in later years: recently a manuscript came to light, with ornamentations to "Una voce poco fà," in Rossini's handwriting, apparently written for Patti.) A woman who would add her own or her coach's fioriture to "Casta diva" is a woman who would stir champagne.

The first of the tenors to become a leading attraction as a singer was Giovanni Battista Rubini, for whom Bellini and Donizetti wrote (but he also, very successfully, sang Rossini: he was the tenor in the Paris productions of *Barber, Otello,* and *L'Italiana in Algeri,* of which Chopin wrote in a letter home to Poland that he had never really heard these works until he heard these performances). With Rubini, again, however, the attraction was essentially in the musical-

An Opening Night

Aficionados wait for hours before standing-room tickets go on sale for Luciano Pavarotti's debut as Radames in Aïda *at the San Francisco Opera (above). Backstage in the tenor's dressing room on the night of the premiere, November 12, 1981 (overleaf ▶), makeup artist Richard Stead helps the new hero get ready, musical coach Antonio Tonini assists at the keyboard during a musical warm-up for the vocal challenges ahead, and trusted friend Giuseppe di Stefano, himself a former Radames, drops by with some last-minute words of advice and encouragement.*

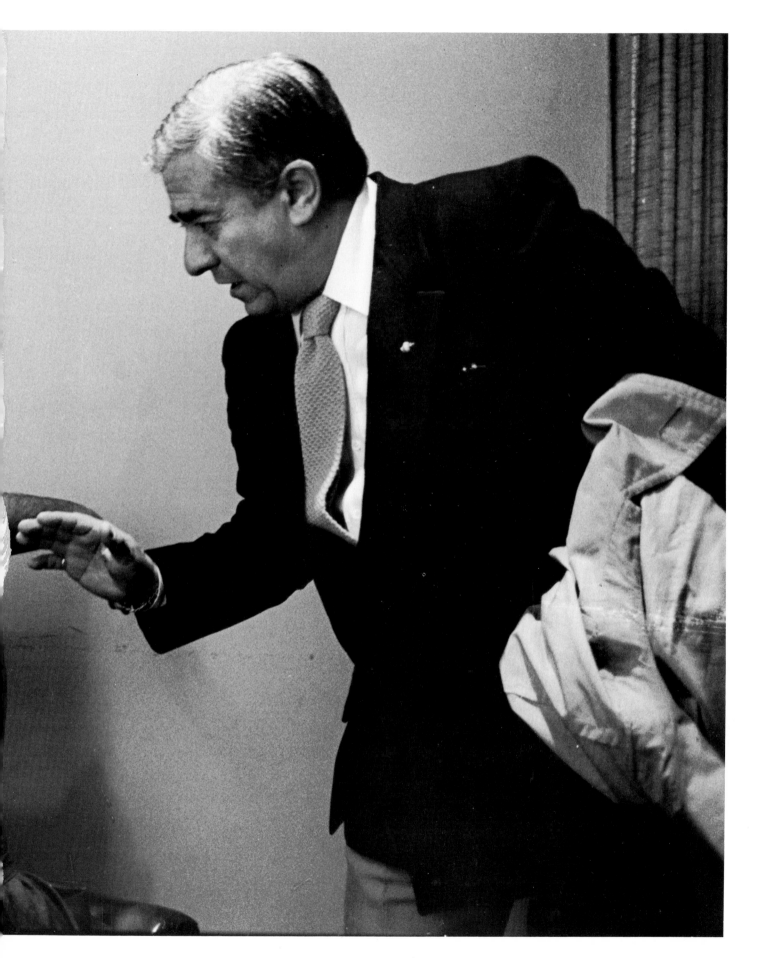

20

ity, though Rossini himself said that by comparison with the castrati, Rubini "owed his talent more to fortunate natural endowment than to training." Rubini's high notes, while loud, were created essentially in the falsetto register, as something separate from the rest of his voice.

The modern tenor voice, with the sound that sets the world to trembling, was the creation of two men: Domenico Donzelli, who created the stentorian role of Pollione in Bellini's *Norma,* a personal friend of Rossini's who was for years his landlord, whose fame rested on the fact that he was the first man known to history to sing an A in full voice—and the Frenchman Gilbert Louis Duprez, who had started in Paris as the lightest of

---

The spectacular Triumphal Scene of Aïda *at the San Francisco Opera, with Kevin Langan as the King of Egypt, Stefania Toczyska as Amneris, and Pavarotti as the victorious Radames (◄ overleaf); and the tenor backstage greeting well-wishers—future San Francisco Opera general director Terence A. McEwen and Giuseppe di Stefano (top) and the retiring general director and veteran conductor Kurt Herbert Adler, his wife Nancy, Mrs. Pavarotti (bottom)*

---

tenors, and began singing all-out in 1831. By the time he created the role of Edgardo in Donizetti's *Lucia di Lammermoor* in 1835, he was known throughout Europe as the man who sang a high C "in the chest voice." Pavarotti observed recently that all tenors have reason to hate the memory of Donzelli and Duprez. Adolphe Nourrit, the leading tenor of Paris before the eruption of Duprez, was the man for whom Rossini wrote *William Tell,* Meyerbeer wrote *Robert le Diable,* and Halévy his *La Juive,* all works that benefit from forceful tenors. He committed suicide in 1839, at the age of thirty-seven, supposedly in despair over Duprez's popularity.

And for a while, indeed, there were few successors to Donzelli and Duprez. Pleasants in his intelligent compendium can find only two tenors to highlight through the years when Verdi was

writing the roles that have since sustained the popularity of the breed—and one of these was Mario, the elegant gentleman who used only the one name because he was an aristocrat, a cavaliere of the house of Savoy, son of a general and trained as an officer, who was concerned initially about the propriety of a life on stage. Mario's triumph was in good part that of demeanor and bearing, sweetness of manner as of voice, rather than anything more elemental. (It did not hurt his chances for engagements, of course, that he was also married to the leading soprano of the time, Giulia Grisi, who preferred him as a partner on stage, too.) Bernard Shaw, one of the best music critics of the late years of the century, believed that Verdi's music had done Mario no good. Written as it is, mostly in the top third of the voice, it promoted, Shaw complained, a method of production he described as "goat bleat," a strained, even pinched tone that generated the notes above the staff in full cry at a sacrifice of beauty and of any emotion other than tension.

The late nineteenth century is the age of the shouting tenor, and of course we still hear some such today. One sees Verdi on occasion trying to escape his tenor problem: all three of the leading characters in Rossini's *Otello* are tenors, but Verdi wrote five operas for a baritone lead *(Nabucco, Macbeth, Rigoletto, Simon Boccanegra,* and *Falstaff)*— to a degree sabotaging his own intent by writing his baritone roles with even more ferocious concentration at the top of that range. It took more than a generation for the teachers and the artists to find the techniques that made Verdi's tenor music as sensuous as that of Bellini and Donizetti. Like the nineteenth-century stars Tamberlik and Tamagno, Pavarotti would rise to public attention as "King of the High C's"—but Pavarotti's C's in Donizetti's *La Fille du Régiment,* the role that catapulted him into the mass media, were round and exuberant.

Even before the tenors had learned to sing Verdi with grace under pressure, opera found

Gio. B. Rubini

DONZELLI
Nell'Opera Norma

LUIGI DUPREZ

Jean de Reszke, the first tenor whose presence on the bill, in any role from any tradition, absolutely guaranteed the sale of all the seats—and whose bargaining position was so strong that he and he alone in the history of New York's Metropolitan Opera could and did demand that his fee include a share of the gate receipts. (The one exception, his bass-baritone brother, Édouard, who signed in tandem with him, does not count; one should note in passing that this aspect of de Reszke's contract wasn't much money, never requiring as much as a ten percent bonus on top of his standard fee—I have seen the books, which still exist, in the Met Archives. Still, the bonus came in the deflationary '90s, when other artists were being pressed to sing for less.) Polish by birth and as

Bel canto predecessors: celebrated tenors of the nineteenth century who excelled in music of Rossini, Bellini, Donizetti: Manuel García, also famous as a teacher, Adolphe Nourrit and his rival Louis Gilbert Duprez (top left to right); Giovanni Rubini in I Puritani, *Domenico Donzelli in* Norma, *and Mario in* L'Elisir d'Amore *(bottom left to right)*

aristocratic as Mario, de Reszke was a baritone originally (Bernard Shaw once wrote in a review that he had heard de Reszke as a young baritone singing Don Giovanni and thought Mozart would have found him a "sympathetic interpreter"); and he did not begin singing tenor roles until he was thirty-four. De Reszke made his early reputation in French opera, that being the language of his childhood, and was hugely successful as Gounod's Roméo, Massenet's Werther, Bizet's Don José in *Carmen*—and then, in the last dozen years of his career, in the Wagner operas, a step that Pavarotti, with true Italian ethnic sincerity, regards as a great error that weakened de Reszke's voice and forced his retirement at the age of fifty-one.

De Reszke was never greatly involved with the Italian repertoire, though he sang Verdi's

Otello and Radames in *Aïda.* From the latter, incidentally, he usually omitted "Celeste Aïda," on
the quite reasonable grounds that it was too difficult to sing before one was properly warmed up,
and also once with the argument that nobody of
significance was in the house for the first act, anyway: Mrs. Astor usually arrived at nine o'clock.
This liberty stirs envy in Pavarotti, a man who
normally—it is one of his great charms—has not
an ounce of envy in his ample body. "The rest of
that role," Pavarotti says wistfully, having added
Radames to his list fairly late in his career, "is
very approachable and very beautiful, no high
C's, just so many B-flats. But that first aria kills."
De Reszke's voice was not by all reports a very
large one—we are not yet into the age of the
phonograph—but de Reszke's ability to suffuse it

---

*Turn-of-the-century idols: the elegant stylist Jean de Reszke as
he appeared during rehearsals (top), the trumpet-toned
Francesco Tamagno in* Guglielmo Tell *(bottom), and their
successor, the golden-voiced Enrico Caruso, in* Aïda *(opposite)*

with the character and emotions of his role ban-
ished all questions. He was beloved by operago-
ers as perhaps no other male singer the stage has
known. When he returned to the Metropolitan in
1900–1, after a year off for reason of vocal indis-
position, the ovation that greeted his first aria
went on for half an hour, the longest ever recorded in New York. When he returned from the
annual tour for the company's farewell gala performance that spring—it would also be, though
no one had been told, his own farewell—the press
estimated five hundred standees on top of a
packed house on a very hot night; and during the
second act of *Tristan und Isolde,* which de Reszke
sang with the American Lillian Nordica, sixteen
women were reported to have fainted.

De Reszke was the most beloved by operago-
ers; his successor Enrico Caruso was the most beloved by mankind. It can probably be said that

Caruso founded an industry, for the early prosperity of the phonograph record both in the United States and in Europe rested to a remarkable degree on Caruso's recordings, which still make a handsome and special sound. Of other artists it has been said that their voices "recorded well" or "lost something in recordings" (as Callas's did, for example, despite all the wonders of later twentieth-century mikes and mixing devices and reverberation chambers). Caruso's was so true, so clearly focused, and so strong that he made the wretched acoustical recording techniques of the years before the First World War seem adequate to their purpose. Each time reproduction technology improves, engineers go back to the Caruso discs and extract more from them.

Caruso died in 1921, and soon there will be no one alive who heard him sing, but the legend

Pavarotti at home during the mid-1970s studying the role of Arturo in Bellini's I Puritani *for the Metropolitan Opera*

is as powerful as ever. Pavarotti refuses all comparison with Enrico Caruso, first because (as he knows) there is no way a living tenor can win this comparison, then also, I suspect, out of a kind of superstition, that God would not like the thought of a mere mortal trying on that particular crown. Even in our age of celebrity and celebrity worship, Caruso's popularity is almost unimaginable. There is a nice story from the years when Toscanini conducted at the Metropolitan Opera, and began a series of Sunday evening symphony concerts with the Met orchestra. These were not announced much in advance, and long lines formed on Broadway behind the Met box office on days when Toscanini was conducting Beethoven. A passerby was quoted in the newspapers as observing the scene with astonishment and with the comment, "I didn't know Caruso sang on Sundays." People who never went to the opera at all

26

would pay scalpers' prices to hear Caruso, though his appearances were not rare: he sang ten and twelve times a month (one year, including the spring tour, one hundred performances just for the Met, in addition to his seasons in London and Buenos Aires).

Toward the end of his career, Caruso sang, as Pavarotti does, for immense crowds outdoors and in sporting arenas, before the days of electronic amplification. Though his two hundred and fifty records are persuasive evidence of a continuously high quality of output, one doubts that the people who came to hear him—most of them, of course, entirely unsophisticated—were there for a musical experience: what they wanted was to bask in the radiance of the presence of Enrico Caruso. Asked once what a man needed to be a great singer, Henry Pleasants reports, Caruso replied, "A big chest, a big mouth, ninety percent memory, ten percent intelligence, lots of hard work, and something in the heart." And this something in the heart, this affection for the audience that brings such an artist such joyful sustenance, is of course the pedestal on which Pavarotti stands. "The public recognition," he says, "is the gasoline that keeps the fire blazing on. How can a person be tired at the end of a Madison Square Garden concert when there are twenty thousand people there and another twenty thousand waiting to get in? There is no way for a person to be tired." One recalls that Caruso at one of his last performances, hemorrhaging from the respiratory abscess that would kill him some months later, had almost to be forcibly restrained from continuing to sing.

A Neapolitan from a background of the deepest poverty (he was his mother's seventeenth child, and the first to survive to adult life), Caruso achieved his perfection step by step. Like Pavarotti, he triumphed first outside of Italy, in Buenos Aires, St. Petersburg, Monte Carlo, and London. He was in a debut season at the Teatro Costanzi in Rome in 1899–1900 when Puccini

wrote *Tosca* for that theater—and decided that Caruso lacked the temperament, experience, and indeed voice to create Cavaradossi. When he sang Rodolfo in *La Bohème* for Toscanini in his Scala debut the next season, the conductor transposed "Che gelida manina" to free Caruso of the high C at the end of the aria, which terrified him. (Francis Robinson, longtime press representative at the Metropolitan Opera and author of the classic picture book about Caruso, once noted that Caruso said he had a glass voice, because it broke on top.) Even his New York debut, as the Duke in *Rigoletto,* was no great shakes (and the Duke was a mascot role for him, which he chose when possible for his first appearance everywhere). Here, incidentally, the Pavarotti parallels are clear though not entirely pleasant for Pavarotti, who

Tenor giants of the 1920s at the Met: Giovanni Martinelli in the title role of Ernani *(opposite) and Beniamino Gigli as Edgardo of Ravenswood in* Lucia di Lammermoor *(left)*

made his youthful march of debuts through the Italian provinces in *Rigoletto,* "because it's very difficult and I could sing it; even today a kid who can sing the Duke can get a lot of engagements." Pavarotti's own mascot role became Rodolfo, his assignment on the matinee of his Metropolitan debut, which he remembers as very difficult: a viral flu had got his voice, and forced him to cancel in the middle of his second performance. (Peter G. Davis, however, then critic for the New York *Times,* thought more highly of Pavarotti's debut than his predecessors had of Caruso's: "Mr. Pavarotti," he wrote, "triumphed through the natural beauty of his voice . . . Any tenor who can toss off high C's with such abandon, successfully negotiate delicate diminuendo effects, and attack Puccinian phrases so fervently is going to win over a *Bohème* audience, and Mr. Pavarotti had them eating out of his hand.")

30

Caruso enjoyed his work, his art, his time off, his eating and drinking, ultimately the American wife he married in his forties and his daughter; and everyone around him enjoyed his presence. He was generous to all, artistically and financially —the worst sucker for a panhandler in New York —and the gods saw to it that his generosity never cost him, that no one wished to be his rival, and that the money flowed in such dimensions that he could afford whatever he wanted to do. The only thing wrong was that he died young: Pavarotti, on the twenty-fifth anniversary of his professional debut, was almost three years older than Caruso was on his last day. He left an estate in eight figures, well over fifty million of today's dollars, and a public that mourned him deeply and sincerely.

Other famous antecedents: Giacomo Lauri-Volpi as Prince Calaf in Turandot *(top), Aureliano Pertile as the painter Mario Cavaradossi in* Tosca *(bottom left), and Tito Schipa as the Chevalier Des Grieux in* Manon *(bottom right)*

And for generations, certainly through Pavarotti's youth (when the legend was restimulated by Mario Lanza's performance as *The Great Caruso,* a film Pavarotti saw and much admired: he lists Lanza among the idols of his adolescence), the story of Caruso is a beacon to peasant and working-class Italians.

Pavarotti's father had longed to be a tenor even after he was firmly established as a baker, and the germ of that hope grew in the breast of the baker's son, who had a sweet voice and a good precise ear. Pavarotti knows all about Caruso but does not talk much about him; for a mature man who has come as close to that ambition as anyone ever has, it seems best not to talk. Every so often he lets slip that while of course there is no comparison, he has, thanks to modern amplification, sung to larger audiences than

Caruso ever reached—and thanks to television has presented his performances to audiences beyond Caruso's dreams.

Pavarotti was of the first generation of singers who found their vocal identity from broadcast and recorded media (and indeed retained it by similar means: "I have tape recordings," Pavarotti said; "I hear myself a lot, which is a terrible thing"). As a wistful former aspirant to the status of solo tenor, Fernando Pavarotti had the family listen religiously to the Martini & Rossi radio broadcasts of vocal recitals, every Monday night, and he kept bringing home recordings of tenors—"Schipa, Gigli, Lauri-Volpi, Pertile, Caruso," Pavarotti recalled in answer to a question at his master classes at New York's Juilliard School in 1979. "My father suffocated me with tenors."

Gigli he met when that master of the glottal stop, not yet sixty, sang a concert in Modena. "I was told he would be vocalizing until eleven," Pavarotti recalls, "so I came at ten. I heard him and then saw him when he was finished. I asked him how long he had studied. He said, 'I stopped five minutes ago.'" But the voice that Pavarotti chose as his model—to the extent that in looking at repertoire he still knows whether or not this tenor ever sang it—was Jussi Björling's.

Pavarotti never heard Björling live—the great Swedish practitioner of Italian art (another who died, incidentally, when younger than Pavarotti is now) did not sing in Italy in the years when young Luciano was an operagoer. But he knew from the recordings, and from listening to his own voice, that this, with hard work and perhaps a little luck, was what he could do. Björling was never an actor: he never pretended to do much more than be where he was supposed to be on stage and sing what he was supposed to sing. This did not mean, of course, that he failed to characterize his roles: Björling singing Rodolfo in

A Teatro

The Duke of Mantua in Rigoletto *has been central to the career of Luciano Pavarotti. He earned his first* bis, *or encore, for "La donna è mobile," during his debut in the part, at Carpi in 1961. Two decades later, the tenor starred in a film version by designer-director Jean-Pierre Ponnelle, who costumed the Duke as Bacchus and made the festivities of the opening scene part of a ribald masquerade (right).*

The Duke was Pavarotti's first Verdi role. His most recent, introduced in 1983 at the Metropolitan Opera, is the bandit hero of Ernani *(first overleaf ▶). The tenor is shown in this Pier-Luigi Samaritani–Peter J. Hall production with Leona Mitchell, who sang Elvira, and Ruggero Raimondi, the Silva (left); in the ensemble "O somma Carlo" with Jean Kraft, the Giovanna, Sherrill Milnes, the Carlo V, and Miss Mitchell (top right); and, finally, during the tragic dénouement with Raimondi and Miss Mitchell (bottom right).*

Only New York has thus far witnessed Pavarotti's Ernani, and so far only San Francisco has seen the tenor as Calaf in Puccini's Turandot, *in 1977. The production by Ponnelle was dominated by an enormous Buddha (second overleaf ▶), and featured Montserrat Caballé (bottom left) as the princess of fire and ice Calaf dreams of conquering during his Act III aria "Nessun dorma" (right).*

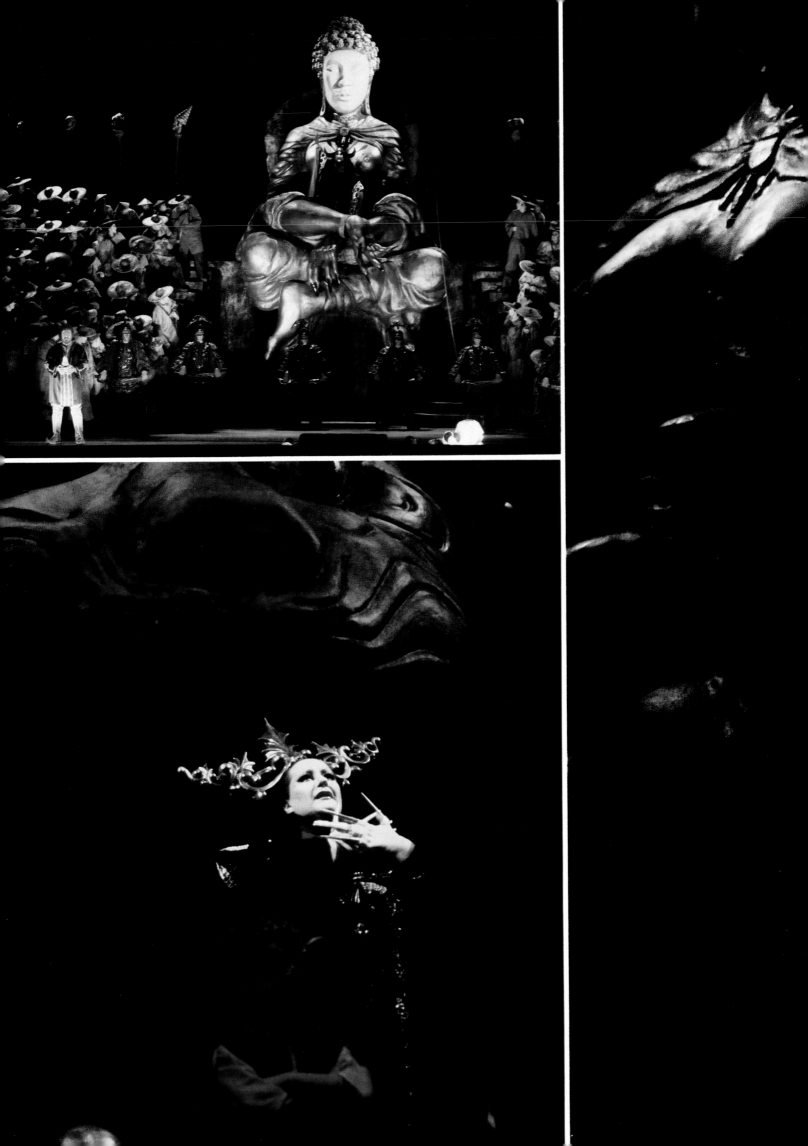

A Teatro

In 1982 at the Metropolitan Opera, Pavarotti returned to Mozart's Idomeneo, a work in which he appeared eighteen years earlier at the Glyndebourne Festival. Now, however, he sang not the youth Idamante, but Idamante's father, Idomeneo, King of Crete, in a monumental Ponnelle production. (◄ overleaf). The episodes pictured capture Idomeneo cast ashore after shipwreck (top left); with members of his court, including Hildegard Behrens as Elettra, John Alexander as Arbace, Loretta Di Franco as a Cretan Woman, Ileana Cotrubas as Ilia, Frederica von Stade as Idamante, and Batyah Godfrey Ben-David as another Cretan Woman (bottom left); and in the concluding aria "Torna la pace" (right).

During summer 1980, Pavarotti sang Enzo Grimaldo in La Gioconda in a spectacular staging at the Verona Arena, and at each performance his aria "Cielo e mar" stopped the show (left). One evening, however, before he could sing it, the performance was rained out. Despite the deluge, the audience refused to leave until the tenor finally came forward under an umbrella and sang—"gargled" is his word—"Cielo e mar." The audience, drenched but happy, then went home.

La Bohème, while clearly the same tenor, by no means makes the same sounds as Björling singing the Duke in *Rigoletto.*

Some of this was Puccini's doing, but some of it was Björling's. And this, too, appealed to Pavarotti, who feels that the approval of a dramatic performance by a singing actor is a direct and unambiguous function of the vocal performance: "I heard di Stefano when he was the greatest actor in the world, full of charm," Pavarotti recalls; "but when I heard him without voice he was a terrible actor."

Pavarotti has always been more than happy to work on understanding his roles. Before the professional debut which this book commemorates he spent six weeks living in a Bohemian ho-

---

Manrico in Il Trovatore, *San Francisco Opera, 1975, with Elena Obraztsova as the old gypsy Azucena (top) and Joan Sutherland as Leonora, the troubador's lady (bottom)*

tel in Reggio Emilia with the rest of an all-debutant cast, mostly studying Murger's *Scènes de la Vie de Bohème* and the ways Puccini and his librettist had altered their source. Among Pavarotti's great strengths as Rodolfo is his *affection* for the character, the chiaroscuro of the reckless poet who burns his verses to heat the room on Christmas Eve and so cleverly and quickly seduces the girl upstairs—and then moves with her into a private world of strong and lasting feelings quite different from the temporary worlds of their friends.

Pavarotti can tell you quite a lot about the private lives of all the characters he sings, and every so often he will bring up a performance memorable for its staging, like the Rome *Rigoletto* of 1969, "a great experience" to which Eduardo di Filippo brought "a global concept; he was very demanding and very paternal, it was difficult to understand why he wanted things before we went

on stage, but once we were there it was very clear. It was a big help, of course, that Giulini was the conductor, and talked to everybody." But he hates the new school of staging that "pretends to be new for the sake of being new," and uses the composer's music to express relationships and situations quite different from those in the libretto. In his early years on stage, he complained that acting as distinct from expressing was an unfair demand on him, partly for the sensible reason that it is hard enough to sing these things, partly because he knew that dramatic verisimilitude had never seriously been asked of Jussi Björling.

When Pavarotti first entered the heavier tenor repertoire, with Manrico in Verdi's *Il Trovatore,* he defended the gamble simply: "Björling sang it. Björling was the best Manrico." Then he found intellectual justification. After all, he told a reporter for a newspaper in San Francisco, where he sang his first Manrico, the presumed gypsy's son is supposed to be only sixteen years old when the opera begins. He should not have a voice that knocks over the stage trees. Later, Pavarotti grumbled that the audiences have been spoiled for his and Björling's sort of Manrico by Mario Del Monaco, another of the heroes of Pavarotti's youth, who got people used to a man of great force and hard tone in the role.

In fact, Del Monaco sang the role very rarely: like the young Caruso, he was basically "a B-flat tenor," very nervous about the dreadfully exposed C in "Di quella pira." What made Del Monaco's Manrico influential was his recording of the role, which Pavarotti studied. And the recording, of course, was not a novel interpretation but a different grand tradition of Manricos: what must have been the finest performance of *Trovatore* ever, the one at the Met for which Toscanini gave himself twenty-six stage rehearsals, featured the trumpet tones of Giovanni Martinelli as Manrico. Pavarotti has mellowed on the subject, and now concedes not only two different Manricos equally correct—that of himself and Björling, that of Del

Monaco and Franco Corelli—but also a third, that of Carlo Bergonzi, "if you are intelligent enough to do something that is entirely your own."

Del Monaco was a hero but vocally not a model: Pavarotti knew from the beginning that Del Monaco's sort of ringing, open sound was not for him. What dazzled the young Pavarotti was the precision of Del Monaco's diction, and the dramatic conviction he brought to the words. When Pavarotti agreed to sing Ernani, he studied the Del Monaco and Bergonzi recordings, and was at first repelled by what he considered Del Monaco's vulgarity; then he listened more, and began to feel that what had at first offended him by its lack of finesse in the end would win him by its force.

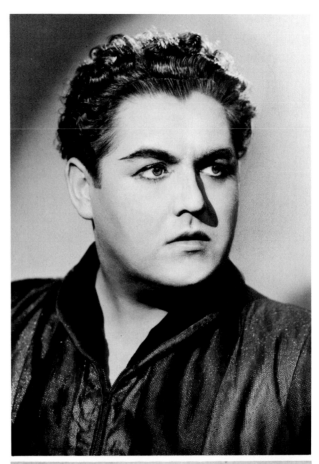

Kings of the 1950s: Jussi Björling as Manrico in Il Trovatore *(top), Giuseppe di Stefano as Nemorino in* L'Elisir d'Amore *(bottom), and Mario del Monaco as the Moor in Verdi's* Otello *(opposite)—all three inspirations for Pavarotti*

Vocally, Pavarotti's admiration for Del Monaco was generalized: other tenors whose work he admired, Pavarotti would say, had an easy job, because they merely had to drive an ordinary little car; but Del Monaco, Corelli, Bergonzi ("the master of masters") were men who "drove a Ferrari, which is much harder to control. All of them got better and better, year after year. Corelli was the best tenor in the world and still he improved. Early he was exciting but not pleasant, but at the end his voice was even pleasant. I was a fan for Corelli; once I made him sing an encore in the Arena in Verona. After the end of the applause, I shouted again in the silence—and everyone started applauding again."

Pavarotti himself these days drives a Maserati, but he does not race it. He told a *Playboy* interviewer once, among other indiscreet things,

that though he was a big man he did not have a big voice. No small part of Pavarotti's attractiveness to the aficionados, which is not quite the same thing as his attractiveness to his fans, is that he has with the passage of time managed to enlarge and strengthen his voice without on his best nights (which admittedly is not quite every night) coarsening it.

For himself and for those he advises (because of the vocal competition for young singers he established in Philadelphia, and because his house in Modena is unusually hospitable, he may hear as many as four hundred aspiring artists a year, and he tries to give each of them a useful word), Pavarotti always counsels prudence. As he told a tenor in the Juilliard master classes, "when you come to

Tenor stars of our time: Franco Corelli in Massenet's Werther *(right), Carlo Bergonzi as the clown Canio in* Pagliacci *(opposite top), and Placido Domingo as hero of Offenbach's* Les Contes d'Hoffmann *(opposite bottom)*

the top, *bite* the voice. Do not let the voice get bigger, or it breaks." Later, in response to a question, he said, "The top is an animal sound. When I think the top of my voice, I think *nothing.*" But this is because he has internalized, beyond consciousness, what he has to do at those moments—or, perhaps he always knew.

Pavarotti is the apostle of the "covered" sound. "If you go back to my debut performance in 1961," he said recently, "and the recording exists [originally a pirate, it can now be bought legitimately in Italy], what you find is the same covered tone I make today. The voice is closed, almost pretentious. I never had a register problem, I always knew where the little hole is to find my resonance. Everything I do today was present embryonically in my singing at my debut. Of course it is the technique of your teacher, but you

take these things on your own. All singers who sing well, with long careers, twenty, thirty years of career, they sing the same—*all* of them."

The man who became Pavarotti's greatest hero, oddly enough, was Giuseppe di Stefano, who took a vocal endowment not entirely unlike Pavarotti's own and ran it into the ground, mostly by never covering a tone and singing out at all times. When he was in his twenties, this daring paid off. Rudolf Bing of the Metropolitan Opera wrote of his year as an observer at the house, before he became general manager, that its "most spectacular moment" was di Stefano's "diminuendo on the high C in 'Salut! demeure' in *Faust;* I shall never as long as I live forget the beauty of that sound." Pavarotti has immense respect for Bing (his own guess as to why Corelli stopped singing, though still in the prime of middle age, was that Bing had left the Met and thus the audience Corelli cared most about was no longer there to hear him), and his recollection of di Stefano's voice squares with Bing's. It was for di Stefano that Pavarotti as a vocal student with little money and less time took buses from Modena to ride more than two hours to Milan and wait in line for standing room tickets at La Scala. But time was beginning to exact a fearful price from di Stefano. "When you are twenty and thirty you can sing open," Pavarotti says sadly, "because you are healthy. Then when you get older you lose control of the voice."

Fifteen years after that "Salut! demeure," Bing, hoping that somehow this hero of his first year could pull himself together for another, now heavier French role, gave di Stefano one performance in a Metropolitan Opera season, and his choice was entirely unsuitable—Hoffmann in Offenbach's *Tales.* Di Stefano failed miserably—it was, as I think he knew, quite impossible that he should succeed—and he left the Met forever. As it happens, I spent some days hanging over a railing on the *Cristoforo Colombo* with di Stefano en route to Naples immediately after that fiasco (which I had heard). He and his American wife and their two children were leaving their home in the United States forever for the house di Stefano had built some years before in a Milanese suburb. The Steinway and the Rolls-Royce were in the hold of the ship.

Circumstance made us companions: his children and mine were the only children in first class. He was bitter and discouraged, not at all looking forward to his next performance, which was, I think, Des Grieux in *Manon Lescaut.* In any event, it was to be in Rome, and the Rome Opera had expected him to fly from New York; and he had decided instead to take the first week of the Rome rehearsals on the ship with his wife and children. Rome would find out where he had been when he arrived. That sort of recklessness was standard operating procedure for di Stefano, made worse by a recklessness in the roles he agreed to sing and the number of times he sang them. In 1965, at the age of forty-four, his triumphs were clearly behind him (though as we left the pier, our cab driver pointed excitedly to the Rolls-Royce at quayside and said, "Do you know who was on that ship with you? The great tenor Giuseppe di Stefano." One of the nice things about opera is that reputation never dies). Not long thereafter, di Stefano acquired a new vocal technique that enabled him to get through almost anything, and because Maria Callas in her farewell tours needed a partner who also didn't make very attractive sounds his career got a kind of wheezing second wind. But what happened to di Stefano was surely not what Pavarotti wanted for himself.

Pavarotti bridled briefly at some of this, for di Stefano had been kind to him both deliberately and inadvertently—deliberately by speaking well of the younger man in places where it mattered and where it occasioned great surprise (for di Stefano was famously jealous of other tenors), and inadvertently by canceling engagements. Pavarotti's debut at Covent Garden, one of the first international opera houses to hire him, was the result of a di Stefano cancellation, and he believes that he first came to La Scala also essentially as a substitute for di Stefano, who had been signed for a series of *Traviatas* he didn't sing. Indeed, the *Traviata* production (by Zeffirelli), which received its *prima* in the fall, had been canceled by the time Pavarotti appeared to be part of the second cast. Karajan substituted *Bohème,* and Luciano once again wowed an audience—but in this case a most sophisticated audience—with his Rodolfo. When I suggested to Pavarotti that di Stefano had changed vocal technique in mid-career to get away from a hopeless problem, his first reaction was to say argumentatively that the change had made di Stefano a better singer, which was doubtless true by comparison with his immediately preceding performances (and true also in that the new technique met Pavarotti's central prescription, because in his forties for the first time di Stefano learned to keep his upper voice covered), but that was not the point.

Then Pavarotti admitted that as early as his student days it had been "unpleasant" to ride the bus and wait on line and buy the ticket and find that di Stefano either had or should have canceled. For the obvious reason: because "he took too many heavy roles too soon." And for a more subtle reason: "When you have difficulty in the beginning, you have some defect, and you learn to fight for survival to cure the defect; when you have no difficulty at the beginning there is a danger, because then when you have a difficulty later you don't know what to do." Still, the sound of di Stefano's youth, especially on records, still rings gratefully in Pavarotti's ears, as it does in those of lesser mortals.

Of his immediate contemporaries, Pavarotti speaks especially enthusiastically about Domingo and Carreras. They have, he says, "goose-pimple voices."

Does he have one too?

"Pavarotti, I cannot judge."

Winning the Game

How does a world-famous tenor spend free time when far from home and family? If good friends are near, and if the tenor in question is Luciano Pavarotti, he might well end up playing a game of poker. One night in the 1970s, Pavarotti challenged a favorite prima donna, Katia Ricciarelli, and a pair of celebrated Spanish tenors, Giacomo Aragall and José Carreras, to try their luck at cards—Italy vs. Spain (above). Pavarotti, as always, kept score, and from the expressions on the faces of the various players, it is clear who was and who wasn't winning the game (overleaf ▶).

41

FROM MODENA TO THE WORLD

odena is one of the string of towns that makes up Emilia Romagna, the province that runs diagonally down the northern section of the Italian boot between the Po River and the Apennines: Piacenza, Parma, Reggio Emilia, Modena, Bologna, Forlì. They are set quite close together: from Reggio Emilia to Bologna is less than thirty miles, and Modena is flat in the middle between them. Nevertheless, each of these towns was an independent duchy literally for centuries and each has its own character. The area as a whole is and has been for a very long time a fat country, prosperous agriculturally, prosperous industrially. People work hard and do well. The cuisine of neighboring Bologna is by popular legend the best in Italy. The wine of the country, unfortunately, is Lambrusco, which Pavarotti is unable to resist.

Pavarotti and fellow citizens of Modena on a chilly winter day in the Piazza Grande outside the Romanesque Duomo

The glory of Modena is its twelfth-century cathedral, a Romanesque structure of some elegance with a bell tower that leans almost as badly as Pisa's. The main streets have arcaded sidewalks, yielding shade for shoppers in the summer, protection from the rain in the winter. Around the cathedral is a considerable area in which a number of the town's eighteenth-century buildings are preserved, rather nondescript and shabby on the street side because the money has been spent inside, not infrequently with snappy boutiques somewhat incongruously flaunting large windows on the ground floor. One of these boutiques the Pavarottis have furnished to satisfy the dream of their oldest daughter, Lorenza (always "Titti"), born in 1962, interested in fashion and herself a very snappy blonde, who comes home and lunches on yoghurt and fruit, complains she is hungry, looks at her father and decides she would

1. S. Pietro, Ord. S. Benedicti.
2. S. Geminiani Suor:
3. PP. Giesuitti.
4. PP. d. S. Agostino.
5. Orologio publico.
6. il Duomo.
7. Chiesa nuova.
8. PP. Carmelittani.
9. Porta Bolognese.
10. Theatini.
11. Suor: Scalzi.
12. PP. di S. Domenico.
13. Palazzo del Duca.
14. Zoccoletti.
15. Viridario del Duca.

MODENA Modena

rather be hungry. The old town is contained within a ring of roadways and thin parks built where the fortress walls once were, and beyond stretches a somewhat haphazard growth of apartment houses and medium-rise office buildings in the unimportant, boxy but not cheerless style of twentieth-century Italian architecture. Pavarotti was born in one of these apartment blocs, but spent the years of childhood and early adolescence a few miles away in Carpi, an agricultural town which was a better place to be in wartime (not much better: the town was bombed). For the modern Italian, Modena is best known as the maker of the nation's two brands of racing car: Ferrari and Maserati.

Because Caruso was Neapolitan, a myth grew up that the Italian singers are from the South, but singers of course come from where they are born, and that can be lots of places. From the previous generation, Emilia-Romagna claimed for its stretch of the Po (maybe inaccurately: the record books differ) Ebe Stignani, perhaps the greatest mezzo of the mid-century, less well known than some in the United States because (shame on us) she never sang at the Metropolitan Opera. I heard her once in Carnegie Hall, then again at La Scala, and at the recording sessions of *Norma,* where she sang Adalgisa with Callas, doing "Mira, O Norma" over and over again for conductor Tullio Serafin and recording director Walter Legge because there was an acoustical quirk in the movie house EMI was using as a studio and the overtones of their thirds, so gorgeous in the flesh, were harsh in the mikes. Stignani was a dumpy housewife by then, but when she opened her mouth, the brickwork shook. Her singing was a flood of vowel sounds—she almost never actually pronounced a consonant—a habit that would have come naturally to her as an Emilian, for Emilia speaks in the mushiest of the Italian dialects. Pavarotti rejects the implied criticism of a goddess of his youth: "It's like with Joan

Sutherland," he says; "if you knew what Stignani was singing, you got the words."

Considering the sounds around him as a boy, the great elegance and exactitude of Pavarotti's Italian diction is a notable and wholly conscious accomplishment. "Women," he says, still refusing any criticism of Stignani (or Sutherland), "can do what they like. For a man there is no substitute for the feeling of idiomatic phrasing in Italian. The composers of the nineteenth century planned everything on that—Rossini, Donizetti, Bellini. F, F-sharp, G, G-sharp, they always put an 'O', or an 'Ah' that can be sung 'O'. They change the structure of the sentence to sing the right vowel, the singer must surround it with the right frame."

On today's stage, Modena boasts not only Pavarotti but also Mirella Freni, arguably (I would so argue) the world's leading lyric soprano, though this is not a category from which it really makes sense to award a single champion's belt. She and Pavarotti were born in the same edge-of-town neighborhood, and in fact shared a wet nurse, as both mothers worked long hours in the same cigar factory. The families saw something of each other when the children were small, but later the children lost touch. They came together again in their twenties, when they both traveled to Mantova, well over an hour away, to work with the same voice teacher. Freni was already married, and sometimes could borrow her husband's car for the trip, and it is the drive and the talk, rather than what was then the vast and for Pavarotti sometimes discouraging difference in their career situations, that they both choose to remember. (The husband, incidentally, was Leone Magiera, who conducted Pavarotti's first *Bohème* in Modena and remains his recital accompanist in Italy.) More important, Freni was already a professional, having made her solo debut at the age of twenty—women start sooner—in Modena's own handsome opera house, with Luciano singing in the chorus. She says she always

knew he would have a big career. Pavarotti himself was not so sure.

Singing was an ordinary part of life in Luciano's family. His father, Fernando, sang in the church choir, and soon after Luciano learned to read music he joined the boy altos. He recalls singing in the courtyard of the apartment house, and most people (but not all) telling him to shut up. What counted for more in his life was sports, especially soccer; Pavarotti first became well-known in his home town as a player in the city's soccer league. The other side of this coin, of course, was that it took a long time before he was known as a singer. For some years, the management of the Teatro Comunale did not invite their native son to sing in their short opera seasons—they thought they could get better out of town. Though there is no more loyal Modenese, Pavarotti still remembers that at a time when they could have been useful to him, the musical city fathers turned their backs. "Maybe," Freni says helpfully, having sung so many times in Modena during her early years, "they just didn't like tenors."

Young Pavarotti went through the neighborhood schools, and at age fourteen was sent to the Scuola Magistrale, a five-year secondary program leading to employment as a schoolteacher in the elementary grades. (It should be noted that the separation of "high school" into three streams—for vocational education, teacher training, and preparation for university—was standard in Europe at the time.) He thought of continuing his training at an Institute that prepared physical education specialists, but it would have meant going to Rome, which young Luciano did not want, and although the Pavarottis had only two children (the second, Gabriella, was five years younger than Luciano), it would have been a fearful strain on a baker's salary. The second option was to get a job in a school and study singing in hopes that lightning would strike.

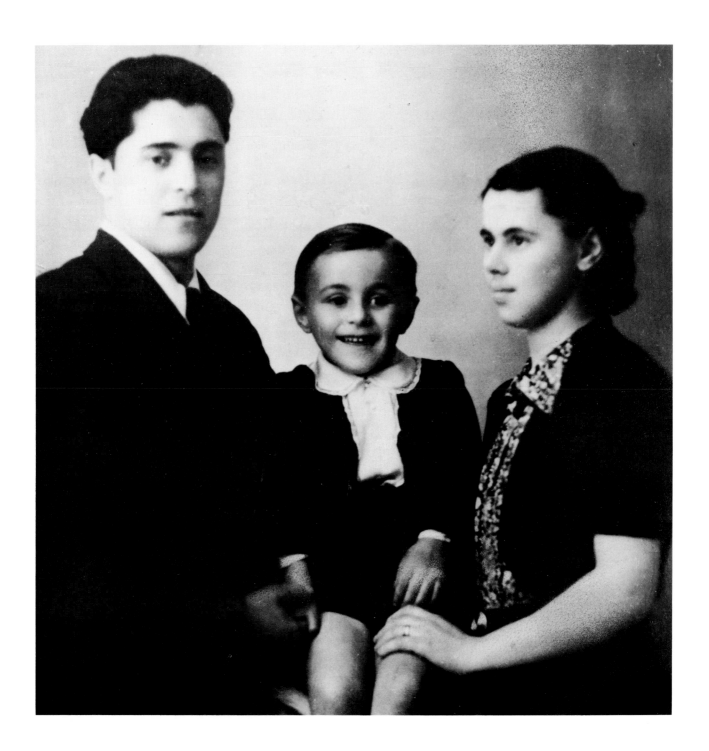

Growing Up

Pavarotti remembers his childhood as "ideal," though in fact his family had very little beyond the necessities of life. His father, Fernando, was a baker by profession and his mother, Adele, found work in a cigar factory. In 1938, at age three, the gregarious Luciano beamed at the camera for a portrait between his proud parents (above). The story goes that on the day Pavarotti was born, as he lay loudly crying on the bed, the doctor exclaimed, "Mamma mia! Che voce di tenore!"

At six, already making music (above); Holy Communion, dressed all in white, 1943 (below); and during school days with classmates in Modena at age fourteen (circled left)

53

As an adolescent with a more or less settled vocal register, Luciano had joined his father in the church choir and in the chorus for the not very frequent productions of opera at the Teatro Comunale—and in the Chorale Gioacchino Rossini, the city's amateur chorus, which sang on public occasions. While Luciano was still in school, the Modena city chorus was invited to compete in the annual *eisteddfod* in Wales—"a fantastic week," Pavarotti recalls, made particularly fantastic because the Modenese, in their first journey ever, were declared the winners. Pavarotti remembers sitting with his father and their friends while the judges read out the rank order of the twenty-two contestants, starting from the back, and the unbearable suspense as Modena's

---

Snapshots: holiday at S. Margherita with sister Gabriella, 1950 (top), and with his champion soccer team, at home in Modena, 1952, with Luciano standing at the far right (bottom)

name was not called, and there were three possible winners, then two . . . and then only one. Pavarotti remembers scenes emotionally—despite the period when he was an enthusiastic painter in a primitive-realist mode, he does not much remember what he has merely *seen*—and the other strong recollection of that trip to Britain thirty years ago is the great disappointment that, after four years of studying English in the Scuola Magistrale ("my best subject"), he couldn't understand a word of what was being said on the streets. Someone took pity on him and told him the locals were speaking Welsh.

None of that was professionalism; and Pavarotti, I think, had an instinctive understanding of what professionalism meant. These days only his father (apart from Pavarotti himself) admits to any doubts about how Luciano's efforts to become a singer would turn out. (Fernando still likes to tease his son by saying he isn't quite as good as his

audiences think he is.) At the beginning it was all very uncertain, and the only fully confident member of the family was Luciano's mother, Adele, who couldn't sing herself but "had an ear." Luciano gives that inherited ear as much credit as the inherited voice for his ultimate triumph. His father had been the kind of choral singer who waited until the fellow next to him began, but once Luciano had the A in his ear the rest was rock solid.

Pavarotti does not lay claim to "absolute pitch"—ask him for an A and he will hit the piano keyboard if it is a serious matter—but he does have perfect relative pitch. "Perfect intonation," he says. "That is something else." Absolute pitch, oddly, would be a handicap to a singer, because even today—though in our age of broadcasts and recordings the variations are much reduced—Vienna tunes lower than New York or London: "When I went to Vienna from Miami for the recording of the *Rigoletto* film for Ponnelle, I thought I was sick; I almost strangled myself. If you give me an orchestra behind a screen, do I know which orchestra it is? Yes—because my throat tells me. But all of them have a tendency to creep to a higher pitch, because it is easier for them." Intellectually, the combination of ear and throat gave Pavarotti the capacity for useful self-criticism. "It is not enough," he likes to say, "to be given a voice by God—even the donkey has a voice."

There was no conservatory in Modena (Pavarotti's gag line is that there had been one once, but the teachers ruined all the voices and they had to close it down). There was, however, a practicing minor-league tenor who took pupils, Arrigo Pola, whom Fernando Pavarotti respected. Luciano, just twenty, sang for Pola, who accepted him as a pupil. Pola's was, apparently, the most traditional of training procedures. The eighteenth century (and some enthusiasts in the nineteenth century, too) loved the story of the instruction of the famous castrato Gaetano Caffarelli by the Ne-

apolitan voice teacher Nicola Porpora, who alleg-
edly wrote out a single sheet of exercises and vo-
calises, kept his pupil working on the contents of
that sheet for six endlessly tedious years, then sent
him forth with the words, "I have nothing further
to teach you. You are the greatest singer in the
world." For most of his first year, Pavarotti
worked with Pola exclusively on vowel sounds
and vocal exercises. He was not studying songs;
he was studying singing. But he was also, non-
trivially, studying music, for much of what he was
doing falls under the heading of solfeggio, training the eye to read and the ear to recognize chro-
matic relationships as well as the usual scales. (Pavarotti had already worked on musical theory at
the Magistrale, and this was, he believes, graduate
study. He is rather vain of his whistling, and says

*Proud day: the Chorale Gioacchino Rossini of Modena wins first
prize at the 1955 international competition in Llangollen,
Wales, with Luciano by trophy, Fernando at front right*

he can whistle the music of Arnold Schoenberg,
"no problem.") When Rudolf Serkin took over
the Curtis Institute of Music two decades ago, the
first thing he did was to reinstitute the study of
solfeggio, for pianists and violinists as well as
singers.

School in Italy ended with lunchtime, so Pavarotti could teach and still have three or four
good hours a day for vocal work. And a little time
left over for a love affair with a very pretty, sol-
idly intelligent and practical fellow teacher, Adua
Veroni, to whom, presently, he became engaged.
This did not necessarily mean as much as that
word sounds in American or northern European
ears, for in provincial Italy in the 1950s it would
have been considered unseemly for a girl to go
out in the evening with a boy to whom she was
not engaged. But this relationship soon was more
serious than the usual Emilian engagement. The

56

57

An old song that Luciano Pavarotti has sung since childhood is called "La ghirlandeina," an apostrophe to the 285-foot tower above the Duomo and Piazza Grande of Modena— "Ghirlandeina, my delight,/how beautiful you are, how lovely!/What a tower! What a marvel!/See, I blow you a kiss!

engagement lasted almost eight years; the marriage is at this writing almost a quarter of a century old, and still strong.

The life of an assistant teacher in an elementary school was not for Luciano Pavarotti: he had no gift for instilling discipline in a wild lot of boys. But the job offered its own rather odd escape hatch, in the form of an arrangement between the school and an insurance company selling life insurance to the parents of young children. While still teaching, Pavarotti became an insurance salesman, following up on leads supplied him by the school itself. This was, after all, the same man who now charms the birds out of

the trees: he became a hugely successful insurance salesman. His commissions from selling insurance were soon many times his salary as a teacher, and he quit the classroom, happily. This is not to say that insurance selling was a bowl of cherries: "In two years I found only one person—one person— who said, 'I have been waiting for you to come.' And it's not like an interview, where people ask the questions, and all you have to do is answer." The three or four hours a day of talking that the job required began to harm Pavarotti's singing, or at least he thought it did. In 1960, gambling all, suddenly, on the voice, Pavarotti resigned the insurance job.

By then Pola had gone off to Japan to make a new career as a singer and teacher in this new and enthusiastic market for Western musical art, and had sent Pavarotti to work with his friend Ettore Campogalliani in Mantova. Now the young tenor was graduated to songs and operatic arias, though not yet to entire roles in operas. In 1957, Luciano made his solo debut, with his church choir, singing the Benedictus in Lorenzo Perosi's *Te Deum*. He once laid out for an interviewer, in English, a collection of adjectives for his voice at that time: "small, subtle, and interesting, mellow, sweet, and round." In 1958, he began to participate in concerts in neighboring towns. Some of these went well, some did not; none yielded any income. Pavarotti has written that it was after a disastrous failure in one of these little concerts that he decided he would quit after he had fulfilled all outstanding engagements—and then, the weight of the future off his vocal cords, he sang so well the next time out that he knew he had made it.

The big break was victory in the tenor category in a contest for debutant singers in the province of Emilia, the prize being an engagement for a performance of *La Bohème* on April 29, 1961, at the Teatro Municipale at the provincial capital of Reggio Emilia, under the baton of one of Italy's foremost conductors, Francesco Molinari-Pradelli. This was a new idea: prior to 1961, the prize had

My Father, My Friend

The Duomo of Modena, with its magnificent bell tower, La Ghirlandeina, was among the locations seen in "Pavarotti and Friends," a television special filmed during 1982. For one episode, Luciano and Fernando Pavarotti blended voices in "Panis angelicus," singing Franck's well-known hymn inside the cathedral (above)—tenors perfectly matched in timbre, father, son, and friends for life.

At the bakery where Fernando once worked (above); backstage after recital at the Metropolitan Opera when they performed a duet as an encore (below); home in Modena (right); by the Duomo (next page ▶)

been a scholarship for further study. Now the study was to be done under the auspices of the theater itself; the winners were gathered together on one floor of an old hotel, "with rooms like dressing rooms," Pavarotti recalls, "and the bathroom at the end of the hall," and every day for six weeks they discussed the opera, practiced ensembles, rehearsed stage action, prepared in each case to give the first professional dramatic stage performance of his or her life. Though it was an Emilian contest, incidentally, it had one non-Italian winner, a young bass named Dmitri Nabokov, the son of the great cosmopolitan Russian critic and novelist, who was studying in Italy. This turned out to be useful to Pavarotti, for an agent came down from Milan to hear this potentially promotable beginner, and wound up signing Pavarotti.

Molinari-Pradelli showed up two days before the performance, and drastically imposed his personality on it. Young Pavarotti, who was pushed around pretty hard, developed a considerable respect for Molinari as a conductor ("the best arm I have ever seen, and he had a great ability to focus me on himself, so in the performance I did not think who was in the hall, who was on the stage, I focused on him")—and also a not inconsiderable distaste for him as a person, because Molinari was nasty to the young singers, the orchestra, and the resident staff who had become family to the kids. Both these attitudes, which are widely shared in the profession, survived further exposure to Molinari, who conducted Pavarotti's debut as a contract singer (rather than a one-shot substitute) at La Scala, his debut at the Met, and his debut in the Arena at Verona.

The *Bohème* played twice in Reggio Emilia, once in Modena. It may be some measure of Pavarotti's success at his debut that he still describes the Teatro Municipale in Reggio Emilia as acoustically the finest opera house he knows: "very tiny, only a thousand seats, and you can hear a piece of paper drop on the stage." The contest

Newlyweds signing the church registry during ceremony, 1961, with maid of honor Gabriella Pavarotti and flower girl Emanuela Maramotti members of the wedding party

attracted some attention from opera managers and agents elsewhere in Italy. The immediate challenge for Pavarotti from his new agent was to acquire roles the agent could offer, and in the three months between his debut and midsummer Pavarotti learned four of them: the Duke in *Rigoletto,* Edgardo in *Lucia di Lammermoor,* Alfredo in *La Traviata,* and Pinkerton in *Madama Butterfly.* Those four plus Rodolfo were the only roles he would sing in his first two professional seasons—indeed, if one skips over the Idamante in *Idomeneo,* which he learned in the hothouse atmosphere of England's countryside Glyndebourne Opera, they were the only roles he sang in his first three seasons. But with five roles to offer and

As a chorister in Tosca, 1957 (above), at Modena's Teatro
Comunale (below), where in 1961 the tenor sang Rodolfo in
La Bohème with Vito Mattioli, the young conductor Leone
Magiera, Bianca Bellesia, Dmitri Nabokov, Polyna Savridi,
Guido Pasella, and Walter De Ambrosis as colleagues (right)

an agent offering them, Luciano had a profession. In mid September he played his first journeyman engagement—as Rodolfo again, to the Mimi of Rosanna Carteri, in Lucca; on September 30 he and Adua were, at last, married.

During the course of the 1961–62 season, Pavarotti sang in four *Rigolettos,* one *Traviata* (in Belgrade, with a touring troupe from Venice), and two *Bohèmes.* One of these *Rigolettos* was for Tullio Serafin in Palermo, Pavarotti's first major opera house. While "falling down old," as Pavarotti puts it, Serafin was an important figure to have as a sponsor: he had been Toscanini's successor at the Metropolitan forty-odd years before, and he had not long ago changed the course of operatic history by persuading Maria Callas, who was singing heavy roles, up to and including Turandot and even Isolde, that her voice was properly placed for the bel canto repertoire. The next season, Pavarotti had his first important assignments outside Italy: a *Lucia* for the Netherlands Opera, a debut in Vienna as a substitute Rodolfo, a Pinkerton in Belfast, and a *Rigoletto* at the Gaiety Theatre of Dublin. This turned out to be a major event, for among those in the audience was Joan Ingpen, a former London artist's agent gone straight as management, who was casting Covent Garden for Sir Georg Solti (as later on she would cast the Paris Opera for Rolf Liebermann, and the Metropolitan for Levine). She not only hired Pavarotti to cover for di Stefano in the 1963–64 season's *La Bohème,* which gave Luciano five performances in a world capital when di Stefano canceled, but specifically commended him to the attention of Richard Bonynge and Joan Sutherland.

It was in the English-speaking world, oddly, that Pavarotti finally perfected his craft and learned his trade. In the summer of 1964 he took his most extended engagement, to sing Idamante in the Glyndebourne Festival production of Mozart's *Idomeneo.* This was interesting casting by someone, for the role was written for castrato, and in the edition most commonly used these days it is sung by a mezzo-soprano. (When Pavarotti returned to *Idomeneo* for James Levine at the Met almost twenty years later, it was in the more robust role of the Cretan king himself; and Idamante was sung by Frederica von Stade.) Pavarotti's predecessor as Idamante at Glyndebourne thirteen years before, when the work had received its premiere professional performance in Britain, had been the light French Canadian tenor Léopold Simoneau. Pavarotti arrived in the English countryside from a season of singing in London and Budapest and Barcelona and Palermo and Genoa, theaters with about five times the cubage of Glyndebourne—and singing, what's more, rather loud, as youngsters will. Glyndebourne's veteran coach Jani Strasser, a

---

Idamante, Mozart's Idomeneo, *Glyndebourne Festival, 1964*

Hungarian with Viennese roots, set himself the task of scaling Pavarotti down to the confines of the theater and of the work as seen by conductor John Pritchard (who has the instincts of a miniaturist, anyway), and it came hard.

Adua was home in Modena, preparing to deliver their second daughter, Cristina, and Pavarotti had found that he spoke much less English than he thought when he finished the Scuola Magistrale. Artists do not get lonely at Glyndebourne, because people are worked collaboratively and arduously and thrown into each other's company at meals, but for Luciano every day was a strain. To the extent that his native optimism and exuberance permitted, he hated every minute of Strasser's coaching, but since the Pola days he had accepted instruction (and, indeed, still does: he once said in an intermission feature on a Met telecast, referring to the relationship between singer and conductor, that "I make the decision,

because my throat must make the voice," but to watch Pavarotti watch James Levine on the podium in a performance at the Metropolitan is to learn a new definition of noblesse oblige). By the time the Glyndebourne performances began, the critics commented that Pavarotti was almost too light to be heard, and the interesting fact is that except for another Idamante in Geneva that fall Pavarotti did not sing in opera again until December—though it was in this period that he went to Moscow, sang in two recitals (one of them televised), and auditioned for Herbert von Karajan to win his engagement at La Scala. What remained from the *Idomeneo* experience—and today Pavarotti is grateful to Strasser—was an ease in singing *piano* that he otherwise might never have acquired.

Ovation following La Sonnambula, Her Majesty's Theatre, Sydney, *the Sutherland-Williamson troupe's farewell to Australia, 1965—Elizabeth Harwood, Pavarotti, Joan Sutherland, Richard Bonynge, Alberto Remedios and Spiro Malas called forth repeatedly to the confetti-strewn stage*

The Sutherland connection would be crucial. Joan Ingpen has written that in recommending Pavarotti to Sutherland she noted that the Australian diva really needed a large partner, and Pavarotti was a big man (not yet overweight, but six feet two, large-boned and muscular). It is an oddity of the world that tenors, and especially Italian tenors, tend to be short. I remember an embarrassing moment in *La Traviata* when the tenor Gianni Poggi got in front of the dying Renata Tebaldi during "Parigi, o cara," and from the depths of her tubercular decline Tebaldi reached out graceful but strong arms and physically lifted him off to one side. Sutherland herself has what Pavarotti likes to call "an important body." So her husband Richard Bonynge came to Pavarotti's Covent Garden audition after his Dublin success in spring 1963. Presently Covent Garden signed Pavarotti for *La Sonnambula* with Sutherland in spring 1965 (other than *Idomeneo,* the first new role he had learned since the rash of study in summer 1961)—and the Bonynges signed him to a four-month tour of Australia with an ad hoc company they were in the process of forming for the coming months.

Especially when they tour the provinces, big stars usually surround themselves with mediocrities whose grayness makes their own bright emergence more striking. To Sutherland's great credit, she has always sought to associate herself with absolutely first-class young people on their way up. For Sutherland's own New York debut in a concert performance of Bellini's *Beatrice di Tenda* in 1961, for example, the Bonynges engaged Marilyn Horne to make *her* New York debut as Agnese. The "Sutherland-Williamson" company formed for this 1965 Australian tour (Williamson was the name of the local impresario firm) was full of people not then well known who would later make worldwide careers: the English soprano Elizabeth Harwood, the English tenor Alberto Remedios, the Australian bass Clifford Grant, the American tenor John Alexander, and the American bass Spiro Malas. And Pavarotti. Moreover, major efforts were made to keep the company happy though very far from home. The Bonynges arranged, for example, to have Adua accompany Pavarotti to Australia. (In the third month, when the company shifted its base from Melbourne to Sydney, Pavarotti reports, Adua went home to Italy. "Then I lived with Spiro Malas," Pavarotti adds. "He was my butler. I was his cook.")

The Australian tour solidified Pavarotti's *Sonnambula* and gave him a new role that would become perhaps his very favorite: Nemorino in Donizetti's *L'Elisir d'Amore.* More important, it put him in a pressure cooker for stage accomplishment: three weeks of vigorous rehearsing, then thirty-nine performances in three months ("a little much"—today Pavarotti may give thirty-nine performances in seven months). Most important

of all, it gave him daily contact with Joan Sutherland: "to have such a partner was a great opportunity for a young singer." She could do things technically that he could not, she could do them hour after hour and day after day, her performances reached the same standard almost every time, and somehow she never showed fatigue. "One day," Pavarotti recalls, "we had a full-dress general rehearsal for *Sonnambula* in the afternoon, and a performance of *Traviata* that night. I saw that lady sing both in full voice, and at the end she was not tired." Pavarotti could not make such claims for himself.

"It had been my problem from the beginning," he says today. "Some days the voice would be pair-fect, other days it was not quite right, and I did not know why. My teachers had told me to make everything 'normal and natural,' but they did not tell me what those words meant. When I was not singing right, they would suggest that I might be tired. Which would be true—I was tired. What I learned from Joan was that when I felt tired it was because I did not control the diaphragm."

Singing in essence is forcing air through a pair of very thin vibrating muscle strands in the throat. Less air than you might think passes through, for the need is to maintain a steady pressure. This can be done in various ways, but the only one that will operate without conscious decision-making is the use of the stomach muscles to push up the diaphragm. It is not easy for women to adopt this procedure, because it involves sticking out the stomach on the intake, and just as Victorian women did not have legs, modern women do not have stomachs. Sutherland understood that her career did not hinge on her figure, and knew that supporting the pressure through the long column of air to the diaphragm would enable her to think about more important things while singing her famously ornate repertoire. Durability is a side benefit: the athletic end of singing, which is of course in large part an athletic

Scaling La Scala

A debut at La Scala, Milan, is the dream of every Italian singer. Pavarotti's dream came true in 1965 as an eleventh-hour replacement for the indisposed Gianni Raimondi in La Bohème, *a performance conducted by Herbert von Karajan. The leading lady that auspicious night was also from Modena, Pavarotti's lifelong friend Mirella Freni. In seasons that immediately followed, La Scala paired them often (overleaf ►): Massenet's Manon and Des Grieux, in Italian (top left); Puccini's Rodolfo and Mimi (top right); Donizetti's Tonio and Maria in* La Figlia del Reggimento *directed by Margherita Wallmann (bottom left and center). Also shown: Pavarotti's Nemorino in* L'Elisir d'Amore, *a part he will sing as long as he sings opera (bottom right).*

activity, becomes less wearing when the basic pressure system is routinized. "A child can cry for the entire night," Pavarotti told his Juilliard master class, "without losing the voice, because he cries with the diaphragm. Of course, he has a great advantage over singers because he chooses the one note on which he cries."

Pavarotti recalls that before the Australian tour, "Sometimes, by instinct, I had been singing from the diaphragm. But my brain did not know how to do it. When I did performances that way, it was fantastic, but I thought it was not necessary to put the brain in control of the diaphragm, and that is the first mechanical part of singing. At first I did not understand what Joan was doing. I would say to Richard, 'Excuse me, but I am going to put my hand on your wife's stomach.' Since then, I know."

From Australia, Pavarotti went on to three triumphant months at La Scala, including his first creation of a role in a new production in Milan, as Teobaldo in Claudio Abbado's controversial edition of Bellini's *I Capuleti e i Montecchi.* Bellini wrote the opera with Romeo as a trouser role for a soprano; Abbado transposed the role for tenor, which necessitated considerable other juggling. Pavarotti's assignment to Teobaldo was not quite the recognition of a star: it was Giacomo Aragall's Romeo that got the top tenor billing. Abbado took his edition, and Aragall and Pavarotti, to the Holland Festival, to Rome, to the Edinburgh Festival, to the Montreal Expo—where Pavarotti also unhappily sat by as second choice, the "cover" tenor in Karajan's astonishing all-star performance of Verdi's *Requiem* (Leontyne Price, Fiorenza Cossotto, Carlo Bergonzi, Nicolai Ghiaurov).

Many were drastically displeased with Abbado's version of the opera: the composer's biographer Herbert Weinstock called the edition "a distortion of Bellini's intentions," and other conductors have remained content with a female Romeo. Understandably, Pavarotti has not sung the role in any other edition. It should be noted, incidentally, that Karajan's preference for Bergonzi in the 1967 *Requiem* did not in the least sour relations between him and Pavarotti. The only picture on Pavarotti's piano in Modena is an autographed portrait of Karajan, who has spoken effusively of Pavarotti, and gave him the palm Pavarotti values more than any other of his honors: the assignment to the special performance of the Verdi *Requiem* Karajan conducted at La Scala in commemoration of the hundredth birthday of Arturo Toscanini. "I had practiced the 'Hostia' from the *Requiem* four hundred times," Pavarotti said, "so when Karajan asked me for it, I was ready."

A reunion with Sutherland at Covent Garden came at the end of the season, when Pavarotti sang French for the first time—absolutely phonetically: he speaks not a word of the language, which he now rather regrets, having become in recent years the toast of *tout Paris.* The occasion was a production of Donizetti's *La Fille du Régiment,* the earliest of that composer's forays into French texts, and outrageously difficult for the tenor (who got revenge on its opening night, apparently, by singing off pitch; nine months after this fiasco, to give you a taste of the sort of trivia that clutters books about opera, this tenor's wife gave birth to a girl who would, thirty years later, as Marie Célestine Galli-Marié, create the role of Carmen for Bizet).

Pavarotti, triumphantly, sang Tonio as Donizetti originally wrote it, throwing off the nine repeated high C's in "Pour mon âme" like rice at a wedding. He repeated this feat six years later at the Metropolitan, and it was Tonio in *La Fille du Régiment* that really established Pavarotti not only in New York but in the United States, for he and Sutherland sang it fifteen times that season, in Boston, Cleveland, Atlanta, Memphis, New Orleans, Minneapolis, and Detroit as well as at the Met, and the associated publicity put Pavarotti in *Life* magazine and on the TV shows. And, less significantly, in the pages of *Esquire* magazine,

King of the High C's

Tonio in Donizetti's La Fiile du Régiment *catapulted Pavarotti to stardom—first at the Royal Opera House, Covent Garden, in 1966, then at the Metropolitan Opera, in 1972. His brilliant singing of the aria "Pour mon âme," with nine successive high C's delivered with astonishing ease, was the stuff of which opera legends are born. Joan Sutherland and Spiro Malas were his partners as Marie and Sulpice in London, during Act II performing a madcap trio (above). In New York (overleaf ▶), makeup artist Victor Callegari helped Pavarotti get ready to go onstage (top right), where he would join the soprano and Fernando Corena, the Sulpice, in a frothy regimental ditty (left), then, during curtain calls with Sutherland, take a breather (bottom right).*

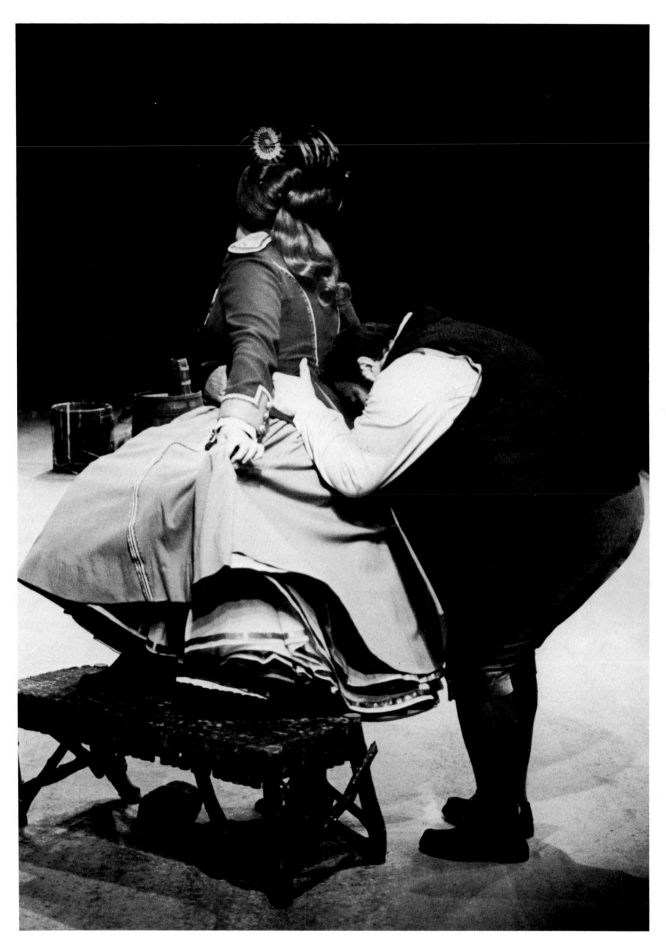

where I wrote an article about him. I commented that part of the joy of this production for the audience was that everybody on stage appeared to be having a good time, which provoked a snort and a shake of the head and a statement that he and Sutherland had been terrified every moment of every performance. Tonio, incidentally, is a role Pavarotti has now abandoned. "Why repeat a very difficult, demanding thing," he told a *Playboy* interviewer, with typical candor, "just to show yourself in worse condition?"

The most significant debut for Pavarotti in the rest of the 1960s was in San Francisco, a *Bohème* with Freni in 1967. Starting in 1972, it would be in San Francisco that Pavarotti would first perform new roles, and a long succession of

---

La Fille du Régiment *at the Metropolitan Opera: chased by a group of soldiers, Tonio seeks refuge behind Marie's skirts —a comic turn that garnered gales of laughter for the stars*

them, too: *Un Ballo in Maschera, La Favorita, Luisa Miller, Il Trovatore, Turandot* ("the first and the only time," Pavarotti notes dreamily), *La Gioconda,* and *Aïda.* "And why not?" Pavarotti says. "Adler [Kurt Herbert Adler, the general director of the San Francisco Opera until 1983] offered me good conductors, good casts, good productions. The city is beautiful, the opera is first-class, *first*-class." It was also for Pavarotti a cheerful situation, because rehearsals in San Francisco, where the season starts early in September, begin before school opens in Italy. His wife and his daughters (with the addition of Giuliana in 1967, there were now three) could and did come with him to the city on the bay. His feelings about San Francisco are so positive, Pavarotti says affectionately, that it's not until he gets on the airplane to go there that he remembers what an awful acoustical beast of an auditorium he will find at the War Memorial Opera House.

Both the management and Pavarotti were thinking of even greater things when Terence McEwen took over as general director in San Francisco in 1983, for Terry and Luciano went back a long way together—McEwen had been the American end of Decca Records ("London Records" in the United States), for which Pavarotti had made virtually all his recordings. A new production of Boito's *Mefistofele* was planned to follow up on Decca's successful recording, a Pavarotti triumph ("It's very interesting," Pavarotti says, "that in Gounod's *Faust* the real center is Méphistophélès, while the tenor is the real center of Boito's opera"). But as the season neared, Pavarotti's learning time was committed to songs and arias for his concerts. A compromise was struck: instead of Faust in *Mefistofele,* Pavarotti will give McEwen his first-ever stage performance of Canio in *Pagliacci,* another role he had very successfully recorded.

The watershed year in Pavarotti's career was 1971–72, the tenth anniversary of his debut. Until then, though he had scored his greatest and most interesting successes outside Italy, he had been primarily an Italian tenor, singing most of the season in Italian opera houses. In 1968–69, for example, there had been a *Lucia* in San Francisco, and the abortive flu-bedeviled one-and-a-half Rodolfos at the Met, but everything else had been in Italy—Lucca, Pisa, Bologna, Genoa, and three productions at La Scala (a grand total, incidentally, of only thirty-five performances for the season). In 1971–72, Pavarotti sang in Tokyo, Hamburg, Berlin, San Francisco, Philadelphia, Miami, the Met and its tour cities, San Sebastián in Spain, and Vienna, appearing in Italy only in the summer, at the Arena in Verona. In no season since has Pavarotti sung more than two productions in Italy, and between March 1983 and December 1985 he did not sing a single performance of opera (there were a few concerts) in his own country. For the

A Casa

It takes only minutes to drive from the center of Modena to the home of Luciano Pavarotti, which in fact is the home of all the Pavarottis. Luciano, Adua, and their three daughters occupy two floors of the main house, once the hub of an elaborate estate, with Adua's sister Giovanna and her family ensconced on the third floor (right). A few steps away, across from the dining room and kitchen, is a long, two-story structure, formerly stables, now housing a studio for the tenor, an archive containing memorabilia of his career and, most importantly, handsome apartments where Pavarotti's parents and sister reside.

A Maserati gleams in the driveway, and Pavarotti might call out an exuberant greeting to approaching guests (overleaf ▶). If visitors are lucky, he might even be singing in the music room, learning new repertory, or going over a song composed by his friend Pippo Casarini. On the Steinway stands a treasured memento—an autographed portrait of Herbert von Karajan.

A Casa

That musician and man of the land Giuseppe Verdi would feel at home in the surrounding fields, flat and verdant, ready to till. One summer day, under the glorious sun of Italy, Pavarotti posed for a now famous photograph near an orchard with Adua, Lorenza, Cristina, Giuliana (◄ second overleaf).

To the rear of the house is a long, imposing avenue of poplars, which lend a particular character to the landscape of Emilia (◄ first overleaf). "I find these trees extremely beautiful, so lean and tall, in such perfect, symmetrical lines," says the singer. "The property just beyond belongs not to me but to the region, but I own other land that is farmed. We grow our own vegetables and fruits, and grapes to make Lambrusco. Who knows, someday, when I no longer sing, I will become a full-time farmer."

While home in Modena, Pavarotti always spends many happy hours with his father, and a favorite game they play is called bocce, a kind of outdoor billiards.

Horses are one of the singer's passions, and he keeps several on his grounds. He loves to ride, especially on Shaughran (left), purchased in Ireland in 1979 and ever since an indispensable member of the Pavarotti family.

past fifteen years, Pavarotti's schedule has been the definition of an international career.

He keeps track of this maelstrom of engagements via a thin, narrow, long, leather-bound datebook that he carries at all times in the inside breast pocket of his jacket. Adua with the assistance of her secretary, Francesca Barbieri, helps Luciano and his secretary, Giovanna Cavaliere, keep up with the massive correspondence. An American and a European manager divide up the work of negotiating terms and conditions. Pavarotti in the end makes all his own significant decisions. In theory, he is tough about the conductor and the soprano, and insists on knowing who they will be before he accepts a booking. In fact, he allows hope to spring eternal, and has accepted engagements to sing for and with people who would not have been his first choice. (I noted that

---

Portraying the hot-tempered Tebaldo in I Capuleti e i Montecchi *at La Scala, 1966, with Mario Petri as Capellio*

a TV tape of a performance in Italy carried a fair amount of booing for his soprano; Pavarotti said, "I tell you, if I had been in the audience there would have been much louder booing . . .") On the other hand, there have been two occasions when Pavarotti dictated to a manager the choice of conductor and soprano, and both times it turned out, he says, to have been a mistake. It is not easy to win this game. Often enough, the managers who engage him, at the largest fees in the world, feel that his presence in itself will sell the tickets, and there is thus no need to put on expensive new productions or stock up with other artists who command high prices. In deciding whether or not to accept an invitation from a theater, Pavarotti remembers what they did to him last time—but if it's the Met or Paris or Vienna or Scala, all of which have one way or another let Pavarotti down in recent seasons, it's hard to hold grudges.

82

For a long time after Luciano's success, the Pavarottis lived frugally. They bought their first house in 1965 (it was the first time Luciano ever signed a check: up to then he had always been paid for his singing in cash, an old tradition in opera houses, and had put what money the family didn't immediately need into a post office giro account, like most European working-class and lower-middle-class households). Luciano spent money to free his father from the early morning hours of the bakery, which also allowed his father to accompany him sometimes on his travels. (Until recently, Adua felt she had to stay home with the three children, first because they were small, then because they were adolescent, finally because, as a traditional Italian mother with unmarried daughters, she worried more than she had thought she would when she was young herself that if she's not around they will get into trouble.) And this was provincial Italy: money had to be saved, with three daughters to endow. As Luciano's fees rose, Adua stopped working as a secretary and became a knowledgeable investor in residential real estate in the Po valley. The Pavarottis bought a vineyard, too, Luciano retaining from the wartime days of his childhood a feeling that some day he might wish to be a farmer. Prices went way up, the stakes grew too high, and eventually Adua sold the properties.

As late as 1975, however, Pavarotti still flew tourist class to and from his engagements, supplementing his fees with the difference between tourist fare and the first-class tickets the opera company paid for. We know that he flew tourist not because he said so (though in fact one can trust what Pavarotti says: he is a guileless man) but because he was in a bad airplane accident in Milan in that year, and the plane broke apart at the wing, right in front of him. Pavarotti has little doubt that at that moment God was personally looking out for his servant Luciano.

Like most highly successful craftsmen, Pavarotti is politically very conservative on the issues that exercise the press. And he is "of course" religious (there may or may not be atheists in foxholes, but there are damned few on opera stages, where singers feel, first, that they have a gift from somewhere, and, second, that they need all the help they can get). Beyond that, and beyond the astrology he takes reasonably seriously (he is a Libra), Pavarotti still looks at the world through the eyes of the baker's son. In summer 1985 he gave a free concert in the town square of Modena for Ferragosto, the mid-August holiday. "Generally everybody is at the beach. The people in Modena then are the people who don't have the money to go to the beach. So we make a beautiful concert for them where they are." Modena is airless and stifling in the summer; Pavarotti is no longer there in the summer, but he remembers.

The first luxury was the fast expensive cars, and then the summer house on the Adriatic just outside Pesaro, acquired in 1974. In 1979, the Pavarottis purchased a fifteen-acre property on the edge of Modena, with a large manor house and several outbuildings, and they have turned it into a sort of Dickensian dream of family propinquity. Luciano and Adua and the three girls, now women, live on the lower two floors of the main house. Adua's sister Giovanna and her husband and four sons live on the top floor; Luciano's sister and her son and his mother and father live in one of the remodeled outbuildings. There is a Steinway for rehearsing, the gift of British Decca on an anniversary, a very large-screen projection-from-the-rear television set, top-of-the-line stereo equipment, and a record collection divided into Luciano's recordings on one shelf, other artists' recordings, often enough the same music, on another shelf.

Away from home, Pavarotti usually does not stay at the very best and most expensive hotels. He likes to have a kitchen where he or a friend or his father or Adua can prepare his meals, and the best hotels want you to use their room service. In New York, Pavarotti recently acquired a permanent residence in one of the city's most elegant apartment-hotels, and one of these days Adua will probably furnish it beyond the rudimentary necessities—beds, piano, desk, couch, and a few chairs—that are now in place. The one improvement completed before he moved in was the luxurious kitchen.

As recently as 1980, Adua was warning that people don't understand how expensive life is for the touring opera singer who has to live in hotels while maintaining his family residence elsewhere, that Pavarotti's true net income was nowhere near what it seemed, and that after all a singer's income-producing life was short. Since then, thanks to the concert tours, Pavarotti's income

---

Pavarotti, Fiorenza Cossotto, Leontyne Price, and Nicolai Ghiaurov, soloists for Verdi's Messa da Requiem *at La Scala, Milan, 1967 (top); the performance onstage, with Shirley Verrett the mezzo (bottom left); Herbert von Karajan conducting this memorial to Arturo Toscanini (bottom right)*

has soared out of sight. But it has not made much difference to the way the family lives. Luciano drives his own car, the family prepares its own food (and Adua serves it), the girls drive little Fiats, there is no entourage, no permanent group of hangers-on, just friends in every port, often enough people Luciano has met on airplanes or at parties and liked.

Pavarotti has the politician's trick of concentrating all his attention on the person to whom he is talking, but it is something more than a trick: he really does relate to people. When he speaks harshly of someone, especially of a conductor or a stage director or opera manager, it is almost always because that person pushes people around, or asserts his superiority to his fellow man in unpleasant ways. The problem with La Scala, Pavarotti likes to say, is that the Scala audience feels a need to select, to pick one artist always rather than another, a Callas rather than a Tebaldi, a Del

Monaco rather than a Corelli—while the genius of the Met, especially under Bing, is that it was inclusive.

There isn't much prima donna to Pavarotti. Though he has been known to be difficult during the final stages of the tailoring process, in principle he wears the costumes designed by the costumer of the production in which he is singing ("I know nobody wants to dress me in white"). He works with the coaches from the opera house (though not, if he can help it, in the basic rehearsals for a performance: "If I were a conductor, I would not allow somebody else to work with the principals, I would want to make my agreement with them right away"). He does not quarrel with the makeup staff. He goes to all the rehearsals he is supposed to go to, and he works hard at them. On the day of a performance he sleeps as late as he can (in an ideal world, he feels, he would always sleep ten hours a night), eats a big lunch, rests again, and gets to the theater early, at least an hour before curtain. "Always the same routine," Pavarotti says. "Boring. For a normal person it's boring. For us it's life or death. I need to breathe the stage from a distance, smell the makeup and the wig and the costumes, and then I have to wake up the voice. Then I don't want to talk, I don't want to see anyone, for at least half an hour before the performance."

There is a ritual of finding a bent nail on the way onto the stage, "the material expression of an idea," Pavarotti says, "that one needs help." After a performance, Pavarotti receives hundreds of people, shakes hands, talks with people, signs autographs. At the Metropolitan, a special table is set up in the Green Room so Pavarotti can be comfortable while greeting his admirers and signing their programs. "If you stay in touch with the audience after the performance," he says, "it keeps the adrenaline flowing." Then, and only then, often more than an hour after the performance, he goes somewhere to eat.

Everyone has a favorite Pavarotti story, and it is almost always a nice story. Mine is from the dress rehearsal for the awful *Ballo in Maschera* at the Met, which Elijah Moshinsky of Covent Garden staged with self-indulgent unconcern for Verdi or the cast. The designer Peter Wechsler had given him an uncomfortably raked stage and a basic set of a bunch of vertical wood slats, like a stockade, which had the acoustical characteristic of swallowing the soprano voices, especially the Oscar of Judith Blegen. (In fairness to Moshinsky, he was no fonder of the set than the cast was.) Pavarotti disliked the director and disagreed with the conductor, but he set his teeth and did the best he could; he had committed for fifteen performances, at the Met and on tour, and by God he sang every one of them. The story, however, is from an earlier moment, before the first performance. In the masked ball scene itself, at the end of the opera, Moshinsky in the last rehearsal came up with a brainstorm, that one of the women at the ball, overcome by excitement, should faint in the crush of dancers around the King (or the Governor of Massachusetts, or whoever he is). The director had, however, neglected to warn Pavarotti. Out of the corner of his eye, Pavarotti saw the lady in question slump to the raked stage.

There are, I can assure you, opera stars who would grimly persist in what they were doing, angry at the chorister for dropping dead in the middle of their rehearsal, hoping that the stagehands will come out soon and cart the body away. Pavarotti has different instincts. He immediately stopped singing, went out of character, and ran to see if he could help the lady. It took a while before the conductor and the director could explain to him that this fainting scene was one of the director's many added bits of business, and he should return to his own betrayal and death. To a great tenor, a chorister is roughly what a sparrow is to God; in his godlike way, Pavarotti unselfconsciously worried that a sparrow had fallen.

Family Man

All his life, Pavarotti has been surrounded by women—and he loves it. Three of unquestioned importance are his daughters, as different from one another as girls can be yet extremely close and caring. In 1972, on the beach at Pesaro, Papà posed with Cristina, Giuliana, and Lorenza, then aged eight, five, and ten (above). At Christmastime 1962, five generations gathered by the tree (overleaf ▶): Luciano, his grandmother Giulia, his great-grandmother Cristina, his firstborn Lorenza, his mother Adele. A 1980 shot finds him at home with wife Adua (top right); another pose, from 1976, shows the singer with Lorenza, Giuliana, and Cristina (bottom right).

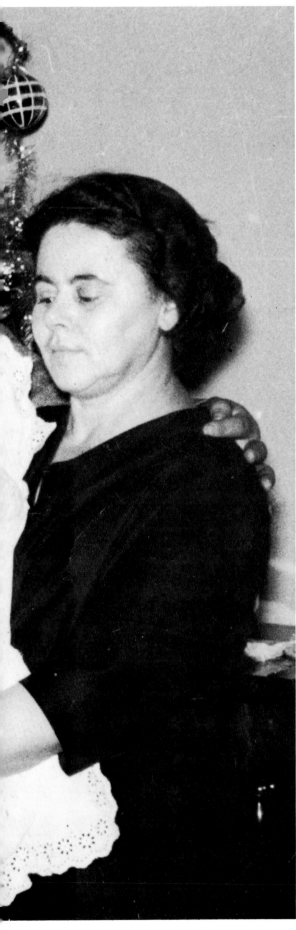

OPERA STAR

"First, of course," says Pavarotti, "you must have the voice. Without the voice, there is nothing."

But what really made Pavarotti's career in opera, I think, was less the voice than the musicality. From the early recordings, it is by no means clear that young Luciano made more beautiful sounds than any of thirty other tenors before the public (and he agrees: "I can name the thirty"). What he had, the late George Movshon wrote in a record review, was "a direct, candid, 'country boy' sort of sound." And his acting in those first years before the public would not have convinced a child. But the phrasing, the sense of legato, were something else. An anonymous vocal coach once told Robert Jacobson of *Opera News* that Pavarotti at work had an attention span of about

Un Ballo in Maschera *at the San Francisco Opera, 1982 —Kathleen Battle as Oscar, Pavarotti as the dying Gustav and Silvano Carroli as Renato, who has murdered the king*

three minutes—but that he was "innately musical and *can't* make a musical mistake." The music critic Irving Kolodin in 1973 put his finger on the quality: "An infallible sense of what some singers still call 'the line,' which is the ability to sustain in perfect order and with no visible vocal strain the spinal cord of any expression to which they attach themselves." Early in the 1970s, when Pavarotti was still quite a fresh face in New York, Harold Schonberg of the *Times* called him "the thinking man's tenor. He sings with style and nuance, and it is hard to imagine any other tenor now before the public who handles Italian music with equal finesse."

Like everything else, this took a while. If one looks, for example, at the four roles Pavarotti learned in that first summer after his debut, two were only moderately useful to him. One of them (Pinkerton in *Madama Butterfly)* he sang only three times in his career, in Belfast in 1962–63, and then in Palermo and Reggio Calabria in 1963–64. The other (Alfredo in *La Traviata*), he sang after 1968 only during one engagement, at the Met in 1970, when he had three different Violettas (Sutherland, Moffo, and Tucci) for three performances. He remembers undertaking the role as a tribute to Robert Merrill, who celebrated the twenty-fifth anniversary of his Met debut with a Germont—but in the end it was Bergonzi who sang on the actual date of the anniversary, though Merrill did two of Pavarotti's three performances. Pinkerton was generally unsuitable for his voice and temperament: composers for some reason write heavier for tenor and especially for orchestra as they get older (compare Otello with the Duke in *Rigoletto,* or Dick Johnson in *The Girl of the Golden West* with Rodolfo, or for that matter Tristan with Lohengrin), and the *Butterfly* orchestra is already edging toward that voice-eating quality that would make *Turandot* a killer for both the lead soprano and the tenor. Moreover, the opera belongs to the soprano, both dramatically and vocally; to say the least, one does not care at the end what happens to Pinkerton. And *Traviata,* as Pavarotti shrewdly observes, is really about the soprano and the baritone, and the tenor is merely their pawn. One does not become a heroic crowd-pleaser as Pinkerton or Alfredo, and from early on that is what Luciano Pavarotti, as a thinking man who was professionally a tenor, had determined to accomplish.

The other two roles in the group of four that he learned after *Bohème,* however, became staples: the Duke in Verdi's *Rigoletto,* which Pavarotti has sung more often than any role except Rodolfo, and Edgardo in Donizetti's *Lucia di Lammermoor,* which he would still be willing to sing except that opera houses are pretty reluctant to pay Pavarotti's fees on top of what they would be charged by a coloratura who could really stand and deliver

the Mad Scene. *Rigoletto* is a great work of musico-dramatic art, its intellectual reputation held down, quite unfairly, by its immense popularity. (Charles Osborne in his book on Verdi's operas reports that *Rigoletto* was the work that first persuaded Rossini of Verdi's genius, and also that Verdi himself told Felice Varesi, his first Rigoletto, that he never expected to write anything better than the fourth act quartet.) From a women's lib perspective, the Duke is a pretty dreadful fellow—but, then, so was Francis I of France, on whom Victor Hugo had modeled the character; and "La donna è mobile" is simply a translation (in the same rhythm) of Hugo's "Souvent femme varie," which was an actual favorite expression of the French king. (Without defending the censors

---

Early Rigolettos: *first outing as the Duke of Mantua, Carpi, 1961 (top left), poster for the much-acclaimed De Filippo staging in Rome (top right), and backstage with the conductor Francesco Molinari-Pradelli, La Scala, Milan, 1965 (bottom)*

who screwed up the dramaturgy of both *Rigoletto* and *Un Ballo in Maschera,* their problem was not that Verdi and his librettist were writing fiction that put royalty into disrepute or trouble but that they were presenting reasonably accurate history for the masses.)

In any event, the role of the Duke, with its high vocal texture and its most utilitarian attitude toward girls, was in every way sympathetic for Pavarotti, who has been cuddled in very feminine surroundings all his life—adoring mother, sister and no brothers, wife and three daughters—and has, as they say, a way with the ladies. Pavarotti has sung it as recently as 1981–82, in the dreadful production mounted by the Met (and made available internationally—alas!—in a telecast: one wonders, sometimes, how the Met decides what productions should represent the company to the world). Like most tenors, Pavarotti adds high

Riposo

For most opera-lovers, the resort town of Pesaro on Italy's Adriatic coast is the birthplace of Rossini and the site of an annual festival in the composer's honor. For Luciano Pavarotti it is that and more— a paradise where he escapes each summer and where, if all work does not exactly stop, it at least proceeds a more leisurely pace. His retreat, named Villa Giulia in memory of his adored grandmother, is a large white house with blue trim and red-tile roof commanding a sweeping hilltop view of sea, town, and verdant skyline—"Cielo e mar."

At Pesaro the tenor pursues pleasures all but impossible elsewhere. Some years ago an admirer gave him a set of oil paints, and he forthwith taught himself to paint. At his easel, which stands on a covered veranda, he creates bold images in blazing colors, and each new canvas has a distinct character and charm of its own (right). Some subjects he takes from postcards of places he has never visited.

There is a relaxed air at Villa Giulia, though visitors are constantly arriving and departing. No one would be amazed to find the tenor eating lunch on his terrace with two dozen guests or so (first overleaf ▶), or casually kibitzing by an upright piano with his daughters, or suddenly bursting into song, perhaps while studying a score with friend and coach Gildo Di Nunzio (bottom left). That would all be part of a normal day.

Riposo

Not far from Pesaro is Gradara, the castle where, in Dante's time, Francesca da Rimini is said to have lived. In 1980, during an engagement in La Gioconda at the Verona Arena, Pavarotti donned an Enzo Grimaldo costume and rode one of his horses through the fields below the ancient fortress, looking very much like an operatic hero come to life (◄ second overleaf).

Among the most popular attractions of Villa Giulia is the king-size swimming pool, and here one might find Il Signor Tenore, as he is sometimes addressed by the house staff, frolicking with his family (◄ first overleaf). He is seen with daughters Lorenza, Giuliana, and Cristina (top left), spouting water like a whale (bottom left) and with wife Adua (right).

At Pesaro, where he can quietly stroll on the shore, Pavarotti finds time to catch his breath, take stock, renew his energies (left). When he leaves, he returns to the breakneck pace of an international career that continues to gain momentum. Little wonder he so needs the serenity of the Villa Giulia.

notes Verdi never wrote, most prominently, the B above the staff, which Verdi wrote an octave lower, at the end of "La donna è mobile." He likes to tell a story of old Serafin approving this interpolation at the dress rehearsal after having banned it earlier, and saying, "Remember, half your applause belongs to me."

Pavarotti's view of the character is softer than that the liberationists would hold: in the culture of his birth and indeed in his own observation the philanderer does less harm than was believed by Hugo and Piave and Verdi (who was faithful to both his wives, probably—and whose second wife, indeed, had been a mirror image of the Duke before their marriage). Pavarotti's Duke is not in the least a sinister fellow. He enjoys himself, and Rigoletto is not just his fool but his foil, the man upon whom he effortlessly places his burdens of deceit and guilt. Significantly, Pavarotti's favorite production of the work was di Filippo's in Rome, which sets the first act, the Duke's boasted seductions of this man's wife and that man's daughter, in the context of a masked ball. Pavarotti also likes the film that Ponnelle made out of *Rigoletto,* which uses the same motif, though in a much more exaggerated and depraved style. In both cases, the interpretation of the Duke does not have to face the damage he is doing in other people's lives; and the fact is, of course, that the only girl the audience actually sees the Duke handling (he keeps his distance from Gilda in Act II, and they are not on stage together in Act III) is the whore Maddalena, the murderer's sister.

One thinks of *Lucia di Lammermoor,* Pavarotti's other choice in that busy summer of 1961, as a showcase for soprano, and of course it is: the work is done when there is a lady to sing the Mad Scene and not when there is a gentleman to sing Edgardo. But the lovely, long first-act duet, which establishes the feeling of the piece, belongs to both equally—and as Herbert Weinstock has pointed out, there is no other opera where the

98

final scene belongs entirely to the tenor, his lady being dead and gone (Juliette and Gilda both manage to revive enough for a little duet on their way out, but Lucia is actually in her coffin with the lid down). The work is, moreover, identified with great tenor figures as well as great sopranos from the past: Duprez sang the premiere in Naples and Rubini sang the Paris premiere. Over the course of twenty years, Pavarotti partnered all the distinguished Lucias: Sutherland, Sills, Scotto, Rinaldi, Zeani, Deutekom, and Serra—and some who were a little less distinguished, too.

Presently there descended upon the young Pavarotti, as there does upon any successful artist, a mob of managers with schemes to use him in their own projects. La Scala was especially importunate, for there were plans afoot to stage a major

Lucia di Lammermoor, Act II, at La Scala, Milan, 1983— Luciana Serra as the heroine, Luciano Pavarotti as Edgardo and Nella Verri as Alisa—a production by Pier Luigi Pizzi

revival of Rossini's *William Tell,* and there were no really suitable Arnoldos around. Pavarotti looked at the Rossini score and said that if he sang Arnoldo he was by no means sure he would ever again be able to sing anything else, provoking the honest if less than assuring response that this would be okay with La Scala. (It is something of an oddity that this very Italian tenor, with his summer home in Rossini's birthplace, and a light voice that was suitable for a number of Rossini roles, never sang in a Rossini opera.) Georg Solti wanted Pavarotti, who had demonstrated that he could sing Mozart in the Glyndebourne *Idomeneo,* to add a Ferrando in *Così Fan Tutte* to his Covent Garden schedule, but the tenor found the role unsympathetic. (One wonders whether Pavarotti would have considered a Don Ottavio in *Don Giovanni,* for various reasons a far more suitable role for him; he sings "Il mio tesoro" exquisitely in his recital.)

Instead, he took the gamble of the repertoire Bellini had written for Giovanni Rubini, very light, very high, requiring great agility. First it was Elvino in Bellini's *La Sonnambula,* a role identified with the likes of Tito Schipa and Dino Borgioli (though Gigli and even Martinelli had sung it), more recently the property of such *leggieri* as Cesare Valletti, the young Nicolai Gedda, and Alfredo Kraus. This was an early example of Pavarotti's faith in Sutherland and Bonynge, whose baby this Covent Garden production was, and it was faith well-placed: though nothing really remains in the memory after a *Sonnambula* except the soprano soaring through the astonishing beauty of "Ah, non credea" and the scintillation of "Ah, non giunge," Pavarotti won ovations both for the loving aria with which he presents

I Puritani *at the Metropolitan Opera, 1976, with Joan Sutherland as Elvira and Luciano Pavarotti as Arturo—* "A te, o cara," *as staged by the producer Sandro Sequi*

the still-undiscovered sleepwalker with his mother's wedding ring and for the confused aria after he repossesses the ring. It is not given equally to all of us to take *Sonnambula* seriously; as the dedicated Herbert Weinstock puts it, key scenes "require a 'suspension of disbelief' which can be won only by the most sensitive acting and stage direction to prove that the director himself believes in what is happening. It is difficult to do. But," Weinstock adds bravely, "it can be done." And perhaps it was done in August 1965 in Australia, when Sutherland and Bonynge and Pavarotti and the bass Joseph Rouleau took *Sonnambula* touring. But not at Covent Garden in spring 1965. I know; I was there.

Pavarotti's most important success in the Bellini repertoire came several years later, in *I Puritani,* which he sang first not with Sutherland but with the elegant Gabriella Tucci at the Teatro

Massimo Bellini in the composer's Sicilian birthplace, Catania, and then with Freni in Bologna and with Beverly Sills in Philadelphia before joining forces with Sutherland and Bonynge at the Metropolitan Opera. The ten performances of *Puritani* at the Metropolitan are I think the month Pavarotti would choose as the operatic high point of his life, especially on those evenings when Sherill Milnes was the spurned Puritan lover and the young James Morris (whose gorgeous bass still rings in Pavarotti's ear) was the affectionate Uncle Giorgio. The mismatch between the historical realities of the English Civil War and the music to which the story is set may be the most extreme in opera, but when everyone is singing well and the pit has the proper lilt one can remember that at least everything comes out all right for these poor stick figures into which Bellini is breathing beauty if not life. And Pavarotti, at least, had the chance to be a Cavalier rather than a Roundhead.

Some New York critics expressed supercilious scorn of this *Puritani,* which everyone engaged in the work considered one of the great performances, and reading these reviews permanently influenced Pavarotti's view of criticism. "Artists are not stupid," he said recently. "I know very few singers who will say after a performance, 'I was *great.*' When a critic makes an analysis, it can be helpful. But it is too easy to be a critic. All you have to say is, 'The tenor was not in good voice,' or 'His acting ruined the character.' What use is that to anybody?"

The second role Pavarotti created under the guidance of Sutherland and Bonynge was Nemorino in Donizetti's *L'Elisir d'Amore,* perhaps his favorite of all. Though I don't disagree with the judgment, it is odd to hear someone as knowledgeable about opera as Pavarotti say that he regards *Elisir* as one of the eternal masterworks. (He is not making an entirely musical judgment here, of course: much of his admiration goes to the poetry as well as the dramatic flow of Roma-

ni's libretto.) Though it has historically been sung most often by light tenors, it is by no means a tenorino role; there is vocal meat in the score, and Caruso among others loved to dig into it. Pavarotti once told an intermission feature interviewer at a Met telecast that it was because the Neapolitan critics made fun of him for singing Nemorino after moving on to a weightier repertoire that Caruso vowed never to sing in Naples again (and he never did).

This was perhaps the first role in which Pavarotti felt full confidence in his ability to portray a character on stage. In his first appearance with the Bonynges (oddly enough, in Miami, whence they had brought him as a substitute for an otherwise engaged Renato Cioni in *Lucia),* Pavarotti had been called aside by the director after the first rehearsal and told he had a lot to do—and he had done it, working one-on-one on the roof of the hotel in the pleasant February sunshine of Miami. Now after a rehearsal of *Elisir* another dramatic coach spoke earnestly to the young tenor about how Nemorino should behave on stage, and Pavarotti waved him away: this person, this poor lovesick country bumpkin, he said, he understood from top to bottom, and he would present him effectively on stage. As indeed he did. And he sang "Una furtiva lagrima" with true pathos, as he still does, his sorrow being not for himself or indeed for Adina, but for all the world of confused young lovers.

What Pavarotti's Nemorino has is a kind of grace. Watching him in this role, or as Tonio in *La Fille du Régiment,* one remembers that he was an athlete. The tragic persona comes hard to Pavarotti, because he has a tendency to bounce on stage, but for the comic characters he can choreograph a convincing presentation. The identification with Nemorino and Tonio, moreover, is quite real: for all his intelligence and his participation in life at the celebrity level, he is not and would not particularly wish to be sophisticated. Asked whether he wasn't uncomfortable in a dra-

A Masterpiece

Nemorino in Donizetti's comic masterpiece L'Elisir d'Amore *and Luciano Pavarotti are inseparable. He has performed this endearing country lad in many a charming production, and among the best was a staging created by designer-director Jean-Pierre Ponnelle for the Hamburg State Opera in 1977. During one rehearsal, the tenor posed with Ponnelle, Bernd Weikl (in costume as Sergeant Belcore), and Hamburg manager August Everding (above). Casting was ideal for every role, with Mirella Freni a captivating Adina, Nemorino's sweetheart (overleaf ▶), and Giuseppe Taddei a droll Dr. Dulcamara, the old charlatan who sells him cheap wine as an elixir of love.*

matic situation where the girl has all the brains (and can read, to boot), he said, only partly as a joke, "No, everyone knows that the dumbest woman is always smarter than the smartest man."

Pavarotti has sung one other Donizetti opera: *La Favorita,* in its Italian version (the work was written to a French libretto, and had its premiere in Paris). This is fairly well stocked with tunes (especially the tenor's "Spirto gentil"), but the fact that the heroine is a mezzo has somewhat inhibited its popularity. Caruso sang it at the Met, though only in one season, and it never came back until Pavarotti seventy years later returned it to that stage with Shirley Verrett. This was one of the works Pavarotti did first in San Francisco (in 1973), with Renato Bruson as the King who renounces his mistress, but an otherwise undistin-

---

The jubilant finale of L'Elisir d'Amore *at the Hamburg State Opera, 1977; Giuseppe Taddei as Dr. Dulcamara, Luciano Pavarotti as Nemorino and Mirella Freni as Adina*

---

guished company. Later that same year *La Favorita* provided the occasion for Pavarotti's absolute worst night ever at La Scala. He and a less than world-class cast had just performed the piece to great acclaim in Bologna, with Molinari-Pradelli conducting. The Scala cast was stronger on paper, including Fiorenza Cossotto and Piero Cappuccilli, but nobody was in very good voice, and the conductor—Pavarotti would rather not have him named, for the man is dead—knew little of *Favorita.* The reviews and news stories the next day make the evening sound like a night of horrors.

"There is no such thing as no reason why these things happen," Pavarotti says, referring to the storm of boos and hisses that greeted the cast at the curtain calls. "There is always a reason. There is such a thing as the audience reacting too much, which can happen at Scala. Whether they

were right or wrong, I don't know, but I certainly gave them the opportunity to disapprove. One of the nice things about an American audience is that it knows that nobody ever goes out on stage with the intent to give a bad performance."

As late as 1972–73, Pavarotti's career was still firmly embedded in the operas of the early nineteenth century. He sang in nineteen productions that year (the most ever), and of the thirteen that were not *Bohème,* six were *Lucia,* with three *Rigolettos,* one *Figlia* and one *Fille* of the Regiment—and two *Ballos,* one in its entirety in Hamburg and one as a single-act contribution to a gala at the Metropolitan. *Ballo* was for Pavarotti the hinge opera, the one that swung open to a heavier repertoire. He had recorded it ("with my head in the score") before attempting it on stage in the first of his San Francisco premieres, in 1971. I think it is fair to say that of all the roles he has acquired since his voice began to darken, Riccardo in *Ballo* is the one for which he feels the deepest affection. The love duet in the second act he considers the greatest example of the genre ever written, an interesting choice, for it is a kind of Verdian Liebesnacht, the expression of a doomed love known to be doomed, and its grand tune is closely related to the love-and-renunciation motif of *Traviata.*

Making sense of *Ballo* has been a challenge to directors since the work was successfully revived (it had pretty much disappeared for half a century) in the Germany of the Weimar Republic. A performance in Berlin established the partnership of conductor Fritz Busch and director Carl Ebert, who would become the artistic founding fathers of Glyndebourne. Here the special moment, which Busch remembered specifically in his delightful memoirs, was the ball scene itself, which Ebert organized in such a way that the audience saw the news of the king's assassination spread slowly through the crowd of dancers, until finally it reached the stage orchestra, and the players one by one fell silent.

The root problem of an effective dramatic presentation of *Un Ballo in Maschera* is in part the idiotic intervention by the papal censors of 1858, who forced Verdi and his librettist Antonio Somma to move the locale from historic eighteenth-century Stockholm to a mythical eighteenth-century Boston. (All English-speaking places have been *very* exotic to Italian opera composers. *Puritani* is set in Plymouth with alleged Devonshire mountains—"beautiful mountains," the libretto says—in the background. Puccini's *Manon Lescaut* ends with the heroine dying in the dreadful desert between New Orleans and Mobile, Alabama. Somma's court for the Governor of Massachusetts, complete with courtiers and chief justices dancing attendance, makes insuperable challenges to credibility.) Verdi sent Somma the list of lines the Roman censors had rejected, and the suggestions he had made, with the comment "If on reading this, you feel a rush of blood to the head, lay it down and try it again after you have eaten and slept well . . ." But the difficulty is really more profound than censorial amendment, and lies in the original libretto written for Auber in 1833 by Scribe, who took the real event of the murder of King Gustav III of Sweden and made it the stuff of conventional, characterless French melodrama. There was one rather strange addition by Scribe to the historical personae: a young page, Oscar, flighty and totally unable to keep a secret, the unwitting betrayer of his master, sung in Verdi's opera by a coloratura soprano, and one of Verdi's favorite creations.

Riccardo, Earl of Warwick, Governor of Boston, is simply too nice a fellow: nobody, not Scribe, not Somma, not Verdi, not the conspirators themselves, gives a reason why there should be a plot against his life, and the love between Riccardo and his best friend's wife, while musi-

cally glorious, does not tie into anything else we are told about either character. What draws Pavarotti to Riccardo, one suspects, is the same chiaroscuro portrait that draws him to Rodolfo and Nemorino: lighthearted men capable of real anguish in the toils of love.

By far the most interesting production of *Un Ballo in Maschera* I have ever seen was that of the Stockholm Opera, which in a sense owns the work (the murder was in their theater). The story was not merely returned to its original Swedish setting, but populated with the real Swedish historical characters. The translation into Swedish, by the nation's poet laureate, interfered less with the flow of the music than any other translation I have ever heard. The king, in the fullness of historical accuracy, sang most of his "public" utterances in French. He was also very, very swish.

"Ma se m'è forza perderti," Riccardo's third-act aria from Verdi's Un Ballo in Maschera, *Metropolitan Opera, 1980*

Charles Osborne in his admirable book on Verdi's operas comments that "to attempt to superimpose the historical Gustavus III onto the character that Verdi has delineated is, of course, immensely harmful to the opera. I have seen a Swedish production in which Gustavus was made to mince about like a revue-sketch homosexual and flirt heavily with Oscar the page. What this has to do with the Riccardo whose great love duet in Act II is, after all, sung not with Oscar but with Amelia, was never made clear." This was, I think, a minority view among those of us who saw that production, though I also think that everyone had at least a little sympathy with the view of Birgit Nilsson, who sang in it, that the concept was a genuine obstacle in the path of a soprano trying to create a convincing Amelia. For me, I must say, it made sense of the opera. We live in a time

when the idea of an AC/DC king delivers only a minor, transient jolt—and the spectacle of the Frenchified Gustav mincing about among the landowners and prelates and military figures of a Swedish court certainly explained the conspiracy to kill him. The production made the operatic reputation of its director, Göran Gentele, and was among the accomplishments that recommended him to the board of the Metropolitan Opera, which presently hired him to be that company's general manager. If Gentele had lived, he would have brought this conception of *Ballo* to New York, and there might have been a real, satisfying scandal.

Pavarotti knows about this production, and greatly admires the tenor who brought it home for Gentele—Ragnar Ulfung, who was part of the group the year Pavarotti was at Glyndebourne. (The two tenors were tennis opponents, and Ulfung taught Pavarotti the difference between an Italian's tolerance for cold weather and a Swede's. Pavarotti, who went without a coat through the European winter—he did wear scarves around his throat—was rather vain of his hardiness. He gave up when he played tennis with Ulfung on a raw day in England, with the temperature in the fifties. At the end of the match, Pavarotti wrapped up in a sweat suit. Ulfung bared his chest and turned to his young son, who had been hosing down the car, and asked the boy to douse him with cold water from the hose to cool him off. Pavarotti does not report who had won the tennis match.) Gentele's and Ulfung's is not an interpretation of Riccardo that Pavarotti could possibly undertake: in all his bulk there is not an effeminate ounce. Nor does he feel any sympathy for Gentele's approach. The production he especially admires is the one John Dexter staged for the Hamburg Opera, with the story set in New Orleans during the Civil War, Riccardo the general commanding the Union forces, Oscar a black slave, Amelia a plantation belle and traitor to her class, her husband an undercover Confederate.

Riccardo for Pavarotti is an uncomplicated man, a true nobleman, distinctly superior to the rest of mankind (note his cheerful scorn for those who believe in prophecy), yet correctly confident in the love of the populace, with the partying instincts to schedule a visit to the oracle by the entire Boston court, for three in the morning, and the gusto to sing to the old witch Verdi's sarcastic fisherman's aria, with its seasick arabesques. He is absolutely torn apart by love—Pavarotti says that the high C in the second act duet is the easiest in the literature, because the passion of the music simply sweeps the voice up to it. And the rest, it should be noted, is relatively easy on the upper voice (the opening aria of love-at-a-distance, "La rivedrà nell'estasi" does not rise above a G-sharp, and the score proceeds for pages with the tenor in the middle and lower sectors of the staff). This does not solve the staging problems, but it gives the director an anchor to windward.

Pavarotti has an extra-special feeling for Riccardo's third act aria "Ma se m'è forza perderti," expressing his determination to save himself and his beloved and his friend by sending both of them far away, where he will never see them again. His first season as a superstar in the United States, after the *Fille du Régiment,* Pavarotti sang a concert in the open air with the New Jersey Symphony, and to my astonishment used this very beautiful but rather intricate and not at all showy aria as an encore piece. Some years later, when the Met restaged *Ballo* in a production Pavarotti honorably denounced in his *Playboy* interview, we came into the second scene of the third act with absolutely no reason to be happy. Suddenly Pavarotti was alone on stage. He fixed what had been a most metronomic conductor with a demanding stare, and he sang "Ma se m'è forza perderti" as he wanted to sing it, leaving the conductor to follow as best he could, and suddenly what had been

a most unsatisfying evening in the opera house became worthwhile.

After *Ballo* came *Favorita,* and then an earlier Verdi, *Luisa Miller* (again in San Francisco). It was an interesting decision by both Pavarotti and the San Francisco management, for this is by no means a tenor showpiece (though the tenor does have the best tune, the affecting "Quando le sere al placido"); the work belongs much more to the soprano and her baritone father (always a key relationship in Verdi) and the two villainous basses (one with the splendid name of Wurm). Moreover, Pavarotti feels that this Rodolfo is essentially "heavier" than Riccardo in *Ballo*—that is, it requires more forceful tones in the lower register

The tormented Fernando in La Favorita, *Metropolitan Opera, 1978 (left), and a year later at the San Francisco Opera for Enzo Grimaldo in* La Gioconda *(overleaf ▶)— rehearsing with Bruno Bartoletti (top), observing colleagues as they practice onstage (bottom), and in the star dressing room, costumed and masked for the Act III ensemble (far right)*

to penetrate what was becoming in Verdi a more complicated orchestration. But he carried it around the world—to Scala in 1976, to Covent Garden and to Spain in 1978, the Met in 1982, Paris in 1983, and Vienna in 1986—and he still lists it in his available repertoire.

Indeed, virtually everything Pavarotti has sung he has done fairly often, mostly, obviously, because managers have rushed to engage him in his new roles. Only twice has he learned an opera and then sung it only in that premiere production. Once it was *Turandot,* for reasons of self-preservation. The other time it was a Verdian oddity, for Rome in 1969, *I Lombardi alla Prima Crociata,* in which he sang the almost sane role of Oronte, the Saracen prince who converts to win the love of a Lombard princess but gets killed in the process (this is dramatically a relatively placid role in this

extremely violent and extremely silly libretto). Though Pavarotti sang his cavatina, his aria, and both of his duets very effectively (there is a pirate recording), the musical high point of this strange piece for me is a duet of two basses, and the brightest of the vocal fireworks is the property of the soprano (the young Renata Scotto, in Rome), who goes off in a fine frenzy about how God does not want these Christians and Muslims to kill each other. Expensive to stage and crude (though fiery) even by the standards of very early Verdi, *I Lombardi* was an opera Pavarotti never had another chance to sing.

One other opera stayed in his repertoire for only three seasons, Massenet's *Manon,* which he did at La Scala in the spring and winter of 1969, with Freni, Peter Maag conducting (the fall revival being obviously a mark of the immense suc-

Katia Ricciarelli as the heroine of Luisa Miller *takes a poisoned cup from Pavarotti as Rodolfo, Covent Garden, 1978*

cess of the spring presentation), and then once more, in Spain, in fall 1970. Massenet's Des Grieux had been one of di Stefano's most admired roles. Unlike di Stefano, Pavarotti sang it only in Italian. Virgil Thomson once reviewed a performance by Ezio Pinza in a French role with the comment that Pinza had not the faintest notion of French style, but being an artist of great taste and distinction in the Italian style he gave total satisfaction; and one imagines that Pavarotti's success as Des Grieux was of that nature. In Modena a while ago, Gerald Fitzgerald regretted to Pavarotti that he had dropped Des Grieux—or, rather, that the world's opera managements had stopped asking him to do it—and the tenor responded by singing "Le Rêve," on the spot, from memory, very beautifully. Clearly, Pavarotti regretted it too.

Future historians of opera will note with admiration the speed and efficiency of Pavarotti's transition from the light lyric to the heavier spinto repertoire once he had determined in the less agitated waters of *Ballo* and *Luisa Miller* that he could —indeed, should—make the move. He added only one role a year—Manrico in *Il Trovatore* in 1975, Cavaradossi in *Tosca* (for the Chicago Lyric Opera) in 1976, Calaf in *Turandot* in 1977. Calaf he sang seven times in San Francisco that season and never again: later he commented that he gave it up because of his feeling that forcing that register would cost him the ability to sing Nemorino, which he wanted to keep beyond all others. There was no question he had been nervous about it from the start; before the first performance, he told Robert Commanday of the San Francisco *Chronicle* that "it has always been a

Luciano Pavarotti as Rodolfo in La Bohème *with three of his many Mimìs: Act I with Madelyn Renée, Australian Opera, Sydney, 1983 (top), Act III with Mirella Freni, Greater Miami Opera, 1978 (opposite), Act IV with Dorothy Kirsten, as staged by the Metropolitan Opera, Tokyo, 1975 (bottom)*

dream of mine that I would sing Calaf. A bad dream." Next for San Francisco came Enzo in Ponchielli's *La Gioconda* in 1979 (another opera where the tenor's role is less than crucial, but he has in "Cielo e mar" the best of the not very impressive bag of tunes: it had been Gigli's role at the Met, and then Tucker's, and then Corelli's).

In 1981 came the gamble with Radames in *Aïda* in San Francisco, less successful in the acoustically dangerous War Memorial Opera House than it would be later in the easier surroundings of Covent Garden, Vienna, and Berlin. It was a triumph in the cavern of Chicago's Lyric Opera, too. In December 1985, Pavarotti opened the Scala season with a new production of *Aïda,* and a few months later he took his Radames to the Met, where he had to fit into that company's unsightly, bargain-basement existing production. ("I found the money for them to do a new production,

too," Pavarotti commented mildly; but a new *Aïda* did not fit into management's plans for spring 1986.) And he will be looking forward to a Paris *Aïda* in 1987. "I am scared already," he said, not joking, in spring 1985. Still, as he once told a *Playboy* interviewer, "I think the best way to be successful is to be constantly scared."

In 1982 there came the eccentric but quite wonderful blustery king in Mozart's *Idomeneo,* an eighteenth-century work that James Levine and Jean-Pierre Ponnelle presented with surprising effectiveness on the larger stage and the larger scale of the Metropolitan, and in 1983 the most dramatic of Verdi's early roles, Ernani, also at the Met, scheduled to be replicated elsewhere but to date, in fact, performed only in New York.

In the first six seasons of the 1980s, Pavarotti sang in forty productions of eleven different operas. Only seven of those productions (five of *La Bohème,* one of *Rigoletto,* and one of *Lucia)* were of operas from the initial batch of five that had been virtually his exclusive repertoire twenty years earlier; eighteen were of works he attempted only after he had tested the waters with *Ballo,* a heavier repertoire than he would have dared in his twenties and thirties. What is most remarkable, I think, is that the voice in this new, somewhat darker and grainier condition is, if anything, even more beautiful than the young man's voice that dazzled us in the 1960s. There was a bad patch in 1981–82, when Pavarotti seemed under serious strain in the upper register, but he came through it triumphantly, and as he neared his fiftieth birthday it was an unalloyed pleasure to be in the same room with him when he sang. It should be noted, as objective evidence of his success in his difficult transition, that the great conductors of the world have been clamoring to work with him: in chronological order in the 1980s, Ozawa, Haitink, Levine, Barenboim, Kleiber, Chailly, Maazel, Mehta. Indeed, of all the major conductors of the last quarter century, the only one with whom Pavarotti has not sung is Leonard Bernstein, and

doubtless the two of them will find a way to fill that gap.

One doubts that Pavarotti will sing any more new roles, beyond his Canio for San Francisco. Not many world-famous artists do, after the age of fifty. Their public, after all, wants to hear them in the roles they are known to do best, and the managers are highly responsive to the public. Pavarotti has, of course, recorded many works he has never attempted on stage, because recording engineers can establish a happier acoustical ambiance for a lighter voice singing a heavier role.

All told, Pavarotti has performed something like two dozen operas, of which the most recent was written and first performed about a decade before his birth. Nor has he been identified, as Callas was, with the revival of a tradition fallen into desuetude until his time—though one can probably credit him with the return of *La Favorita,* which had not been done for some time, and certainly the renewed popularity of *La Fille du Régiment* can be traced in large part to the delight of his "Pour mon âme." If the operatic career were all that Pavarotti had to show, he would be a major figure in the history books of the musical theater, for the remembered (and recorded) quality of his voice and his musicianship, for his longevity as a great singer, for his all but unique mastery of the transition from youth to experience (and here the comparison with Caruso can legitimately be made). But there is something beyond the operatic career, for Pavarotti has become one of those artists—again like Caruso, and also like Heifetz, or Paderewski, or Paganini, or Liszt—whose appeal far transcends their art. We live, as has been sourly noted by many, in the age of the celebrity (brilliantly defined by the historian Daniel Boorstin as "a person who is well-known for his well-knownness"). But there are still a few whose appearance tears up all the cardboard structures of the press agents and TV networks, and reaches directly to the hearts of a heterogeneous public. And Pavarotti is one of those.

Diva and Divo

Montserrat Caballé and Luciano Pavarotti met in 1971 during a series of La Bohèmes *at Barcelona's Gran Teatre del Liceu, the first of many memorable collaborations. "Luciano is the only one, everybody knows that," the soprano says, with disarming candor, adding, "He's something very rare, a kind of genius. You simply cannot give a score or a grade to such perfection. I have many wonderful colleagues whom I love and respect, but Luciano is truly different, unique—so natural, so positive, so clever in a good way, and a friend who always understands. The public, of course, sees us in a frame—a diva and a divo in the stage frame—but, believe me, inside that picture for each other we are something else . . . two very human spirits." This series of photographs (above and overleaf* ► *) were taken in 1979, when Caballé and Pavarotti were in the midst of long rehearsals for the San Francisco Opera's opening-night* Tosca. *At one point, weary of the camera, the tenor playfully disappeared under a towel to escape its lens.*

PERSONA

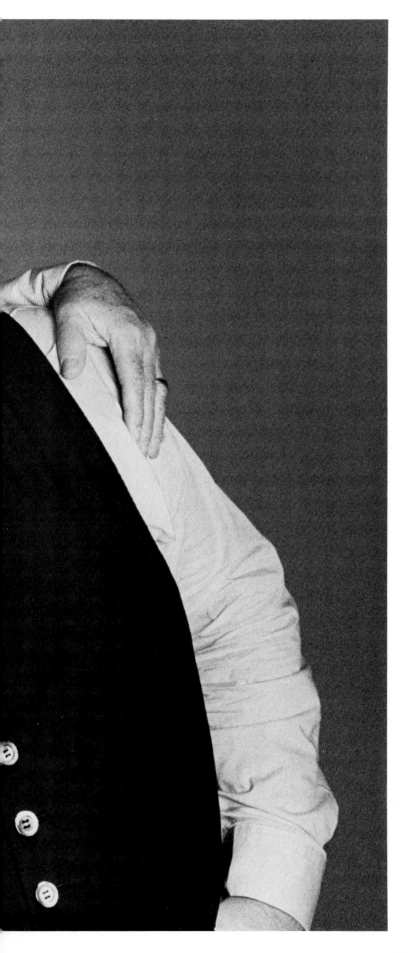

"Luciano Pavarotti!" said Robert DeStefano, the golf pro at the Gardiner's Bay Country Club on Shelter Island, about a hundred miles from New York City. "Sure! When you see him, will you tell him we always use his recipe for spaghetti sauce? I was watching one of those morning talk shows, and he was on, and they asked him about cooking. So he described what he put in his spaghetti sauce, and then he said that he never put it on the fire. When you cook spaghetti sauce, you lose all the flavor, he said. You make it cold. When the spaghetti comes out of the pot, piping hot, you pour the sauce over it. The spaghetti heats the sauce, and you keep all the flavor. I came home last night,

---

With Frank Sinatra, a good friend who has twice shared the bill with Pavarotti at New York's Radio City Music Hall— gala benefits that have raised millions for cancer research
Photograph by Francesco Scavullo

said, 'What are we having for dinner?' and my wife said, 'Spaghetti with your favorite sauce.'"

The connection between culinary accomplishment and opera goes back a long way. We have Tournedos Rossini, and Pêche Melba, and Chicken Tetrazzini. But those were advertised by the restaurateurs who served the great their favorite dishes. There is as yet no famous dish named for Luciano Pavarotti, perhaps because he has made the name a symbol of *alta cucina* without the help of anybody promoting a restaurant. The feeling is that if Pavarotti hadn't been an opera singer, he could have been a celebrity as a chef. We have also had, very prominently in the magazines and newspapers and even occasionally on television, Pavarotti the horseback rider, mounted triumphantly on a handsome, large animal, most spectacularly in 1980 when he rode ahead as Grand Marshal of the Columbus Day parade in New York, resplendent in a broad-brimmed Borsalino and a gorgeous poncho-sized scarf made from fabric handwoven for him by his cousin Lotaria. And Pavarotti the painter, putting the final touches on a street scene while waiting for a call in his dressing room. And Pavarotti the tennis player, truly dominating the net with a large racket. At all times, Pavarotti the celebrity, who is also, and it means a lot to that public that honors celebrity, a regular guy. All true, oddly enough. But it is also true, of course, that Pavarotti lays out his days and his years "to play what he does best"—as Hubert Saal put it in a cover story in *Newsweek* in 1978—"a version of himself in a big Hollywood production called 'The Great Pavarotti.'"

"You know why I grow a beard?" Pavarotti commented recently. "Because I was doing a crossword puzzle in a book, a book called *Strange But True* that gives you little bits of information with the puzzles, and it said that if you start shaving at seventeen and keep shaving every day until you are seventy, you spend two months of your life before the mirror. I thought, 'Let's see how a beard would look. I'd rather spend those two months somewhere else.' And the beard was very good for me. Before, the face [as neutral here as "the voice"] was very uninteresting. And the stage beard was very uncomfortable. Now the face is interesting, and the beard is very good for dukes and poets."

In his discussion of his first big-city success, in London, Pavarotti puts great emphasis on the fact that he was summoned at the last minute to replace Giuseppe di Stefano, who had canceled this engagement as well as his Covent Garden Rodolfos, on the popular TV show "Sunday Night at the Palladium." "The audience," he wrote, "went wild. I think that TV studio audience was more open-minded than some opera audiences and certainly more so than some opera professionals. They had never heard of me, they were not opera lovers, but they went crazy . . .

That one television performance made me known in England." Pavarotti came to the United States too late for the sort of variety show that once gave occasional attention to opera stars, and one suspects that the television appearance that made the difference in America was not of the general-audience shows, not "Today" or "Tonight," both of which made time for Pavarotti after his giant success in *La Fille du Régiment*, but an opera performance, the *Bohème* "Live from the Met" on public television in 1977, the first time since the early days of black-and-white TV that the Metropolitan Opera had telecast a performance.

This was in every way a heartwarming occasion. It was, to begin with, an astonishingly good performance, with both Pavarotti and Renata Scotto at their best. One had not thought of either as an especially convincing actor. Because an opera stage is so big, character creation imposes a very broad style of acting, and requires the suppression of detail effects that might be valid in other contexts. Pavarotti and Scotto both have a tendency toward irrelevant movements of both hands and feet that distract from their characterizations, and can give audiences in the house a feeling that they are *seriously* involved only with their vocal performance. The television camera, with its penchant for closeups, does not notice the movement of extremities. In this *Bohème,* the home screen showed the singers' surprisingly expressive and mobile facial gestures—which are quite invisible to the opera audience, and do indeed demonstrate their artistry (like the artistry of the medieval stonemasons who finished the backs of the statues at the church portals though no mortal would ever see them), their involvement with the characters they portray.

Pavarotti the bearded poet was seductively handsome from the neck up and convincingly grieving when the time came for grief; Scotto was vulnerable and touching. Both sang very beautifully, and voices, as the early pre-electric record-

The Big Parade

Everyone was smiling at New York's Columbus Day Parade in 1980, even the police, for the Grand Marshal was none other than Luciano Pavarotti, who quite incidentally was celebrating his forty-fifth birthday (above). Crowds thronged Fifth Avenue to greet the singer (overleaf top ▶), who did some greeting himself at the official reviewing stand, where a bevy of political bigwigs awaited his arrival—Mario Biaggi, former President Jimmy Carter, Mario Cuomo, and Ed Koch among them (bottom). It was a great day for all, including Maverick, a steed on loan from the New York City Police Department, and no one enjoyed this big parade more than Luciano Pavarotti.

ings show, come over well even on the sort of very limited sound reproduction equipment available on television sets. (For the small fraction of audio fanatics, the opera was simulcast on FM, and of course sounded even better.) And the live performance, or live-on-tape, which is in this context the same, has an immense advantage over filmed opera, because the sound and the picture are being generated together and the voices and lips are always in synch.

The novelty of the occasion and the popularity of the opera combined to give the telecast an audience of more than four million households (more, one notes in passing, than "Today" or "Tonight"). *Opera News,* a publication of the Metropolitan Opera Guild, was permitted to offer a sample issue to the television audience, free of

---

charge, and more than thirty-five thousand people wrote in for it—this at a time when the total circulation of the magazine was under eighty thousand. In New York in 1978, Pavarotti's live recital from the Met tripled the audience for Channel 13, the local Public Television station. Every year since, the Public Broadcasting Service stations have sought to include a Pavarotti performance in their musical series; if they can't get him in an opera, they'll settle for a recital; if they can't get him live, they'll take a film.

Ultimately, it is the recital end of the career that makes Pavarotti a unique phenomenon in the musical-entertainment scene. Other opera singers have, of course, been recitalists. Some, like John McCormack and Elisabeth Schumann, and Lotte Lehmann toward the end of her life, became only occasional participants in opera, with many more engagements in their calendar for solo appear-

ances. But Italian singers do not have the resource of art song available to their French and German colleagues. The *arie antiche,* the seventeenth- and eighteenth-century semi-popular *canzone* that are the staple of the Italian recital, do not hold up very well on repeated use, and the singing of operatic arias to piano accompaniment is considered rather vulgar by the cognoscenti (who are not entirely wrong: the orchestration is inescapably part of the aria). Pavarotti did not attempt a recital until 1973, and then only at the urging of his new manager, Herbert Breslin, who was convinced that Pavarotti's special kind of projection would work particularly well in the psychologically more individual, more one-to-one atmosphere of the concert hall. Everybody was worried about this, and Pavarotti made his first attempt at the new form far from the madding crowd of critics, at William Jewell College in the town of Liberty, Missouri, where a benefactor had endowed a concert series.

Pavarotti liked it, the audience liked it, and Breslin tried again, still relatively cautiously, in Dallas, where if he bombed the noise could be muffled. The crowded hall was another piece of evidence that a recital career was a lively possibility for Pavarotti. That November, Pavarotti was interviewed in Chicago, where he was making a local debut in (of course) *La Bohème,* and said that in addition to his work at the Lyric Opera he hoped some day to give a solo recital in Chicago. The *Tribune* reporter made the mistake of warning him in a kindly way that vocal recitals don't sell, and provoked one of the few examples of belligerence on the Pavarotti ledgers: "My plan," he said flatly, "is to sing here in a concert with the house full. That is my plan. Okay?" And indeed he did, in Louis Sullivan's gorgeous late nineteenth-century Auditorium, which, he said recently, "has the best acoustic I know of any large theater in the world."

These were essentially recitals of art songs, in Italian, with a few operatic excerpts and encore

132

pieces. In London, for example, Pavarotti sang a program that included Beethoven's "In questa tomba oscura," Gluck's "Che farò senza Euridice" (an opera excerpt, but not from an opera Pavarotti could sing), and Liszt's vocally murderous and musically complicated settings of Petrarch sonnets. John Huggins of the London *Times* described the concert as in many ways a throwback to Victorian times, when singers did programs quite like Pavarotti's, and thought it a triumph: "Two hours," he wrote, "of total professionalism, another very Victorian virtue." But in the end, especially as one moved into the larger halls, this was not an art song audience, come to ponder the revelations of a new lieder

Bantering with Johnny Carson during "The Tonight Show" of June 25, 1985, Pavarotti's eleventh guest appearance on the late-night program (left). On the next pages he is shown arriving on the West Coast for another engagement (overleaf opposite ▶) and about to board the private jet that sometimes helps him get to destinations on time (top). We also see what the tenor would have viewed had he flown over Boston's Hatch Memorial Shell on June 27, 1981—some 100,000 music-lovers gathered for one of his concerts (bottom), this one filmed by MGM for a sequence in the motion picture Yes, Giorgio

singer's *Winterreise;* it was a Pavarotti audience, come to bask in the effulgence of his projection. So it was natural for him to sing popular pieces as encores, even Neapolitan pieces like " 'O Sole Mio" and "Torna a Surriento," and it was noted that the audience went even wilder than usual. Di Stefano had unashamedly and very successfully (in both financial and artistic terms) made discs of Neapolitan songs and of Italian pop standards. Now Pavarotti began making records of these materials, partly because he sang such music very well and enjoyed doing it, partly because there was lots of money in it.

Breslin sold out Carnegie Hall for Pavarotti's first New York recital with one small ad in the Sunday *Times:* all the tickets were gone by Wednesday, including well over a hundred seats

133

134

on stage. Increasingly, orchestras began to ask for Pavarotti for their pension fund benefit concerts (the two for the New York Philharmonic were televised, with Zubin Mehta at his most charming; on the first of them, the violinist Itzhak Perlman sang the few bars of the jailer's commentary in the build-up to "E lucevan le stelle" in *Tosca).* Pavarotti sold tickets at the highest prices these orchestras had ever charged. There was ever-increasing publicity: a cover story in *Time* as well as *Newsweek,* a "Sixty Minutes" story, repeated appearances with Johnny Carson and with Phil Donahue (which was where he taught golf pros how to make spaghetti), even a movie, *Yes, Giorgio,* which did not do very well and did not deserve to do very well (it's been fun to watch The Great Pavarotti in real life, but there's not much point in watching him play himself in the guise of a fictional character in a film), but which heightened the feeling that here was someone unlike anyone else. Especially after Pavarotti's Duke in *Rigoletto* in New York's Central Park drew an audience over a quarter million strong onto Sheep's Meadow—the largest crowd in the history of the Met's summer presentations—it became inevitable that the recitals would move out of the traditional concert halls and into the outsize barns, the Masonic temples, convention centers and such that most cities have.

Finally, in August 1984, Pavarotti at Breslin's urging took the plunge, into the sports arena world, at the best known of all of them, Madison Square Garden—in August, which is not prime time for culture. What was offered was a concert with orchestra, divided roughly equally into celebrated operatic arias, popular *canzone* (as orchestrated by Henry Mancini, with whom Pavarotti had made a best-selling record) and pops-concert warhorses for the orchestra alone to give Pavarotti a few minutes to catch his breath. (Several of the orchestral pieces, in a very nineteenth-century tradition, featured a solo flute-player, a gifted young musician from Reggio Emilia, Andrea Griminelli, who also teamed up for some numbers with Pavarotti.) Prices were set ambitiously high, to a $50-per-ticket top, and the place sold out virtually on the day the tickets went on sale, permitting the addition of a duplicate concert in the same place two months later. The first of the two was televised live by PBS in a fund-raising drive, and taped to be shown again during the stations' next campaign. The gate receipts were the highest for any single event in the history of Madison Square Garden. Pavarotti is extremely proud of the sequence *Bohème,* Met recital, Madison Square Garden concert by which he reached the largest paying audience any tenor has ever attracted. "It's like Daniel Boone," he said recently. "I am the pioneer, the first to do these things. Some day there will be others." The financial rewards have been unbelievable. Hasn't changed him a bit.

There are three secrets here—three "mysteries," as the Middle Ages had it, referring to the arcane skills by which professionals make a living.

The one that gets noted most is Pavarotti's conscious and imaginative creation of the persona. "When you put together a *personaggio* for the public," he says, "you have to put in everything—the qualities and the defects. The problem is that the defects the public remembers more." The aspects of the persona that get noticed least are those associated with Pavarotti's very considerable intelligence: the beauty of his Italian diction, for example, and the size of his English vocabulary. "Is not so great," he argues, brushing off a compliment on his English; "if you listen carefully, you notice all the words are from Latin, I still don't know much of the German side of English"—but he also admits that sometimes in Italy, to his embarrassment and occasional annoyance, he finds himself thinking in English because the English word is more clearly denotative than

Strawberry Hill

Luciano Pavarotti has presented song recitals in various settings—concert halls, opera houses, movie palaces, sports arenas—but without question the most beautiful place he ever performed was in the formal gardens of Strawberry Hill, the estate of Barrie and Ada Regan in Hillsborough, near San Francisco. The musical program resembled many another Pavarotti has offered; however, as day turned to evening, all present were swept away by the glorious combination of nature and song. During "Ave Maria" the tips of the trees took on a halo glow from the sun and, unexpectedly, a dove flew over. It was sheer magic, for audience and performers alike. Sharing the stage with Pavarotti, as he has so often, was a cherished associate, pianist John Wustman (above). Other moments from this unforgettable event are on the following pages (overleaf ▶).

140

its more inclusive but less precise Italian equivalent.

In constructing a persona today, the celebrity is largely at the mercy of his interlocutors. Speaking in a filmed interview for "The Today Show" —which was off to spend Easter Week in Rome and was picking up Italian tidbits higgledy-piggledy—Pavarotti noted that Verdi's special position with the Italian people had come because he wrote "at the time of Italian unification, and the generation who lived that experience, you understand, are all dead. People of my father's generation, ninety-nine percent of them do not give any special importance to Verdi, just as they do not know that Mozart was the genius of geniuses and always will be. I know music not because I am Italian but because I was a teacher. But if you

---

Strawberry Hill, September 23, 1979: with pianist John Wustman (top), and with the Regans and wife Adua on occasion of his recital on the grounds of a California estate

---

know music it does not mean you'll be a good singer—I know people who know music and cannot put four notes together, just as I know singers who don't know music. The way singers are trained, there are twenty in the conservatory, and the teachers pick the top three, who then study only singing, not music." One does not often hear Pavarotti talking that way, about the subjects of greatest interest to him, when he appears on television, because television tends to seek out what fits the stereotypes.

The Pavarotti stereotype, of course, starts with the weight, and Pavarotti, wisely or otherwise, has used it himself over the years as part of what people are to remember. In the rash of interviews after the great success of *La Fille du Régiment,* he posed for the accompanying cameramen wearing things like Japanese kimonos that called attention to his bulk (with gold chains around the neck, yet). His old friend Freni says it's useless to look for psychological explanations of why Luciano got so large; the reason is that he just likes to eat. Personally, I saw him overeat only once, after a performance in Chicago, when the late Carol Fox, the manager of that company, took him out for supper with a group of her most important supporters, to a private room in a restaurant, The Italian Village, that was for mysterious reasons Miss Fox's special favorite, and Pavarotti loaded up—no lesser term will do—on some not very good pasta. But there's no doubt that left to his own devices, in the absence of restraint by his doctors or loved ones, he does overeat.

He says himself that the reason lies in the athleticism of his youth: when he was eighteen and nineteen, and not fat, he was a soccer player running up and down the field three and four hours a day, and he worked off a very high food intake. Moving to the less active life of the singer, he did not change his eating habits, and the result was a steady accumulation of bulk. Other aspects of his career also may have something to do with it. Another seriously overweight artist, Marilyn Horne, has talked about the problem of living in hotel rooms: "You're lonely, and you compensate, you order up a quart of ice cream." Pavarotti denies that he gets lonely—but one of the reasons he can make that argument is that he eats out a lot, often enough at banquets associated with the money people of the opera companies.

In the mid-1970s, Pavarotti became tired of being so heavy, and took off eighty-five pounds in less than a year. By then he had grown so large that even this drastic weight loss did not change the persona of the jolly fat man, though it did allow him to do much more of the horseback riding and tennis playing he enjoys. In the 1980s, unfortunately, after his film, he let himself go, to the extent that he began to lose his agility on stage. "When I did *Elisir* in Hamburg," he said regretfully, "only a few years ago, I could jump into the tree on stage, but in Vienna this year I could not have done that." At the weight Pavarotti had acquired by spring 1985, sedentary habits develop. I had been warned that among the hazards of visiting the Pavarottis was a very stupid old German shepherd who thought that unless visitors were accompanied by a member of the family the best thing to do was to bite them. So when I finished an interview session with Luciano and prepared to go across the courtyard to the archive where the newspaper clippings and memorabilia were kept, I asked him to walk me over. "Adua!" he called. "Could you take Martin to the library?" She called back cruelly but necessarily, "Do it yourself. It's good for you to get on your feet."

Las Vegas, March of 1984, with a souvenir he was given before a concert he was to perform at the Riviera Hotel

Pavarotti says that the physical ailments that forced him to cancel a number of opera engagements in spring 1985 were not the result of overweight—"my doctor says I have the blood of a kid; it is just that I think young and I do not want my body to tell me I cannot do the young things I want to do"—but the fact is that he finally put himself on a tough diet, eating only those items approved by his doctor (which include a limited quantity of pasta weighed before cooking on a very precise scale), and, most important, eating alone, joining his family only for black coffee at the end of the meal, so that he is not tempted to graze upon other people's plates. His hope in mid-1985 was to lose no less than a hundred pounds before mid-1986. That would still leave him large, but happier, and no doubt healthier. And it would eliminate the risk that his face, too, might lose its contours, which has not yet happened: indeed, the handsome head on the oversized body has been part of the *personaggio.*

Concerti

Luciano Pavarotti had appeared in concerts before 1973, but never had he given a solo song recital— a lone singer, a pianist, and an audience. This test he first attempted out of the spotlight, in far-off Liberty, Missouri, and at once Pavarotti found the new forum very much to his and his public's liking.

Without doubt, the most nerve-racking recital of his career took place at the Metropolitan Opera House on February 12, 1978, telecast "Live from Lincoln Center," with an audience of twelve million viewers. A few days before, the tenor overcame his apprehension and posed by the poster proclaiming the great event (right). Just before the performance, however, in a cold sweat of fear, Pavarotti worried, "I know they love me now, but will they still love me by the time this concert is over?" In fact, he scored a triumph, becoming one of PBS's most prized attractions.

To date there have also been two "Live from Lincoln Center" telecasts uniting Pavarotti with Zubin Mehta and the New York Philharmonic. With this singer and this conductor rehearsals could only be both serious business and great fun (first overleaf ▶).

HERBERT H. BRESLIN
PRESENTS

LUCIANO PAVAROTTI

JOHN WUSTMAN - Pianist   TENOR

SOLD OUT

GREAT PERFORMERS AT LINCOLN CENTER
METROPOLITAN OPERA HOUSE
SUN. FEB. 12 - 4:00 PM

HERBERT H. BRESLIN INC. 119 W. 57th St. New York, N.Y. (212) 581-1750

Concerti

The extraordinary concert of August 1984 that attracted twenty thousand music-lovers to Madison Square Garden was also telecast by PBS. The appearance gave Pavarotti an opportunity to personally reach more of the public that knows him principally through TV. His colleagues for this event were conductor Emerson Buckley and the New Jersey Symphony Orchestra (◄ second overleaf).

The Metropolitan Opera Centennial Gala of October 22, 1983, was a signal experience, and to conclude this seven-hour marathon of exceptional voices, Leontyne Price and Luciano Pavarotti sang the love duet from Un Ballo in Maschera. The stage had been decorated with a brilliant red drop from Marc Chagall's Die Zauberflöte, and behind the performers sat rows of honored guests, singers of other days, including Zinka Milanov, Erna Berger, Eleanor Steber, Kitty Carlisle, Nell Rankin, and Gabor Carelli, who joined the audience in applauding the ecstatic soprano and tenor (◄ first overleaf).

In August 1985, Pavarotti offered an outdoor concert for fellow citizens of Modena in Piazza Grande, beside the Duomo, a homage to his hometown. For several songs he was accompanied by flutist Andrea Griminelli, a native of Reggio Emilia, and now Pavarotti's frequent collaborator (left).

The second of Pavarotti's mysteries is his intense professionalism. This sort of thing is, I think, an instinct rather than an accomplishment, part of what Pavarotti means when he says that "I was born for this profession; from the moment I went on the stage I knew I should be there." The quality shines brightest not in the opera house—where there are conductors and directors, managers (though these tend to be timid with big-name artists) and colleagues who can insist if not always enforce that a singer will arrive knowing his role, will come on time for rehearsals, and will cooperate in the ensemble—but on the concert stage, where the performer is king, and like a king can demand that his whim is law regardless of the in-

During preparations for a Pavarotti concert at the Market Square Arena in Indianapolis, Indiana, as some of the many loudspeakers are about to fly aloft (opposite), Drew Serb, who designed and owns the equipment used, goes over technical details with Roger Gans, an amplification and sound-effects expert (top). Later, James Lock, an audio wizard from Decca International, oversees the control panel—assisted by Gans— checking volume, balances, and tonal quality (bottom)

convenience to others. In an opera house, moreover, it is important to the people he lives with that an artist cares, for his performance affects all other performances, and if he grows inattentive or sloppy, word of it will get out to colleagues elsewhere and to managers. In the concert setting, especially out in the boondocks far from the musical marketplaces, an artist who is bored with delivering the same program for the fifteenth time can loaf through his night's work in relative safety. I assure you I have seen it done—and by great artists, too.

With Pavarotti, this would be absolutely unimaginable. He gives to every audience, every time, everything he has. At the sports arenas, where a major part of the problem is getting the sound lifelike in a space not well suited for music, he sings a rehearsal the afternoon of a perfor-

146

mance, full out for the full program, enabling the engineers to note the adjustments that must be made at this moment and that to keep his voice and the orchestra correctly balanced. Part of Pavarotti's professionalism is that he takes as much responsibility as he can for how his voice and his performance will sound, all of the time. In the case of the large auditorium and arena concerts, this means a unique attention to the possibilities of electronic amplification. A Pavarotti concert sounds better than anything else that has ever been done in a sports arena, because more care and attention has gone into the sound than anyone else has ever devoted to such matters.

The audio quality at Pavarotti concerts rests on the work of three men: James Lock, the recording director for British Decca, very English, wearing a jacket and tie to sports arena rehearsals; Roger Gans, amplification and sound-effects expert for the San Francisco Opera (which does a certain amount of outdoor work); and Drew Serb, a young, mustachioed San Francisco designer of sound equipment. Pavarotti started his insistence on good sound in large halls as a matter of self-defense, after an overexcited engineer in the Miami Convention Center brought up the sound to the point of feedback and then in terror turned off the system while Pavarotti was singing. For the rest of the evening Pavarotti tried to fill this hemispherical, plushly carpeted, oversized five-thousand-seat hall with his own unassisted voice. "It was miserable," he recalls, adding the singer's special horror: "I could not hear myself."

Not until several days later could Pavarotti be entirely sure he had not done himself permanent damage, and he decided that if he was going to continue auditorium engagements he needed a professional sound man at his side. He put in a call to Lock, the engineer on nearly all his records, who was in Chicago working with Solti and the Chicago Symphony, and Lock caught up with him in Montreal. As it happens, Lock arrived while Pavarotti was holding a press conference, which meant that the world knew about Lock's role in the tenor's concerts from the beginning (Pavarotti saw him enter the room, and called out, "I am very 'appy to see you, Jimmy"). All hell broke loose among the local electrical unions, but Pavarotti was insistent, and each hall or arena now squares its unions in its own way.

For the first engagements with Pavarotti, Lock used recording-studio equipment, which was not entirely satisfactory. In San Francisco, he met Gans and Serb ("God looked down upon us," Lock says), and they formed "an agency: no name, just the Three Musketeers." Their first job was a concert in a large tent in Atlantic City behind the Resorts International hotel/casino, with no place to hang the speakers; they put up a pole before the stage. In the second half of the concert a wind blew up, the tent billowed, the ropes creaked, two thousand members of the audience fled—and Luciano kept right on singing, and it sounded pretty good. Since then, Lock and friends have been *de rigueur* at a Pavarotti concert in a big space. When a local group in the United States wants Pavarotti (the sports arena concerts are invariably benefits for some local cause), they call Herbert Breslin, who negotiates the terms and then tells them that the arena or convention hall will also have to engage Lock. This is done by mail to and from London, with Gans flying in from San Francisco to examine what Lock calls "the venue—if we think the venue is impossible, which hasn't happened yet, we reserve the right to refuse, which would mean that Pavarotti has the right to cancel."

The equipment used is state-of-the-art plus a little: Schoeps microphones from Germany, custom-designed loudspeakers from John Meyer in San Francisco, what Lock calls "sixth generation" amplification equipment from Drew Serb. Gans designs the layouts, which include shallow umbrellas ("plates") spotted in the orchestra to reflect the sound down to their mikes (and keep it out of Pavarotti's), and speakers facing in all di-

148

The Great Team

Grisi and Mario, Melba and De Reszke, Farrar and Caruso, Flagstad and Melchior—to these add Sutherland and Pavarotti (above), glorious voices made more glorious through association. The team of Sutherland and Pavarotti was born in 1965, less than four years after the tenor's professional debut in opera, a Lucia di Lammermoor for the Greater Miami Opera. The rest is history at opera houses in London, Australia, San Francisco, Chicago, and New York. Countless London/Decca records document the duo's feats, and on occasion they have given spectacular joint concerts—the first in January 1979, telecast "Live from Lincoln Center." That was a night of musical joy, ovations, and floral tributes that recalled the Golden Age of Singing (overleaf ▶).

149

152

rections. The equipment belongs to Serb, "all new technology, I don't know anyone else who uses it," and it arrives in a sixty-four-foot monster tractor-trailer truck with his name on the sides. Installing the system takes eleven or twelve hours; Pavarotti's rehearsal is normally three in the afternoon, so Serb's crew gets to work immediately after the previous night's attraction leaves the arena (then they dismantle right after Pavarotti finishes, to get the truck back on the road by five or six the next morning: professionalism exacts a price from many people).

What the audience receives is in most parts of the hall something as close as can be imagined to the real sound of orchestra and voice, close up —maybe a little loud, but not at all artificial. Lock

---

During the first Sutherland-Pavarotti concert in 1979, television director Kirk Browning of "Live from Lincoln Center" watches multiple screens to select the shot to be transmitted to home screens (top), and a bow on the stage of Avery Fisher Hall by the four participating musical artists—soprano Madelyn Renée, conductor Richard Bonynge, and the Great Team (bottom)

---

does an occasional double check, arriving in time to catch Pavarotti's first rehearsal with orchestra, which is in a concert hall the day before the concert, to make sure he has the real live sound in his ears when he pulls the levers at his console. One other singer has bought the services of Lock & Co. Placido Domingo, who was engaged for the Miami Convention Center, had heard of Pavarotti's troubles on his first appearance there and also of Pavarotti's triumphant return two years later with the new sound system. He called and asked Luciano whether there would be any objection to his using Pavarotti's audio team and their equipment, and Pavarotti of course said he would be delighted.

Pavarotti hears himself in the arena through two very small speakers at his feet when he stands at the mikes. And it is "mikes," plural: a pair of them, about eight inches apart, each covering a hemisphere of sound. For the system to work right, Pavarotti must stand absolutely motionless with his mouth between the two of them. "It's not a problem," he says; "anyone who has made recordings can do it." But the result is that he is completely deprived of body English in putting over a song. The voice must do all the work, and it does.

The voice, and the third mystery: Pavarotti's intense feeling for his audiences, which they understand and love. I had never been to one of these sports arena concerts before I signed on to write the text for this book, and I told Doubleday that I would have to see and hear one of them before I could undertake the job. If the experience turned my stomach, and I thought it might, I was out. Breslin, whom I have known since he was a high school teacher with an impossible dream of managing musical artists, confidently urged me on; he couldn't be sure I would like it, but he was quite certain it wouldn't nauseate me. So I tootled off to Philadelphia, to the Spectrum, where the Flyers play hockey and the 76ers play basketball, and banners hanging from the rafters attest to their championships. I watched the afternoon rehearsal in the empty arena, the expert veteran conductor Emerson Buckley owlishly licking into shape the free-lance orchestra of the Opera Company of Philadelphia, Lock sometimes standing at his consoles and sometimes wandering the far reaches of the huge hall, Pavarotti perched on a high stool, listening to himself and the orchestra very intently, beating time, checking the sounds, conferring every so often with Buckley.

Then I went back that night, to watch the dressed-up contributors to the Opera Company of Philadelphia (the beneficiary of the benefit) enter down the long, steep aisles of the arena and sit on the floor where usually the athletes frolic; and to mingle a bit with the very different audience in the less expensive seats, mostly but by no means exclusively Italian, for whom this evening was something they would some day brag about to their grandchildren. The concert was half an hour late in starting; these arenas are not designed to fill up at just one given moment, and every seat was not just sold but occupied. The orchestra had been sitting for a while on its brightly lit raised platform when Buckley, bent and bald, with white goatee and mustache, arrived with Pavarotti, resplendent now in white tie and tails. Pavarotti was adding to his printed program the "Ingemisco" from Verdi's *Requiem* in honor of Eugene Ormandy, conductor emeritus of the Philadelphia Orchestra, who had died that day. He sang it exquisitely, no sobs, no scoops, and it is a very difficult aria, then shook his head at the applause that followed and left the stage. Pavarotti had sung with Ormandy only once (Or-

Lights! Action! Master Class!: Pavarotti as teacher during a stint at the Juilliard School in New York, January 1979, an event television later made available to the world at large. The pianist is John Wustman, the student Christine Radman

mandy's operatic experience had been restricted to *Fledermaus* at the Met), but he knew Ormandy was a major musical figure who was entitled to mourning; and he mourned.

The rest of the program was, in reality, as serious-minded as the "Ingemisco." Jimmy Lock has talked with Pavarotti about why these concerts are so important to him (after all, Pavarotti in effect pays half the cost of Lock and his crew and equipment, and it's many thousands of dollars a night). "He feels," Lock reports, "that he's touching an audience here way beyond what he can reach in opera houses." For this audience, then, he sings the two big tenor tunes from *Rigoletto* (the audience gasps with glee at the big-guitar orchestral opening chords of "La donna è mobile"), Edgardo's third-act aria from *Lucia,* "Ah, sì, ben mio" and "Di quella pira" from *Trovatore,* "Amor ti vieta" from Giordano's *Fedora* and the big number from *Pagliacci*—and six Italian *canzo-*

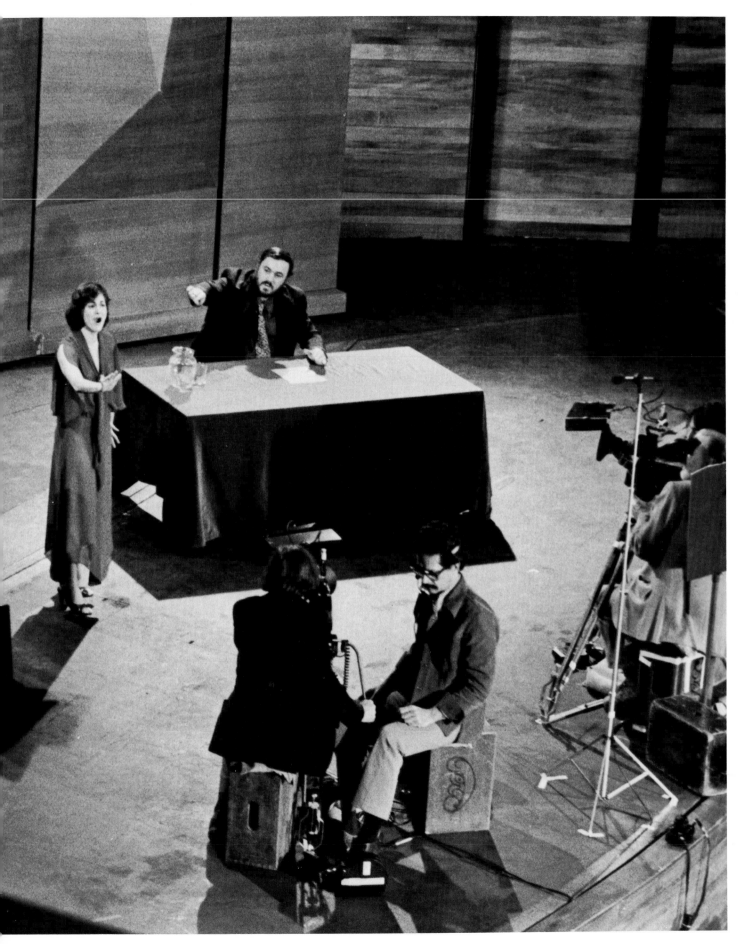

nette. Everything is done *a punto,* a touch rare but not bloody, the socko high notes held but not exaggerated. On each entrance there was a gleeful acceptance of the applause from the audience, and a special bow to the people who sat behind the platform in the oval auditorium (in concert halls where stage seats are sold, Pavarotti will usually sing one encore facing this group). This is not the audience that goes to "arts" events; it is an audience Pavarotti is reaching, on his own motion, as the great tenors of the 1930s and '40s reached out through radio to his father and his father's friends. No question this Philadelphia audience was moved: nineteen thousand of them stood and cheered and cheered for encores, and Pavarotti loved them for it.

George Kalinsky says that the wildest enthusiasm he ever saw at Madison Square Garden, where he is official photographer, was for the first Pavarotti concert there; it beat out the Michael Jackson Victory Tour, which was the same summer. "In terms of intensity the Pavarotti concert was in the top five events that we've ever had in this building. The sound of the people, the aliveness of that audience, the tone of the arena—especially during the encores—it was a crescendo of excitement you could compare only to the evenings when the Knicks were winning their championships."

This was not in truth an occasion for the sophisticated critic. Many years ago at a recording session of *Norma,* I let slip to Lady Troubridge, who was a groupie for Tullio Serafin when not posing for word portraits by Radclyffe Hall, that large stretches of *Norma* bored me. She told Serafin, of course, and as he walked into the next session he stopped by my chair and said in Italian, "You don't like Bellini? God will punish you." I felt I was committing a similar blasphemy by attending this occasion in a skeptical, almost sociological mode. But certainly I did not find it offensive: the fact was that, in a somewhat different way, I was moved, too. I came home and began

telling my wife about it, and she said, "You really *liked* it, didn't you?" And I said, "Yes, I did." I had been part of Pavarotti's audience; he had been singing for *me;* and if I had gone to the stage door afterwards, as hundreds did, he would have signed my program.

There is one other audience that Pavarotti cherishes: the young artists, those who are studying as he did, alternately worshiping and distrusting their teachers, smuggling themselves somehow into as many performances as they can hear, and wondering how they are going to get started. "Master class," Pavarotti said jokingly, entering into his televised Juilliard teaching episode. "The word by itself already scare me . . . The TV here gives a lot of public-

---

---

ity to these students, and I hope it doesn't take any credit away from me." But he was serious about helping these kids, if he could. One of the students in the master class, Madelyn Renée, became Luciano's only private pupil, working also as his personal secretary until she moved on to a full-time career in 1985; a mezzo, she has sung the beauteous Helen of Offenbach's *La Belle Hélène* in Paris, Zerlina in *Don Giovanni* in Berlin, and Siébel in Ken Russell's travesty *Faust* for Vienna.

Like many people who have done well in the world, Pavarotti believes in the route he followed, which means the competition with the prize of a public performance. And such matters were particularly in his mind in 1979, the year of the Juilliard classes, when he was filling out his book for 1981 and thinking of the twentieth anniversary of his own debut. Among those trying to

engage him for the 1981 season was Margaret Anne Everitt, general director of the Opera Company of Philadelphia. Pavarotti had sung several times for one of the two predecessor companies of this organization, and especially liked the Philadelphia Academy of Music, the oldest surviving opera house in the United States, built before the Civil War, and acoustically still one of the best. He had never sung for Everitt, and there was no way she could afford both his fees and a production to his standards. But just because the company was struggling and half-new, it could offer what the Teatro Municipale in Reggio Emilia had offered two decades earlier: the promise of a performance engagement for the winners of a competition. Between them, Everitt and Pavarotti cooked up The Opera Company of Philadelphia/ Luciano Pavarotti International Voice Competition.

This would not be for absolute beginners, as the Emilian competition had been. Reggio Emilia is a provincial city with a bandbox of an opera house that seats eleven hundred people, while Philadelphia is the fourth largest city in the United States, with an opera house larger than La Scala or Covent Garden, that seats more than twenty-eight hundred and has been for a hundred and thirty years home to a great operatic tradition. It is no kindness to beginners to ask them to fill that much space with their voices, or to reach for the level of expectation of a Philadelphia audience. Still, Pavarotti set a ceiling age of thirty-five for men and thirty-three for women, and a requirement that their experience should not include engagement by a major company. The prize would be a performance with Pavarotti himself, who would sing the tenor lead, which would guarantee the winners an audience—as it turned out, indeed, the largest audience public television has ever gathered for an opera, the combination of Pavarotti, *Bohème* (again), and contest being irresistible.

The stage director, very important for kids, was no less than Gian Carlo Menotti. The coach was Antonio Tonini, a veteran *maestro* at La Scala, who had been the accompanist for Pavarotti's audition in Milan many years before, and had recently worked with him in his preparation for his first Radames in *Aïda.* Tonini, whom Pavarotti made one of the jury that would choose the winners, would take responsibility for their stylistic security in performance. The conductor would be another grand old-timer, Oliviero de Fabritiis, a dominant figure at the Rome Opera for half a century; this *Bohème* would be, in fact, his swan song, his last engagement before his death only a few months later.

Five hundred singers applied, from all over the world, and Pavarotti made time to hear them in widely scattered auditions. The finals were in Philadelphia itself, and produced two major discoveries: Mary Jane Johnson and Susan Dunn. Miss Johnson, a blond voice teacher from a small Texas college with virtually no professional experience, is now singing starring roles in great houses in the United States and Europe. Pavarotti was the only one of the judges who thought her a winner, he recalls, and finally he said to his fellow judges, "This competition is a democracy, but it carries my name, and with my vote she wins." Miss Dunn rose to public prominence a little later, substituting for Montserrat Caballé in the Verdi *Requiem* at New York's Carnegie Hall for the Richard Tucker Foundation; and then on to an Aïda at La Scala. Both were featured in "Pavarotti Plus!" the television show Luciano organized to showcase for a large public a group of significant American singers.

For the competition that came to fruition in spring 1986, for Pavarotti's silver jubilee, there were seventy-seven finalists singing in Philadelphia in the period September 26 to October 7, 1985. This sort of thing costs endless money, to fly in so many candidates, give them room and

Prize Song

Winning the Opera Company of Philadelphia/Luciano Pavarotti International Voice Competition has become a goal of aspiring young singers throughout the world. European auditions for the second competition were held in the Teatro Comunale of Modena during winter 1985 (above), with the finals taking place at the Academy of Music in Philadelphia the subsequent fall (overleaf ▶). Winners included American mezzo-soprano Alteouise DeVaughn (top left) and Italian tenor Bruno Beccaria (bottom left). Principal judges, as they had been for the first competition in 1981, were Margaret Anne Everitt, general director of the Opera Company of Philadelphia, Antonio Tonini, and Pavarotti (center). Among those winning in 1981 were American soprano Mary Jane Johnson (top right) and Bulgarian bass Laszlo Polgár (bottom right), who were later featured as Musetta and Colline in Pavarotti's Emmy-winning telecast of La Bohème, *staged by Gian Carlo Menotti.*

board, pay the orchestra, hire the hall, host the parties, etc. Pavarotti himself in effect pays many of these bills, donating his time and performances, singing the benefit concerts, luring the television money, and helping out in the acquisition of corporate sponsors. One of the objections to the first competition was that because Pavarotti was singing in the performances there wasn't any opening for a tenor under the main tent (though in fact one of the tenor winners, Dénes Gulyás, now sings at the Metropolitan, and major roles, too), so in 1986 there were three works: a Verdi *Requiem* and a *Ballo in Maschera* with Pavarotti himself in the cast, and *Bohème* again, with Pavarotti cheering from the other side of the foot-

---

Fiamma Izzo D'Amico in La Bohème *with Luciano Pavarotti, her prize as a winner of the 1986 Opera Company of Philadelphia/Luciano Pavarotti Voice Competition. They appeared together in Philadelphia and in Modena, performances marking the silver anniversary of the tenor's professional debut, April 29, 1961*

lights. In 1987–88, several of the winners will appear in Philadelphia's production of Bellini's *La Sonnambula;* Pavarotti hopes to be present for this one, too, in the audience.

Pavarotti cares, much more than one would expect, about what happens in Philadelphia. As he travels around the world, he still lives in hotel rooms and spends a lot of time watching television, musical programs where available. If he hears a singer he likes, he gets on the phone to Breslin and asks him to check this artist out, see if he wishes to become part of "my competition."

Away from his audiences, Pavarotti is not ebullient. He answers questions precisely and intelligently, and when he volunteers information that goes beyond the four corners of the question, you can always see the chain of reasoning that led him there. He sits at his desk (really a table, in Modena and in New York: he does not like having things in drawers), and sharpens a pencil with a big Swiss army knife, and answers quickly because he is quick-witted and honest and never has to worry about what he said before in answer to some similar question. Pavarotti does not create fables. He drinks adulation when on stage, but does not seem to wish it —let alone demand it—in a private setting. His daughters are easy with him and tease him in the manner of upper-middle-class young ladies everywhere (the Pavarottis are rich, of course, but during the years when the girls were acquiring their attitudes Luciano's net was upper middle class). Luciano's father, always "Babbo," wanders circumferentially, a delegate from another world to the luxe of his son's present life, clearly Luciano's best friend. But there are lots of friends, especially in Modena, where it is not just a case of people who went to school with Pavarotti, but of people he will tell you he went to school with. And Adua his wife, like her mother-in-law before her—but much more decoratively, partly because this is one of the things you can buy with money, partly because she was always something of a beauty—presides over the family.

The house is full of gifts and souvenirs—cushions embroidered with the symbols of Pavarotti's roles, portraits, decorated handkerchiefs and scarves. Adua and her secretary answer the mail. When home, Luciano rides a bicycle around the roads of his property, and rides horses when he gets his weight down a little, and works at least a little every day, learning new songs for recordings or for concert tours, reviewing roles he has contracted to sing, reading. He talks a great deal on the telephone, especially on a portable cordless, a favorite toy that he loves to carry around with him.

Every so often, a voice teacher in the Emilian region or one of its neighbors calls to ask Luciano if he could make time to hear a pupil, and if he's home he almost always does. (Among Pavarotti's

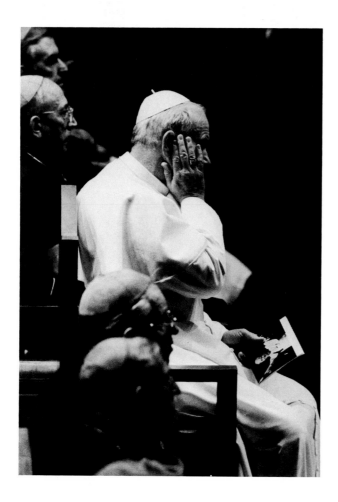

As His Holiness Pope John Paul II listens (above), Luciano Pavarotti and tenor Frank Little (right) perform during a concert offered in the pontiff's honor at Holy Name Cathedral in Chicago during the fall of 1979. Pavarotti performed the Ave Maria of Schubert and, with Little, Franck's Panis Angelicus

few fantasies is that he will some day find a young tenor "of good quality" whom he would teach himself.) Sometimes the Pavarottis dine with friends, or Luciano takes a daughter to the opera in nearby Bologna, or they catch a concert or a movie. Movies with musical referents are favorites: Pavarotti hugely enjoyed and admired *Amadeus.* In the summer, there is the seaside home in Pesaro, with its large swimming pool and a parade of guests. But, of course, Pavarotti is away most of the year, living in hotels, most fre-

quently alone. "If a week after you leave 'ome you get 'omesick," he says, "you should not be in this business. I do not get 'omesick. I have my work to do, music, colleagues—and great cities to see." Pavarotti was born not only for the stage but for tourism: he is a man of extensive, quirky curiosities.

Some commentators feel that Pavarotti (or, rather, Breslin, who is easier to blame) has been greedy, that he has pushed solo fees over the limit of the payable, placing an unnecessarily low ceiling on what can be paid to others in an enterprise where he is active, and setting unreasonably high goals for the fund-raisers. Managers, by and large, don't feel that, because they see the difference in the box office not only for individual productions but for the sale of season subscriptions when Pavarotti is on the schedule, and also because they know that by the traditions of the past, the Carusos and Chaliapins, what Pavarotti receives is a reasonable match for his extraordinary popularity. "A truly good tenor," Kurt Herbert Adler once said—a conductor and impresario paying tribute—"is the best box office."

In the end, Caruso's contribution was the packed houses the Metropolitan Opera enjoyed not only while he was in the casts but through the 1920s, after his death—that, and a new middle-class habit of purchasing and repeatedly listening to vocal recordings. Caruso got the tired businessman accustomed to going to the opera and playing records for his friends. Similarly, the books will not close for many years on Luciano Pavarotti's contribution. Obviously, many who come to hear Pavarotti will not come for anything else, but in the cult following of a great entertainer like Luciano Pavarotti there is always a saving remnant, the converts not just to his aura but to his art. On the twenty-fifth anniversary of his almost accidental debut, Luciano Pavarotti still cares most of all about that art, and the seriousness of his purpose makes all else sweet.

CAREER CHRONOLOGY AND RECORDED REPERTORY

Curtain call after Tosca *at La Scala, Milan, 1980, with Raina Kabaivanska and conductor Seiji Ozawa sharing the cheers*

Opera Chronology

This chronology of Luciano Pavarotti's stage career spans twenty-five years and over a thousand performances, from the tenor's debut in *La Bohème* at the Teatro Municipale in Reggio Emilia, on April 29, 1961, to the silver anniversary of that historic performance at the Teatro Comunale in Modena on April 29, 1986. The information was gathered from programs, posters, brochures, and clippings saved by the tenor through the years, now preserved in an archive at his home in Modena. This data was then double-checked with all the theaters at which Pavarotti has sung, most often with total success, but not always. The exact dates of Pavarotti's debuts at La Scala, Milan, the Teatro di San Carlo of Naples, and Genoa's Teatro Margherita could not be documented by those theaters. At each he sang on short notice, as a replacement, and somehow his appearance as the young unknown was not registered in official company records. No evidence of a *Rigoletto* in San Remo could be found, though Pavarotti recalls the performance, and the cast of another *Rigoletto* in Bari eluded every search. Happily, most theaters could supply full casts and dates, and memories of colleagues further helped make these listings as complete and accurate as humanly possible. In effect, this chronology sums up, at least factually, Pavarotti's work in opera, but in so doing, it also celebrates the many singers, conductors, and theaters that have been part of the Pavarotti career.

1960–61

April 29
LA BOHÈME
A. Pellegrini/Gianotti/Savridi,
  Bellesia/Iotti;
Mattioli, De Ambrosis, Nabokov;
Molinari-Pradelli/Sabbioni/Magiera
Teatro Municipale, Reggio Emilia (2)
Teatro Comunale, Modena (1)

1961–62

September 14
LA BOHÈME
Carteri, Davini;
Iori, Carbonari, Novelli;
Ferraris
Teatro Comunale del Giglio, Lucca (2)

November 1
RIGOLETTO
Ferracuti, Bortoluzzi;
Meliciani, Ventriglia;
Balardinelli
Teatro Comunale, Carpi (2)

December 3
LA TRAVIATA
Zeani;
Sereni;
Gracis
National Theater, Belgrade (1)

January 24
LA BOHÈME
Carteri, Manni Iottini;
Iori, De Ambrosis, Riccò/Ventriglia;
Rapalo/Magiera
Teatro Municipale, Reggio Emilia (2)
Teatro Comunale, Modena (2)

March 4
RIGOLETTO
Fusco, Mongelli;
P. Guelfi, Novelli;
Gerelli
Teatro Grande, Brescia (1)

March 15
RIGOLETTO
D'Angelo, Zannini;
Bastianini, Campi;
Serafin
Teatro Massimo, Palermo (4)

May 9
RIGOLETTO
Ferracuti, Cattelani;
MacNeil, Ferrin;
Molinari-Pradelli
Teatro Margherita, Genoa (2)

1962–63

October 9
LA TRAVIATA
Moffo;
Fioravanti;
Savini
Teatro Astra, Forlì (1)

October 14
RIGOLETTO
Cast unavailable
Teatro Piccinni, Bari (1)

October 23
RIGOLETTO
Guglielmi, Di Stasio;
Meliciani, Foiani;
Guarnieri
Teatro Sociale, Rovigo (2)

December 27
RIGOLETTO
Benvenuti, Casadei;
Protti/D'Orazi, Di Stasio;
Morelli
Teatro Duse, Bologna (1)

January 10
RIGOLETTO
Guglielmi, Vighi;
Fioravanti/Protti, Bergamonti;
Campori
Teatro Municipale, Piacenza (2)

January 18
LUCIA DI LAMMERMOOR
Zeani;
Forgione, Gaetani;
Guarnieri
Nederlandse Opera: Amsterdam,
  Utrecht, Den Haag,
  Rotterdam (5)

February 5
RIGOLETTO
Vanni, Vighi;
Cappuccilli/Meliciani, Foiani;
Marini
Teatro Sociale, Mantua (3)

February 13
LA BOHÈME
Zeani/Otta, Leoni;
D'Orazi, Mineo, Maddalena;
Morelli
Teatro Grande, Brescia (3)

February 24
LA BOHÈME
Carlyle/Jurinac, Coertse/
  Lotte Rysanek;
Wächter, Braun/Evans, Guthrie/Cava;
Hollreiser/Prêtre
Staatsoper, Vienna (2)

March 31
LA TRAVIATA
Carteri;
Alberti;
Rapalo
Teatro Massimo, Cagliari (2)

April 27
RIGOLETTO
Coertse, Lilowa;
Bastianini, Kreppel;
Verchi
Staatsoper, Vienna (1)

April 28
LA BOHÈME
Tyler, Van Doesburg;
Bijnen, Van der Bilt, Van den Berg;
Bauer-Theussl
Stadsschouwburg, Tilburg (1)

May 7
MADAMA BUTTERFLY
Yamaguchi, Di Stasio;
Pasella, Vezzosi;
Annovazzi
Grand Opera House, Belfast (3)

May 27
RIGOLETTO
M. Rinaldi, Di Stasio;
Cappuccilli, Clabassi/Mazzoli;
Ziino
Gaiety Theatre, Dublin (5)

July 4
RIGOLETTO
Ferracuti, Contigiani;
Cappuccilli, Sisti;
Boccaccini
Arena della Fiera, Ancona (2)

1963–64

September 21
LA BOHÈME
Carlyle, Vaughan/Collier;
Glossop, Ronald Lewis, Robinson;
Sillem
Royal Opera, London (5)

October 19
LA BOHÈME
Alper/Aydan, Sökmen/Sergen;
Yildiz, Gurkoc/Köpük, Iktu/
 Girginkoc;
De Rosa
Devlet Tiyatrosu, Ankara (2)

October 23
RIGOLETTO
Laszlo, Komlossy;
Radnay, Body;
Kerekes
Hungarian State Opera, Budapest (1)

October 26
LA TRAVIATA
Matyas;
Palocz;
Kerekes
Hungarian State Opera, Budapest (1)

November 16
LA TRAVIATA
Zeani;
Cappuccilli;
Wolf-Ferrari
Gran Teatre del Liceu, Barcelona (1)

January 21
LA BOHÈME
Scotto/Benetti, Vanni;
Stecchi, Bordoni, Bergamonti;
Parenti
Teatro Sociale, Mantua (3)

February 6
MADAMA BUTTERFLY
Stella, Cattelani;
Basiola/Mazzini, Scarlini;
De Fabritiis/Machì
Teatro Massimo, Palermo (4)

February 23
LA BOHÈME
Carteri, Fusco;
Basiola, Meletti, Cava;
Scaglia
Teatro di San Carlo, Naples (1)
[Pavarotti recalls his Naples debut taking
place in March, after an engagement in
Reggio Calabria. The Teatro di San Carlo
has no record of the tenor ever singing in
La Bohème on its stage, conceding he may
have appeared in the final of three
performances during February, replacing the
indisposed Gianni Raimondi. There are no
records for March performances of La
Bohème in Naples. The date given here is
that of the final La Bohème of the season
recorded by the theater.]

February 29
MADAMA BUTTERFLY
Amedeo, Urano;
Forgione, De Julis;
Morelli
Teatro Comunale "F. Cilèa,"
 Reggio Calabria (1)

April 10
LA BOHÈME
Scotto, Zanolli;
Bruscantini, Borgonovo, Cava;
Capuana
Teatro Margherita, Genoa (3)

May 19
LA BOHÈME
Tosini, Sinnone;
D'Orazi, Oro, Mazzoli;
Annovazzi
Gaiety Theatre, Dublin (4)

May 23
LA TRAVIATA
M. Rinaldi;
G. Taddei/Bardelli;
Guarnieri
Gaiety Theatre, Dublin (4)

July 24
IDOMENEO (Idamante)
Janowitz/L. Elias, Tarrés;
Richard Lewis, Taylor, Hughes;
Pritchard
Glyndebourne Festival (12)

1964–65

October 20
IDOMENEO (Idamante)
Stich-Randall, Berowska;
Richard Lewis, Mollet, Olsen;
Baud-Bovy,
Grand Théâtre, Geneva (5)

December 1
LA TRAVIATA
Fabbri;
Olsson;
Martelli
Koninklijke Vlaamse Opera,
 Antwerp (1)

Arrigo Pola with pupils Bindo Verrini, Pavarotti, 1957; with Tullio Serafin, Palermo Rigoletto;
in Lucia di Lammermoor *with Virginia Zeani, Holland; Pinkerton in* Madama Butterfly, *Palermo*

January 15
RIGOLETTO
M. Rinaldi/Núñez-Albanese,
  Bortoluzzi/Antonini;
Cappuccilli/Iori, Foiani/Uto;
Bartoletti
Teatro Municipale, Reggio Emilia (3)
Teatro Comunale, Mirandola (1)
Teatro Comunale, Modena (2)
Teatro Comunale, Ferrara (2)

February 7
LA TRAVIATA
Freni;
D'Orazi;
Patanè
Teatro Comunale, Modena (1)

February 15
LUCIA DI LAMMERMOOR
Sutherland;
Sordello, Cross;
Bonynge
Greater Miami Opera (3)
Fort Lauderdale Opera (1)

March 15
LA TRAVIATA
Scotto;
Mittelmann/Glossop/O. Kraus;
Cillario
Royal Opera, London (7)

April 28
LA BOHÈME
Freni, Martino;
Sereni, Maffeo, Vinco;
Karajan
Teatro alla Scala, Milan (1)

May 26
LA SONNAMBULA
Sutherland, Woodland;
Rouleau;
Bonynge
Royal Opera, London (5)

July 15
L'ELISIR D'AMORE
Harwood/Elkins/Mammen, Yarick/
  Mammen/Hayman;
Allman/Maconaghie/Opthof, Malas/
  Rouleau;
Weibl/Krug
The Sutherland Williamson
  International Grand Opera Company
Her Majesty's Theatre: Melbourne (3),
  Adelaide (2), Sydney (7),
  Brisbane (1)

July 20
LA TRAVIATA
Sutherland/Mammen;
Opthof/Allman;
Bonynge/Krug
The Sutherland Williamson
  International Grand Opera Company
Her Majesty's Theatre: Melbourne (3),
  Adelaide (2), Sydney (4)

July 28
LUCIA DI LAMMERMOOR
Harwood/Sutherland;
Opthof/Allman, Cross/Malas/
  Rouleau;
Bonynge
The Sutherland Williamson
  International Grand Opera Company
Her Majesty's Theatre: Melbourne (3),
  Adelaide (1), Sydney (1),
  Brisbane (2)

August 3
LA SONNAMBULA
Sutherland/Harwood, Harwood/
  Yarick/Mammen;
Rouleau/Malas;
Bonynge
The Sutherland Williamson
  International Grand Opera Company
Her Majesty's Theatre: Melbourne (5),
  Sydney (5)

1965–66

December 9
RIGOLETTO
M. Rinaldi, Lazzarini/Di Stasio;
Glossop, Zaccaria;
Molinari-Pradelli
Teatro alla Scala, Milan (6)

January 27
LA BOHÈME
Freni/Novelli, Galli/Leoni;
G. Guelfi/Panerai, Maffeo, Vinco/
  Zaccaria;
Sanzogno
Teatro alla Scala, Milan (3)

March 26
I CAPULETI E I MONTECCHI
Scotto;
Aragall, Petri/Zaccaria, Giacomotti;
Abbado
Teatro alla Scala, Milan (5)

Arrival for U.S. debut, Miami; as Alfredo in London La Traviata; *Elvino to Joan Sutherland's Amina, Royal Opera* La Sonnambula

April 24
LA BOHÈME
Güden, Rothenberger;
Kerns, Holecek, Ganzarolli;
Klobučar
Staatsoper, Vienna (1)

June 2
LA FILLE DU RÉGIMENT
Sutherland, Sinclair;
Malas;
Bonynge
Royal Opera, London (7)

June 24
I CAPULETI E I MONTECCHI
M. Rinaldi;
Aragall, Petri, Monachesi;
Abbado
Holland Festival: Den Haag,
    Amsterdam, Rotterdam, Utrecht (6)

July 31
LA TRAVIATA
Zeani;
D'Orazi;
Bartoletti
Terme di Caracalla, Rome (5)

1966–67

September 8
LA BOHÈME
Freni, Sinnone;
Scalco, Mori, Solomonov;
Magiera
Teatro Comunale of Modena:
    Narodno Pozoriste, Sarajevo (2)

October 18
RIGOLETTO
Guglielmi, Bonato;
Schiavi, Zerbini;
Wolf-Ferrari
Teatro Donizetti, Bergamo (3)

November 19
RIGOLETTO
Scotto, Bortoluzzi;
Paskalis, Washington/Pugliese;
Giulini
Teatro dell'Opera, Rome (7)

December 16
RIGOLETTO
Scotto, Laghezza;
Paskalis, Washington;
Giulini
Teatro Comunale, Florence (4)

December 30
RIGOLETTO
M. Rinaldi/Guglielmi, Lane/Bonato/
    Di Stasio/Maddalena;
Glossop, Zaccaria;
Molinari-Pradelli/Zamboni/Gavazzeni
Teatro alla Scala, Milan (16)

February 16
L'ELISIR D'AMORE
Pauli, Grigolato;
Bordoni, Dara;
Masini
Teatro Comunale, Modena (2)

April 8
I CAPULETI E I MONTECCHI
M. Rinaldi;
Aragall, Petri, Monachesi;
Abbado
Teatro dell'Opera, Rome (5)

June 18
LA TRAVIATA
Sgourda;
Mittelmann;
Erede
Opernhaus, Zürich (1)

June 24
LA FILLE DU RÉGIMENT
Sutherland, Sinclair;
Malas;
Bonynge
Royal Opera, London (5)

August 30
I CAPULETI E I MONTECCHI
Moffo;
Aragall, Foiani, Monachesi;
Abbado
Edinburgh Festival (4)

1967–68

October 7
I CAPULETI E I MONTECCHI
Scotto;
Aragall, Ferrin, Giacomotti;
Abbado
Teatro alla Scala, Milan:
    Salle Wilfrid Pelletier, Montréal (3)

November 11
LA BOHÈME
Freni, Scovotti;
Wixell, Bryn-Jones, Estes;
Bernardi
San Francisco Opera (5)

Home in Italy rehearsing with Margherita Rinaldi, La Scala Rigoletto; *with Giacomo Aragall,* I Capuleti e i Montecchi *in Milan; with Gabriella Tucci in Catania for* I Puritani, *1968*

Giovedi 20 Novembre 1969 - ore 21
Prima rappresentazione in abbonamento alle "PRIME SERALI" (recita n. 1)

INAUGURAZIONE DELLA STAGIONE

I LOMBARDI
ALLA PRIMA CROCIATA

Dramma lirico in tre atti di Temistocle Solera

Musica di GIUSEPPE VERDI

(R. Ricordi & C.)

personaggi e interpreti

Arvino } figli di Folco, signore di Rò	UMBERTO GRILLI
Pagano }	RUGGERO RAIMONDI
Viclinda, moglie d'Arvino	ANNA DI STASIO
Giselda, sua figlia	RENATA SCOTTO
Pirro, scudiero d'Arvino	MARIO RINAUDO
Priore della città di Milano	FERNANDO JACOPUCCI
Acciano, tiranno d'Antiochia	ALFREDO COLELLA
Oronte, suo figlio	LUCIANO PAVAROTTI
Sofia, moglie del tiranno d'Antiochia	SOFIA MEZZETTI

Claustrali - Priori - Sgherri - Armigeri nel Palazzo di Folco
Ambasciatori Persi, Medi, Damasceni e Caldei - Cavalieri e Guerrieri Crociati - Pellegrini
Donne lombarde - Donne dell'Harem

La scena Atto 1° in Milano - Atto 2° in Antiochia e sue vicinanze
Atto 3° presso Gerusalemme

Maestro Concertatore e Direttore

GIANANDREA GAVAZZENI

Regia di   Scene e costumi di
LUIGI SQUARZINA   PIER LUIGI PIZZI

Maestro del Coro
TULLIO BONI

Direttore dell'allestimento scenico   Realizzatore delle luci
GIOVANNI CRUCIANI   ALESSANDRO DRAGO

Direttore musicale del palcoscenico   Maestro collaboratore   Maestro rammentatore
Luigi Ricci   Alberto Paoletti   Alberto Leone

Assistente alla regia   Maestro d'armi
Marcello Aste   Enzo Musumeci Greco

Scene realizzate da   Costumi realizzati nella sartoria del Teatro diretta da
Giovanni Cruciani - Ettore Rondelli   Carla Jacobelli

Assistente per la scenografia   Assistente per i costumi
Giovanni Agostinucci   Vittoria Guaita

December 29
LA BOHÈME
Freni, Di Rocco;
D'Orazi, Mori, Gaetani;
Magiera
Teatro Comunale, Modena (2)

January 8
I CAPULETI E I MONTECCHI
Scotto;
Aragall, Ferrin, Giacomotti;
Abbado
Teatro alla Scala, Milan (4)

February 26
LA FIGLIA DEL REGGIMENTO
Freni/Cioni, Di Stasio;
Ganzarolli;
Sanzogno
Teatro alla Scala, Milan (5)

March 22
I PURITANI
Tucci, Magnaghi;
Protti, Raimondi;
Quadri
Teatro Massimo Bellini, Catania (4)

April 11
LUCIA DI LAMMERMOOR
Scotto;
Bruson, Ferrin;
Bartoletti
Teatro Massimo, Palermo (5)

April 24
RIGOLETTO
M. Rinaldi/Bonifaccio, Bonato;
Protti, Amore;
Rosada
Teatro Massimo, Palermo (5)

May 27
LUCIA DI LAMMERMOOR
Scotto;
Bruscantini, Cava;
Peloso
Teatro Margherita, Genoa (4)

June 16
LA TRAVIATA
Rothenberger;
Mittelmann;
Erede
Opernhaus, Zürich (1)

June 19
LA BOHÈME
Sgourda, Rohner;
Justus, Holecek, Rohr;
Santi
Opernhaus, Zürich (1)

July 23
LA TRAVIATA
Zeani;
Sereni;
Urbini
Terme di Caracalla, Rome (6)

1968–69

September 16
LA BOHÈME
Sighele, Di Rocca;
Rinaldi, Mazzini, Clabassi;
Verchi
Teatro Comunale del Giglio, Lucca (1)

October 25
LUCIA DI LAMMERMOOR
M. Rinaldi;
Braun, Grant;
Patanè
San Francisco Opera (4)

November 23
LA BOHÈME
Freni/Stojanovic, Boky/C. Carson;
Guarrera/Sereni, Christopher, Hines/
    Macurdy
Molinari-Pradelli
Metropolitan Opera, New York (2)
[At the second performance illness forced
Pavarotti to cancel after Act II.]

January 25
LA BOHÈME
Freni/Novelli/Sighele, Adani/
    Martelli/Leoni;
Sereni/Panerai/Boyer, Maffeo/
    Mantovani, Vinco/Zaccaria;
Sanzogno
Teatro alla Scala, Milan (6)

February 11
LA FIGLIA DEL REGGIMENTO
Freni, Di Stasio;
Ganzarolli;
Sanzogno
Teatro alla Scala, Milan (4)

March 8
RIGOLETTO
A. Arena, Bocca;
Cappuccilli, Bergamonti;
Morelli
Teatro Comunale "G. Verdi," Pisa (2)

Preparing La Scala Manon with Mirella Freni, 1969; poster announcing Pavarotti's only engagement in an early opera by Verdi; Gianandrea Gavazzeni, who conducted this production

March 18
I PURITANI
Freni, Lago;
Alberti, Pagliuca;
Savini
Teatro Comunale, Bologna (5)

April 12
LA BOHÈME
Freni, Adani;
Saccomani, Borgonovo, Pagliuca;
Wolf-Ferrari
Teatro Margherita, Genoa (4)

May 31
MANON
Freni;
Panerai, Zerbini, Ricciardi, Morresi;
Maag
Teatro alla Scala, Milan (4)

1969–70

September 20
LA BOHÈME
Kirsten, Boky/Moser;
Bruscantini/Wixell, Blankenburg/
   Monk, Berberian;
Coppola
San Francisco Opera (4)

October 7
L'ELISIR D'AMORE
Grist, Matsumoto;
Wixell, Bruscantini;
Patanè
San Francisco Opera (4)

October 23
LA BOHÈME
Sighele, Higareda;
Darrenkamp, Bañuelas, Hecht;
Ochoa
Teatro de Bellas Artes,
   Mexico City (1)

October 28
LUCIA DI LAMMERMOOR
Sills;
Bañuelas, Hecht;
Guadagno
Teatro de Bellas Artes,
   Mexico City (1)

November 20
I LOMBARDI ALLA PRIMA
   CROCIATA
Scotto, Di Stasio;
Grilli/Castellana, Raimondi;
Gavazzeni
Teatro dell'Opera, Rome (7)

December 19
MANON
Freni/Maliponte;
Panerai/Mantovani, Foiani, Ricciardi,
   Morresi;
Maag/Verchi
Teatro alla Scala, Milan (7)

March 10
LA BOHÈME
Berdini/Goltara, Mezzetti/Meneghini;
Zecchillo, Manelli, Ventriglia/Clabassi;
Magiera
Teatro Comunale, Bologna (3)
Teatro Consorziale, Budrio (1)

May 2
LUCIA DI LAMMERMOOR
Deutekom;
Trimarchi, Pagliuca;
Franci
Teatro di San Carlo, Naples (4)

May 21
LA BOHÈME
Freni, Orán;
G. Taddei, Carta, Ariè;
Sanzogno
Teatro de la Zarzuela, Madrid (2)

1970–71

September 3
MANON
Freni;
Maffeo, Pagliuca, Poli, Carta;
Magiera
Teatro Coliseo Albia, Bilbao (1)
Teatro Campoamor, Oviedo (1)
*[In Oviedo, Freni fell ill and the
performance ended after Act I.]*

September 9
L'ELISIR D'AMORE
Freni, Galvano;
Maffeo, Dara;
Savini
Teatro Coliseo Albia, Bilbao (1)
Teatro Campoamor, Oviedo (1)

September 26
RIGOLETTO
Scotto, Little-Augustithis;
Cappuccilli, Kreppel;
Franci
Staatsoper, Vienna (2)

October 15
LUCIA DI LAMMERMOOR
Scotto/R. Peters;
Sereni/Guarrera, Raimondi;
Franci
Metropolitan Opera, New York (4)

October 22
LA TRAVIATA
Sutherland/Moffo/Tucci;
Milnes/Merrill;
Bonynge/Molinari-Pradelli
Metropolitan Opera, New York (3)

December 8
L'ELISIR D'AMORE
Bonifaccio/Vernocchi/Maliponte,
   Vernocchi/Zotti;
A. Rinaldi/Capecchi, Montarsolo;
Patanè
Teatro alla Scala, Milan (6)

January 12
LA BOHÈME
Caballé, Stokes;
Sardinero, Galindo, Del Bosco;
Cillario
Gran Teatre del Liceu, Barcelona (3)

January 28
LUCIA DI LAMMERMOOR
Deutekom;
Galindo, Del Bosco;
Ferraris
Gran Teatre del Liceu, Barcelona (3)

March 2
LUCIA DI LAMMERMOOR
Guglielmi;
Bordoni, Fissore;
Zani
Teatro Carani, Sassuolo (1)

March 10
LA BOHÈME
Kirsten/Amara/Maliponte, De Paul/
   Boky;
Sereni/Walker, Goodloe/Gibbs,
   Hines/Díaz/Macurdy/Tozzi;
Cleva
Metropolitan Opera, New York (4)

March 31
RIGOLETTO
M. Pellegrini, Bainbridge;
Paskalis, Langdon;
Downes
Royal Opera, London (8)

May 7
RIGOLETTO
M. Pellegrini, Laghezza;
Mastromei/Saccomani, Gaetani;
Toffolo
Teatro Massimo Bellini, Catania (4)

1971–72

September 7
RIGOLETTO
Russell, Di Stasio;
Glossop/Monachesi, Raimondi/Vinco;
Matacic
NHK, Metropolitan Hall, Tokyo (5)

October 3
RIGOLETTO
Geszty/Scovotti, Boese;
Glossop, Moll;
Janowski
Staatsoper, Hamburg (2)

October 10
RIGOLETTO
Jasper/Köth, Little-Augustithis/
    Scherler;
Mastromei/Murray/Wixell, Sardi/
    Von Halem/Mazura;
Patanè/López-Cobos
Deutsche Oper Berlin (3)

October 27
UN BALLO IN MASCHERA
Arroyo, Donath, Dalis;
Bordoni;
Mackerras
San Francisco Opera (5)

November 12
LA BOHÈME
Papantoniou, Stokes;
Darrenkamp, Fiorito, Del Bosco;
Guadagno
Philadelphia Lyric Opera (1)

November 21
LUCIA DI LAMMERMOOR
Scotto;
Mittelmann, Moll;
Patanè/Ziino
Staatsoper, Hamburg (3)

January 11
LA BOHÈME
Krilovici, Jasper;
Dooley, Röhrl, Lagger;
Amaducci
Deutsche Oper Berlin (1)

January 18
I PURITANI
Sills, E. Shade;
Quilico, Plishka;
Guadagno
Philadelphia Lyric Opera (1)

January 24
LA BOHÈME
Scotto, Sena;
Sardinero, Darrenkamp. M. Smith;
Buckley
Greater Miami Opera (3)
Fort Lauderdale Opera (1)

February 17
LA FILLE DU RÉGIMENT
Sutherland, Resnik/Sinclair;
Corena/Gramm;
Bonynge
Metropolitan Opera: New York,
    Boston, Cleveland, Atlanta,
    Memphis, New Orleans,
    Minneapolis, Detroit (15)

March 30
LA BOHÈME
Marimpietri, Rothenberger;
Kerns, Bunger, Lackner;
Varviso
Staatsoper, Vienna (1)

April 29
LA BOHÈME
Amara/Tucci/Zylis-Gara, Boky;
Manuguerra/Cossa, Goodloe/Gibbs,
    Díaz/Macurdy;
Molinari-Pradelli
Metropolitan Opera: Boston,
    Cleveland, Atlanta, Minneapolis (4)

June 10
RIGOLETTO
Sutherland, Godfrey/Grillo;
Milnes/Manuguerra, Raimondi/Vinco;
Bonynge
Metropolitan Opera, New York (4)

July 22
UN BALLO IN MASCHERA
Orlandi-Malaspina, Mazzuccato-
    Meneghini/Cappellino, Lazzarini;
Zanasi;
Molinari-Pradelli
Arena di Verona (5)

August 30
LA BOHÈME
Sinnone, Zotti;
Schiavi, Serra, Del Bosco;
Malaval
Teatro Victoria Eugenia,
    San Sebastiano (1)

1972–73

September 3
LA FIGLIA DEL REGGIMENTO
Freni, Di Stasio;
Cesari;
Magiera
Teatro Coliseo Albia, Bilbao (1)
Teatro Campoamor, Oviedo (1)

September 7
LUCIA DI LAMMERMOOR
Bonifaccio;
Carroli, Foiani;
Ruisi
Teatro Coliseo Albia, Bilbao (1)
Teatro Campoamor, Oviedo (1)

September 11
LA BOHÈME
Freni, Zotti;
Cesari, Carta, Foiani;
Magiera
Teatro Coliseo Albia, Bilbao (1)
Teatro Campoamor, Oviedo (1)

November 8
LUCIA DI LAMMERMOOR
Sills;
Wolansky, Grant/Estes;
López-Cobos
San Francisco Opera (6)

December 1
LA BOHÈME
Scotto/Maliponte, Weidinger/Boky;
Guerrera/Sereni, Goodloe, Flagello/
    Plishka;
Behr/H. Lewis
Metropolitan Opera, New York (2)

December 2
LUCIA DI LAMMERMOOR
Scotto/Boky;
Sereni, Michalski;
Molinari-Pradelli
Metropolitan Opera, New York (2)

December 31
LA FILLE DU RÉGIMENT
Sutherland, Resnik/Sinclair;
Corena/Gramm;
Bonynge
Metropolitan Opera, New York (6)

February 6
RIGOLETTO
Grist, Grillo;
Wixell, Macurdy;
Levine
Metropolitan Opera, New York (2)

February 10
UN BALLO IN MASCHERA, Act III
E. Ross, G. Robinson;
Manuguerra;
P. H. Adler
Metropolitan Opera, New York (1)

February 13
RIGOLETTO
Brooks, Marsee;
Glossop, Dworchak;
Guadagno
Philadelphia Lyric Opera (1)

March 1
LA BOHÈME
Ricciarelli/Sighele, Robson/Scovotti;
Bañuelas/Krause, Krekow/
    Grundheber, Sotin/K. C. Kohn;
Santi/Patanè
Staatsoper, Hamburg (3)

March 4
LUCIA DI LAMMERMOOR
Núñez-Albanese;
Mittelmann, Moll;
Patanè
Staatsoper, Hamburg (3)

March 18
LA BOHÈME
Sighele, Paniagua;
Bordoni/Sardinero, Carta, Pagliuca/
    Foiani;
Ferraris
Teatro Pérez Galdós, Las Palmas (2)

March 20
LUCIA DI LAMMERMOOR
Núñez-Albanese;
Sardinero, Pagliuca;
Ferraris
Teatro Pérez Galdós, Las Palmas (1)

April 1
UN BALLO IN MASCHERA
Santunione/Bosabalian, Marheineke,
    Boese/C. Smith;
Milnes/Braun;
Santi
Staatsoper, Hamburg (9)

May 4
RIGOLETTO
Eda-Pierre, Boese;
Ohanesian, Moll;
Janowski
Staatsoper, Hamburg (1)

May 16
LUCIA DI LAMMERMOOR
Sutherland;
Quilico, Howell;
Bonynge
Royal Opera, London (8)

June 14
LA BOHÈME
Kirsten/Lorengar, Boky;
Sereni, Goodloe, Hines;
H. Lewis
Metropolitan Opera, New York (2)

August 5
LA BOHÈME
Scotto, Zilio;
Sereni, Maffeo, Vinco;
Maag
Arena di Verona (4)

1973–74

September 7
LA FAVORITA
Nave/Killebrew, Bybee;
Bruson, Giaiotti;
Cillario
San Francisco Opera (6)

October 13
L'ELISIR D'AMORE
R. Peters/Blegen/Boky, Weidinger/
    Di Franco;
Sereni/Reardon, Corena/Flagello;
Rudolf
Metropolitan Opera, New York (10)

November 11
LUCIA DI LAMMERMOOR
Moser/Deutekom;
Bordoni/Bañuelas, Díaz/Stamm;
Verchi/López-Cobos
Staatsoper, Hamburg (2)

November 13
LA BOHÈME
Ligabue/Mauti-Nunziata, Martikke/
    Peacock;
Bañuelas/Workman, Workman/
    Grundheber, Stamm/Krekow;
Verchi/Patanè
Staatsoper, Hamburg (2)

November 28
LA BOHÈME
Cotrubas, Zilio;
Patrick, Giorgetti, Washington;
Bartoletti
Lyric Opera of Chicago (6)

Philadelphia I Puritani *with Beverly Sills; visiting Regina Resnik, Metropolitan Opera* La Fille du Régiment;
with Sherrill Milnes, Hamburg Un Ballo in Maschera; *in* La Bohème *with Pilar Lorengar*

January 5
LA FAVORITA
Baglioni/Mazzieri, Colla/Cervo;
Bruson/D'Anna, Rinaudo;
Molinari-Pradelli
Teatro Comunale, Bologna (5)

January 28
LA FAVORITA
Cossotto, Macchinizzi;
Cappuccilli, Vinco;
Verchi
Teatro alla Scala, Milan (1)

March 9
LA BOHÈME
Zylis-Gara, Moser;
Sereni, Holloway, Macurdy;
Segerstam
Metropolitan Opera, New York (3)

April 2
LA BOHÈME
N. Shade, Rogers;
Ellis, Wagner, Ramey;
De Almeida
Philadelphia Lyric Opera (1)

April 27
UN BALLO IN MASCHERA
Orlandi-Malaspina, Nazario/Pizzo,
  Laghezza/Anastasijevic;
Sereni;
Sanzogno
Teatro la Fenice, Venice (5)

May 11
LA BOHÈME
Sinnone, Baleani;
Manuguerra, Daniele, Liendo;
Veltri
Teatro Municipal, Caracas (1)

May 14
LUCIA DI LAMMERMOOR
Dal Piva;
Manuguerra, De Narké;
Veltri
Teatro Municipal, Caracas (1)

May 23
LA BOHÈME
Sighele, Orán;
Sardinero, Bermudez, Washington;
Sanzogno
Teatro de la Zarzuela, Madrid (2)

May 30
UN BALLO IN MASCHERA
Gulin, Arregui, Silva;
Sardinero;
Sanzogno
Teatro de la Zarzuela, Madrid (2)

June 8
RIGOLETTO
Nawe, Schwenninger;
Mittelmann, Sotin;
Guadagno
Staatsoper, Hamburg (1)

June 17
UN BALLO IN MASCHERA
Scotto, Marheineke, Boese;
Mittelmann;
Santi
Staatsoper, Hamburg (1)

July 14
RIGOLETTO
Pizzo, Di Stasio;
Milnes, Zerbini;
Franci
Arena Sferisterio, Macerata (3)

1974-75

September 25
LA BOHÈME
Ricciarelli, Sarroca;
Bisson, Bona, Soyer/Soumagnas;
Patanè
Opéra, Paris (8)

September 29
LA BOHÈME
Freni, Scovotti;
Bañuelas, Krekow, Stamm;
Magiera
Staatsoper, Hamburg (1)

November 13
LUISA MILLER
Ricciarelli, Tourangeau;
Quilico, Tozzi, Weller;
López-Cobos
San Francisco Opera (5)

January 7
LA BOHÈME
Cotrubas/Freni, Guglielmi/Pediconi;
Panerai, Maffeo, Washington;
Prêtre
Teatro alla Scala, Milan (4)

With Giorgio Tozzi in Luisa Miller, *San Francisco; greeting Richard Thomas, San Francisco* Il Trovatore;
opposite Joan Sutherland in Chicago Lucia di Lammermoor; *Metropolitan Opera* La Bohème *with Ingvar Wixell*

January 23
LA BOHÈME
Moffo, Fisk;
Edwards, Shapp, Sgarro;
Moresco
Connecticut Opera, Hartford (1)

February 20
LA BOHÈME
Lorengar, Peacock/Jasper;
Fortune, McDaniel, Lagger;
López-Cobos
Deutsche Oper Berlin (2)

March 1
UN BALLO IN MASCHERA, Act II
E. Ross;
Quilico
LA FAVORITA, Act IV [concert form]
M. Dunn;
Morris
LA BOHÈME, Act I
Lorengar;
Goodloe, Boucher, Plishka;
H. Lewis
Metropolitan Opera, New York (1)

March 10
L'ELISIR D'AMORE
Blegen, Cavendish;
Sereni, Malas;
Buckley
Greater Miami Opera (3)
Fort Lauderdale Opera (1)

March 22
LA BOHÈME
Freni, Holm;
Panerai, Maffeo, Washington;
Karajan
Easter Festival, Salzburg (2)

May 30
LA BOHÈME
Kirsten/Maliponte, Costa;
Reardon, Boucher/Christopher, Díaz;
Segerstam
Metropolitan Opera: Tokyo (3)

July 12
UN BALLO IN MASCHERA
Santunione/Zampieri, Ferracuti,
  Gonzáles;
Salvadori;
Franci/Campori
Arena Sferisterio, Macerata (3)

August 5
LA BOHÈME
Scotto, Zilio;
Romero, Giorgetti, Zardo;
Zani
Teatro all'Aperto, Torre del Lago (2)

1975–76

September 12
IL TROVATORE
Sutherland, Obraztsova/Verrett;
Wixell, Grant;
Bonynge
San Francisco Opera (5)

October 21
LA BOHÈME
Freni, Weidinger;
Bañuelas, Krekow, Stamm;
Mackerras
Staatsoper, Hamburg (1)

October 24
LUCIA DI LAMMERMOOR
Uhrmacher;
Bañuelas, Stamm;
Weikert
Staatsoper, Hamburg (1)

October 26
LA BOHÈME
Freni, Peacock;
Kerns, Röhrl, Van Dam;
Gómez-Martínez
Deutsche Oper Berlin (2)

November 12
LUCIA DI LAMMERMOOR
Sutherland;
Saccomani, Ferrin;
Bonynge
Lyric Opera of Chicago (7)

January 2
LA BOHÈME
Mauti-Nunziata, Herbé;
Sordello, Abello, Pagliuca;
Wolf-Ferrari
Théâtre de l'Opéra, Nice (2)

January 15
LA BOHÈME
Te Kanawa, M. Pellegrini;
Allen, Harling, Van Allan;
Stapleton
Royal Opera, London (5)

February 25
I PURITANI
Sutherland, Munzer;
Milnes/Opthof, Morris/Flagello;
Bonynge
Metropolitan Opera, New York (10)

March 8
DER ROSENKAVALIER
Troyanos, Zylis-Gara, Blegen, Love;
Berry/Edelmann, Dooley/Meredith;
Levine
Metropolitan Opera, New York (6)

March 27
LA BOHÈME
Caballé, Niska;
Sereni, Monk, Plishka;
Levine
Metropolitan Opera, New York (1)

May 12
LUISA MILLER
Caballé/Maliponte, Baglioni/Jori;
Cappuccilli/Salvadori, Zardo/
  Washington, Del Bosco/
  Michalopoulos;
Gavazzeni
Teatro alla Scala, Milan (5)

June 21
UN BALLO IN MASCHERA
Arroyo, Grist, Payne;
Bruson;
Downes
Royal Opera, London (4)

July 24
LUCIA DI LAMMERMOOR
Deutekom/Devia;
Bruson/Zancanaro, Rinaudo/Zardo;
De Fabritiis
Arena di Verona (4)
*[In the performance of August 10 Gaetano
Scano replaced Pavarotti in Act III.]*

1976–77

October 11
IL TROVATORE
Scotto, Verrett;
Manuguerra/Quilico, Morris;
Gavazzeni
Metropolitan Opera, New York (8)

November 26
TOSCA
Neblett;
MacNeil, Tajo, Giorgetti, Andreolli;
López-Cobos
Lyric Opera of Chicago (7)

February 23
LA BOHÈME
Scotto, Niska;
Wixell, Monk, Plishka;
Levine
Metropolitan Opera, New York (7)

April 11
TOSCA
Kabaivanska;
Glossop, Hammond-Stroud, Langdon,
  Dobson;
Stapleton
Royal Opera, London (4)

May 8
IL TROVATORE
L. Price, Ludwig;
Cappuccilli, Van Dam;
Karajan
Staatsoper, Vienna (3)

May 19
DER ROSENKAVALIER
Schwarz, Leonie Rysanek/Beckmann,
    Ihloff, Fredricks;
Moll, Gutstein;
Stein
Staatsoper, Hamburg (5)

May 30
TOSCA
Kabaivanska;
Constantin, Stern, Yoshie, Müller;
Patanè
Staatsoper, Frankfurt (1)

June 18
L'ELISIR D'AMORE
Freni/Mazzucato, Michael;
Weikl/Romero, G. Taddei;
Giovaninetti
Staatsoper, Hamburg (6)

August 4
TOSCA
Kabaivanska;
Mastromei, Giorgetti, Malfatti, De Julis;
Sanzogno
Teatro all'Aperto, Torre del Lago (2)

1977–78

September 23
L'ELISIR D'AMORE
M. Rinaldi, Brown;
Romero, Evans;
Bartoletti
Lyric Opera of Chicago (8)

October 29
TURANDOT
Caballé, L. Mitchell;
Tozzi, Duesing, Corazza, Frank;
Chailly
San Francisco Opera (7)

December 30
UN BALLO IN MASCHERA
Verrett/Zampieri, Mazzucato/Anelli,
    Obraztsova/Payne;
Cappuccilli/Sarabia
Abbado
Teatro alla Scala, Milan (8)

January 26
LA BOHÈME
Freni, Holm;
Brendel, Grumbach, Hillebrand;
Kleiber
Bayerische Staatsoper, Munich (1)

February 21
LA FAVORITA
Verrett, A. J. Smith;
Milnes, Giaiotti;
López-Cobos
Metropolitan Opera, New York (6)

March 13
L'ELISIR D'AMORE
Blegen, Di Franco;
Sereni, Corena;
Caldwell
Metropolitan Opera, New York (2)

April 10
LA BOHÈME
Freni, Moser;
Palmer, Griffin, M. Smith;
Buckley
Greater Miami Opera (3)
Fort Lauderdale Opera (1)

June 19
LUISA MILLER
Ricciarelli, Connell;
Nucci/Zancanaro, Lloyd/Howell,
    Van Allan;
Maazel
Royal Opera, London (5)

July 13
IL TROVATORE
Ricciarelli, Cossotto;
Cappuccilli/Boyagian, Ingram;
Gavazzeni
Arena di Verona (4)

July 26
DER ROSENKAVALIER
Minton, Janowitz, Popp, Soffel;
Moll, Gutstein;
Dohnányi
Salzburg Festival (2)

1978–79

September 3
LUISA MILLER
Gulin/Di Rocco, Jori;
Zancanaro, Giaiotti, Furlanetto;
De Fabritiis/Lauret
Teatro Coliseo Albia, Bilbao (1)
Teatro Campoamor, Oviedo (1)

Rehearsing Hamburg L'Elisir d'Amore *with Giuseppe Taddei; with Shirley Verrett in Metropolitan Opera* La Favorita;
after Tosca *at Met with José Carreras, Placido Domingo; in Met Elisir with Judith Blegen*

September 7
UN BALLO IN MASCHERA
Parazzini, Arregui, Anghelakova;
Bordoni;
De Fabritiis
Teatro Coliseo Albia, Bilbao (1)
Teatro Campoamor, Oviedo (1)

October 14
TOSCA
Caballé/G. Jones;
G. Taddei, Davià, Hudson, Egerton;
Peloso
San Francisco Opera (6)

December 13
TOSCA
Verrett/Olivero/Leonie Rysanek;
MacNeil/Glossop, Corena/Tajo,
    Cheek, Velis/Anthony;
Conlon
Metropolitan Opera: New York,
    Cleveland, Boston, Memphis, Dallas,
    Detroit, Philadelphia (15)

February 13
L'ELISIR D'AMORE
Freni/Ferrarini, Ratti/Fabbri;
Nucci/Noli, Montarsolo/Trimarchi
Giovaninetti
Teatro alla Scala, Milan (6)

March 22
LA BOHÈME
Cotrubas, Popp;
Cappuccilli/Saccomani, Giorgetti,
    Nesterenko/Zardo;
Kleiber
Teatro alla Scala, Milan (7)

1979–80

September 7
LA GIOCONDA
Scotto, Toczyska, Lilowa;
Mittelmann, Furlanetto;
Bartoletti
San Francisco Opera (6)

October 12
RIGOLETTO
Blegen, Kuhlmann;
Manuguerra, Gill;
Chailly
Lyric Opera of Chicago (7)

December 2
UN BALLO IN MASCHERA
Arroyo, Conwell, Wulkopf;
Cappuccilli/Nucci;
Gómez-Martínez
Bayerische Staatsoper, Munich (5)

February 4
UN BALLO IN MASCHERA
Ricciarelli/Cruz-Romo, Blegen/
    R. Peters/Norden, Berini/Payne;
Quilico/Nucci;
Patanè/Veltri
Metropolitan Opera: New York,
    Washington, Cleveland, Atlanta,
    Memphis, Dallas, Detroit,
    Boston (15)

March 15
TOSCA
Marton/Kabaivanska;
Wixell, Mariotti/Tadeo, Zerbini/
    Giacomotti, Romani/Porzano;
Ozawa/Amner
Teatro alla Scala, Milan (8)

April 15
L'ELISIR D'AMORE
G. Robinson/Blegen, Di Franco;
Sereni, Trimarchi;
Rescigno
Metropolitan Opera: New York,
    Washington, Cleveland, Atlanta,
    Boston (6)

May 29
LA BOHÈME
Soviero/Renée, Nielsen;
Derksen, Raftery, Hale;
Rigacci
San Diego Opera (5)

July 10
LA GIOCONDA
Dimitrova, Nave/Toczyska, Payne/
    Jori;
Cappuccilli/Manuguerra, Giaiotti;
Guadagno
Arena di Verona (5)

1980–81

November 26
UN BALLO IN MASCHERA
Scotto, Battle, Payne;
Nucci;
Pritchard
Lyric Opera of Chicago (7)

In Salzburg Der Rosenkavalier; *with Danny Kaye bussing Montserrat Caballé, San Francisco* Tosca;
after Milan La Bohème *with Carlos Kleiber, Ileana Cotrubas;* Tosca *at La Scala with Raina Kabaivanska*

January 19
UN BALLO IN MASCHERA
Caballé, Kenny, Payne;
Manuguerra/Bruson;
Haitink
Royal Opera, London (7)

March 2
L'ELISIR D'AMORE
Blegen, Wohlafka;
Ellis, Bruscantini;
Rescigno
Metropolitan Opera, New York (4)

April 6
TOSCA
Neblett;
Wixell, Flagello, Bogart, Frank;
Buckley
Greater Miami Opera (3)
Fort Lauderdale Opera (1)

April 29
TOSCA
Marton;
Nurmela, Rohr, Stachel, Peter;
Rescigno
Opernhaus, Zürich (1)

1981–82

October 5
L'ELISIR D'AMORE
Buchanan, Harman-Gulick;
Sereni/Duesing, Montarsolo;
Bartoletti
Lyric Opera of Chicago (4)

November 12
AÏDA
M. Price/L. Price, Toczyska;
Estes, Rydl/Furlanetto;
Navarro
San Francisco Opera (6)

December 4
UN BALLO IN MASCHERA, Act II
and "Ma se m'è forza perderti"
Zylis-Gara;
Quilico;
Levine
Metropolitan Opera, New York (1)

December 9
RIGOLETTO
Eda-Pierre, I. Jones;
Quilico, Berberian;
Levine
Metropolitan Opera, New York (3)

January 20
LUISA MILLER
Ricciarelli/Maliponte, Berini;
Nucci/Sereni, Plishka, Vernon/Cheek;
Santi
Metropolitan Opera, New York (4)

March 22
AÏDA
Varady, Toczyska;
Fischer-Dieskau, Salminen;
Barenboim
Deutsche Oper Berlin (4)

April 25
LA BOHÈME
Tsukada/Guimaraes, M. J. Johnson;
Cimino/Sioli, Ellison/Konsulov,
    Caforio/Polgár;
De Fabritiis
Opera Company of Philadelphia (3)
)

May 7
L'ELISIR D'AMORE
Kim/M. J. Johnson, Clancy;
Konsulov, Del Carlo/Barbosa;
De Fabritiis
Opera Company of Philadelphia (2)

1982–83

September 10
UN BALLO IN MASCHERA
Caballé, Battle, Baldani;
Carroli;
K. H. Adler
San Francisco Opera (1)

September 29
DER ROSENKAVALIER
Troyanos, Te Kanawa, Blegen, Kraft/
    Conrad;
Moll, Hammond-Stroud/Meredith;
Levine/Tate
Metropolitan Opera, New York (5)

October 14
IDOMENEO (title role)
Cotrubas, Behrens, Von Stade/Catania;
Alexander, Jenkins;
Levine
Metropolitan Opera, New York (7)

January 27
LA BOHÈME
Renée, Bruce;
Allman, Myers, Shanks;
Cillario
Australian Opera, Sydney (3)

Opposite Kathleen Battle in L'Elisir d'Amore, *Vienna; after Milan* Aïda, *celebrating with Renata Tebaldi;*
Metropolitan Opera Tosca *co-star Cornell MacNeil; Met* Aïda *with Anna Tomowa-Sintow*

March 15
LUCIA DI LAMMERMOOR
Serra;
Miller/Saccomani, Federici;
Maag
Teatro alla Scala, Milan (5)

April 11
UN BALLO IN MASCHERA
Zylis-Gara, Rolandi, Chookasian;
Wangerin/Quilico/Boyagian;
Buckley
Greater Miami Opera (3)
Fort Lauderdale Opera (1)

May 30
LUISA MILLER
Ricciarelli/Maliponte, Denize;
Cappuccilli, Cheek, Curtin;
Guadagno
Opéra, Paris (8)

July 14
LA BOHÈME
Freni, Guglielmi;
Brendel, Janssen, Rootering;
Kleiber
Bayerische Staatsoper, Munich (2)

July 28
IDOMENEO (title role)
Popp, Connell, Schmidt;
W. Lewis, Jenkins;
Levine
Salzburg Festival (6)

1983–84

September 23
AÏDA
Tomowa-Sintow, Cossotto;
Wixell, Giaiotti;
Bartoletti
Lyric Opera of Chicago (5)

November 18
ERNANI
L. Mitchell/Negri;
Milnes/Elvira, Raimondi;
Levine
Metropolitan Opera, New York (9)

January 30
UN BALLO IN MASCHERA
Tomowa-Sintow, Borst, M. Dunn/
   Baldani;
Cappuccilli;
Chailly
Grand Théâtre, Geneva (7)

April 18
L'ELISIR D'AMORE
Battle, Sima;
Helm, G. Taddei;
Bareza
Staatsoper, Vienna (3)

April 30
AÏDA
Chiara/Troitskaya, Vergara;
Weikl/Pola/Boyagian, Bogart;
Maazel
Staatsoper, Vienna (6)

June 2
AÏDA
Ricciarelli/Plowright, Toczyska;
Wixell, Burchuladze;
Mehta
Royal Opera, London (6)

1984–85

December 6
TOSCA
Behrens;
Bacquier, Courtis, Soumagnas,
   Sénéchal;
Conlon
Opéra, Paris (6)

January 18
LA BOHÈME
Freni, Guglielmi;
Brendel, Mori, Rydl;
Kleiber
Staatsoper, Vienna (3)

January 29
L'ELISIR D'AMORE
Battle, Sima;
Wixell, G. Taddei;
M. Arena
Staatsoper, Vienna (3)

February 12
TOSCA
Dimitrova;
Wixell, Mazzola, Bunger, Nitsche;
M. Arena/Buckley
Staatsoper, Vienna (3)

June 11
TOSCA
Kabaivanska;
Wixell, Lang, Sardi, Driscoll;
López-Cobos
Deutsche Oper Berlin (1)

1985–86

September 23
TOSCA
Caballé/Zschau;
MacNeil, Tajo/Malas, Courtney/
   Darrenkamp, Velis;
Cillario
Metropolitan Opera, New York (10)

December 7
AÏDA
Chiara, Dimitrova;
Cappuccilli/Pons, Ghiaurov;
Maazel
Teatro alla Scala, Milan (5)

February 18
LUISA MILLER
Gasdia, Yachmi/Gall;
Bruson/Brendel, Burchuladze; Rydl;
Guadagno
Staatsoper, Vienna (4)

February 24
LA BOHÈME
Kincses, Renée;
Sólyom-Nagy, Póka, Polgár;
Saccani
Hungarian State Opera, Budapest (1)

March 21
AÏDA
Tomowa-Sintow, Cossotto;
Manuguerra/Quilico, Kavrakos/
   Rouleau;
Levine
Metropolitan Opera, New York (5)

April 14
UN BALLO IN MASCHERA
Pierson/Williams, Focile/Iauco, Berry;
Rucker;
Buckley
Opera Company of Philadelphia (2)

April 21
LA BOHÈME
Esperian/Izzo d'Amico, Cassello/
   Pacetti;
Mattsey/Servile, D. Carter/Servile,
   DuPont/Monici;
Saccani
Opera Company of Philadelphia (2)

April 29
Twenty-fifth Anniversary of
Luciano Pavarotti's Debut
LA BOHÈME
Izzo d'Amico, Pacetti;
Mattsey, Servile, DuPont;
Magiera
Teatro Comunale, Modena (1)

Salzburg Festival recital, August 1985

Recital and Concert Chronology

As with the preceding opera chronology, the listing that chronicles Luciano Pavarotti's work in concert and recital was drawn from materials in the archives at the tenor's home in Modena. This particular record was prepared in close collaboration with Mrs. Pavarotti and her sterling associate Francesca Barbieri. After the available data had been logged, the chronology was checked for omissions against all contracts and engagement records extant in the office of Herbert Breslin, Pavarotti's American manager. This done, copies of the chronology were corrected by a number of associates long involved with the Pavarotti career: John Coast, his agent in London, pianist John Wustman, conductor Emerson Buckley, and soprano Madelyn Renée, who for several years worked as secretary to the singer. Many other generous people offered assistance to the task, and the accuracy of the chronology reflects their contributions.

In contrast to Pavarotti's opera career, his emergence as a major name in the concert field was measured. Among the milestones, both of which brought significant change to his artistic life, were the addition of Verdi's *Messa da Requiem* to his repertory in 1967 and his first full-length solo recital in 1973. Most important during the 1980s are the orchestral concerts presented in vast sports arenas, where an evening with Pavarotti might attract as many as twenty thousand music-lovers.

1961–62

May 16
RECITAL
Breda;
La Macchia
Righi, piano
Gioacchino Rossini Chorale
Borri
Teatro Comunale, Modena

July 30
IL NATALE DEL REDENTORE
   (Perosi)
Vercelli, Di Stasio;
Dondi
Chorus and Orchestra of the Maggio
   Musicale Fiorentino
Capuana
Basilica della S.S. Annunziata, Siena

1962–63

March 28
RECITAL
Ferrari, Iotti;
Mattioli
Campogalliani, piano
Conservatorio Musicale Arrigo Boito,
   Parma

May 13
RECITAL
Bersiani, Como, Yamaguchi, Di Stasio;
Tei, D'Orazi, Vezzosi, Gambelli,
   Pasella
Annovazzi, piano
Town Hall, Dundalk

1963–64

September 6
RECITAL
Núñez-Albanese, Pesarini;
Manicelli
Campogalliani, piano
Residenza Municipale, Mantua

April 20–27
CONCERTS
Azuma, Malvisi, Bortoluzzi;
De Ambrosis, Mazzieri
Philharmonic Orchestra of Pomerania
Masini
Bydgoszcz, Wrozwawek, Grudgionz,
   Torun (5)

August 17
IDOMENEO
Janowitz, Tarrés;
R. Lewis, Neilson, Taylor, Hughes
Glyndebourne Festival Chorus
London Philharmonic Orchestra
Pritchard
Royal Albert Hall, London

1964–65

September 26
RECITAL
Guglielmi, Novelli
Ventura, piano
TV Studio, Moscow

September 27
RECITAL
Guglielmi, Tucci, Vajna;
Zaccaria
Tonini, piano
Kremlin Theater, Moscow

March 3
CONCERT
Freni, Domínguez
Orchestre Philharmonique
   del'O.R.T.F.
Santi
Salle Pleyel, Paris

1966–67

January 16, 18
MESSA DA REQUIEM (Verdi)
L. Price, Cossotto/Verrett;
Ghiaurov
Chorus and Orchestra of La Scala
Karajan
Teatro alla Scala, Milan (2)

March 25
MESSA DA REQUIEM (Verdi)
De Osma, C. Smith;
Hines
Chorus and Orchestra of the Maggio
   Musicale Fiorentino
Abbado
Teatro Comunale, Florence

May 14, 16
MESSA DA REQUIEM (Verdi)
G. Jones, Soukupova;
Talvela
London Symphony Chorus and
   Orchestra
Solti
Royal Festival Hall, London (2)

June 30
LUCIA DI LAMMERMOOR
Scotto;
Cappuccilli, Ferrin
Chorus and Orchestra of Radio Italiana
Molinari-Pradelli
RAI Auditorium, Turin

1967–68

December 12
RIGOLETTO
M. Rinaldi, Lazzarini;
Cappuccilli, Zaccaria
Chorus and Orchestra of Radio Italiana
Rossi
RAI Auditorium, Turin

December 22
STABAT MATER (Rossini)
Zylis-Gara, Verrett;
Zaccaria
Chorus and Orchestra of Radio Italiana
Giulini
RAI Auditorium, Rome

February 1
CONCERT
Stella
Orchestra of Radio Italiana
Bonavolontà
RAI Auditorium, Rome

May 19, 20, 21
MESSA DA REQUIEM (Verdi)
Arroyo, Ludwig;
Talvela
Singverein der Gesellschaft der
   Musikfreunde, Vienna
Vienna Symphony
Abbado
Musikverein, Vienna (3)

1968–69

July 8
I PURITANI
Freni, Fiorentini;
Bruscantini, Giaiotti
Chorus and Orchestra of Radio Italiana
Muti
RAI Auditorium, Rome

July 17
LA BOHÈME
Freni, Talarico;
Bruscantini, Maffeo, Ghiuselev
Chorus and Orchestra of Radio Italiana
Schippers
RAI Auditorium, Rome

1970–71

October 10
MESSA DA REQUIEM (Verdi)
Scotto, M. Horne;
Ghiaurov
Choruses of Radio Italiana, Rome and
    Milan
RAI Orchestra of Rome
Abbado
Chiesa di S. Maria sopra Minerva,
    Rome

1971–72

April 22
RUDOLF BING FAREWELL GALA
Amara, Arroyo, Caballé, Crespin,
    Kirsten, Lorengar, Moffo, Nilsson,
    R. Peters, L. Price, G. Robinson,
    Leonie Rysanek, Stratas, Sutherland,
    Tucci, Zylis-Gara, Bumbry, Dalis,
    R. Elias, Resnik;
Corelli, Di Giuseppe, Domingo,
    Konya, McCracken, Tucker, Vickers,
    MacNeil, Merrill, Milnes, Sereni,
    Stewart, Corena, Flagello, Hines,
    Macurdy, Plishka, Raimondi, Siepi
Metropolitan Opera Chorus, Orchestra
    and Ballet
K. Adler, Böhm, Bonynge, Levine,
    Molinari-Pradelli, Rudolf
Metropolitan Opera House, New York

June 17
CONCERT
New Jersey Symphony Orchestra
H. Lewis
Garden State Arts Center, Holmdel,
    New Jersey

1972–73

November 9
FOL DE ROL
Mandac, Sills, Resnik, Verrett;
Domingo, Mittelmann, Yarnell, Estes;
San Francisco Opera Orchestra and
    Ballet
Woitach
Civic Auditorium, San Francisco,
    California

January 9
LUNCHEON RECITAL
Masiello, piano
Waldorf-Astoria Hotel, New York

February 1
RECITAL
Kohn, piano
John Gano Memorial Hall, Liberty,
    Missouri

February 3
RECITAL
Kohn, piano
McFarlin Auditorium, Dallas, Texas

February 15
CONCERT
Denver Symphony Orchestra
Priestman
Auditorium Theatre, Denver, Colorado

February 18
RECITAL
Kohn, piano
Carnegie Hall, New York

February 21
RECITAL
Kohn, piano
Theatre of the Performing Arts,
    New Orleans, Louisiana

April 24
TRIBUTE TO CARUSO
Atlantov, Del Monaco, Gedda,
    Ferruccio Tagliavini, Vanzo
Orchestra of the Teatro di San Carlo
De Fabritiis
Teatro di San Carlo, Naples

June 18
RIGOLETTO
R. Peters, Ewing;
Quilico, Morris
Philadelphia Orchestra
Levine
Robin Hood Dell, Philadelphia,
    Pennsylvania

June 21
CONCERT
Festival Casals of Puerto Rico
Tevah
Carnegie Hall, New York

June 24
CONCERT
New Jersey Symphony Orchestra
H. Lewis
Wolf Trap Farm Park, Vienna, Virginia

Ettore Campogalliani, one of Pavarotti's teachers; frequent colleague Claudio Abbado; during San Francisco concert with Licia Albanese; with pianist for first song recitals, Eugene Kohn

August 25
LA BOHÈME
Ricciarelli, Weidinger;
Edwards, Myrvold, Lawrence;
Los Angeles Philharmonic
Foster
Hollywood Bowl, Hollywood,
    California

1973–74

September 2
CONCERT
Albanese
San Francisco Opera Orchestra
K. H. Adler
Golden Gate Park, San Francisco,
    California

September 23
RECITAL
Kohn, piano
Royce Hall, Los Angeles, California

October 3
CONCERT
Dallas Symphony Orchestra
Rudolf
Music Hall, Dallas, Texas

October 7
RECITAL
Kohn, piano
Northrop Memorial Auditorium,
    Minneapolis, Minnesota

October 15
RECITAL
Kohn, piano
Academy of Music, Philadelphia,
    Pennsylvania

October 23
RECITAL
Kohn, piano
Loew's Theater, New Rochelle,
    New York

October 28
RECITAL
Kohn, piano
Whitman Hall, Brooklyn, New York

December 9
RECITAL
Kohn, piano
Massey Hall, Toronto, Ontario

February 27
RECITAL
Kohn, piano
Hill Auditorium, Ann Arbor, Michigan

March 2
RECITAL
Kohn, piano
C. W. Post Center Auditorium,
    Brookville, New York

March 11
RECITAL
Kohn, piano
Municipal Auditorium, New Orleans,
    Louisiana

March 18
RECITAL
Kohn, piano
Van Wezel Performing Arts Hall,
    Sarasota, Florida

March 29
RECITAL
Kohn, piano
Avery Fisher Hall, New York

June 13, 15
MESSA DA REQUIEM (Verdi)
Ricciarelli, Pecile;
Ghiaurov
Chorus and Orchestra of La Scala
Abbado
Concert Hall, Tchaikovsky
    Conservatory, Moscow (2)

June 24
MESSA DA REQUIEM (Verdi)
Freni, Ludwig;
Van Dam
Singverein der Gesellschaft der
    Musikfreunde, Vienna
Berlin Philharmonic Orchestra
Karajan
Musikverein, Vienna

August 20, 21
MESSA DA REQUIEM (Verdi)
Arroyo, Cossotto;
Ariè
Edinburgh Festival Chorus
London Philharmonic Orchestra
Giulini
Usher Hall, Edinburgh (2)

Among Pavarotti's maestri: Carlo Maria Giulini, Sir Georg Solti, Riccardo Muti, Daniel Barenboim, James Levine

1974–75

October 21
RECITAL
Kohn, piano
Staatsoper, Hamburg

October 24, 25, 27
MESSA DA REQUIEM (Verdi)
Arroyo, M. Dunn;
Raimondi
Los Angeles Master Chorale
Los Angeles Philharmonic
Mehta
Dorothy Chandler Pavilion,
    Los Angeles, California (3)

November 21
FOL DE ROL
Malone, Ricciarelli, Tomowa-Sintow,
    Gingold, Turner;
Frank, Thomas, Quilico, Malas, Soyer,
    Tozzi, Weller
San Francisco Opera Orchestra and
    Ballet
A. Lewis
Civic Auditorium, San Francisco,
    California

November 26
RECITAL
Kohn, piano
Royce Hall, Los Angeles, California

November 28
TONIGHT SHOW
Kohn, piano
Bishop, host
NBC Studios, Burbank, California

December 1
RECITAL
Kohn, piano
Auditorium Theatre, Chicago, Illinois

December 6
LUISA MILLER
Cruz-Romo, Angelakova;
Manuguerra, Ariè, Mazzoli;
Chorus and Orchestra of Radio Italiana
Maag
RAI Auditorium, Turin

December 14
CONCERT
Orchestra
Giovaninetti
Opéra, Marseilles

January 15
RECITAL
Magiera, piano
Teatro alla Scala, Milan

January 25
CONCERT
Verrett
Zuckerman, violin
Philadelphia Orchestra
Ormandy
Academy of Music, Philadelphia,
    Pennsylvania

January 28
RECITAL
Kohn, piano
Spaulding Auditorium, Hanover,
    New Hampshire

January 31
RECITAL
Kohn, piano
Symphony Hall, Boston, Massachusetts

February 2
RECITAL
Kohn, piano
Massey Hall, Toronto, Ontario

March 4
RECITAL
Kohn, piano
Indiana University Auditorium,
    Bloomington, Indiana

April 7
RECITAL
Kohn, piano
Edwin J. Thomas Performing Arts
    Hall, Akron, Ohio

April 11
CONCERT
Denver Symphony Orchestra
Priestman
Auditorium Theatre, Denver, Colorado

April 15
RECITAL
Kohn, piano
John Gano Memorial Hall, Liberty,
    Missouri

April 19
RECITAL
Kohn, piano
Colden Center for the Performing
    Arts, Flushing, New York

April 24, 26, 30
MESSA DA REQUIEM (Verdi)
L. Price, Minton;
Howell
Chicago Symphony Chorus and
    Orchestra
Solti
Orchestra Hall, Chicago, Illinois (2)
Carnegie Hall, New York (1)

May 2
RECITAL
Wustman, piano
Mershon Auditorium, Columbus, Ohio

May 4
RECITAL
Wustman, piano
Virgil M. Hancher Auditorium,
    Iowa City, Iowa

May 6
TONIGHT SHOW
Wustman, piano
Carson, host
NBC Studios, Burbank, California

May 10
RECITAL
Wustman, piano
Carnegie Hall, New York

May 13
RECITAL
Wustman, piano
Salle Wilfrid Pelletier, Montréal,
    Québec

May 16
RECITAL
Wustman, piano
National Arts Centre, Ottawa, Ontario

May 23
RIGOLETTO D'ORO
Eoli, Sato;
Kogima, Moubayed
Campogalliani, piano
Friends of Music Club, Mantua

June 10
RECITAL
Magiera, piano
Grosser Saal, Vienna

June 28
RECITAL
Zanlari, Stara;
Bernardi, Vezzani, Casarini
Magiera, piano
Palazzo dei Principi, Correggio

July 14
RECITAL
Magiera, piano
Faenza Lirica, Faenza

1975–76

September 14
CONCERT
Wixell
San Francisco Opera Orchestra
K. H. Adler
Golden Gate Park, San Francisco,
  California

September 24
RECITAL
Wustman, piano
Ambassador Auditorium, Pasadena,
  California

September 25
TONIGHT SHOW
Carson, host
NBC Studios, Burbank, California

October 5
RECITAL
Wustman, piano
Queen Elizabeth Theater, Vancouver,
  British Columbia

October 8
RECITAL
Wustman, piano
Auditorium Theatre, Denver, Colorado

October 10
RECITAL
Wustman, piano
El Camino College Auditorium,
  Via Torrance, California

October 18
RECITAL
Magiera, piano
Teatro Carani, Sassuolo

November 1
RECITAL
Wustman, piano
Whitman Hall, Brooklyn, New York

November 26
RECITAL
Wustman, piano
Academy of Music, Philadelphia,
  Pennsylvania

December 4
RECITAL
Wustman, piano
Dade County Auditorium, Miami,
  Florida

December 7
CONCERT
Orchestra
Brown
Theatre of the Performing Arts,
  New Orleans, Louisiana

December 10
RECITAL
Wustman, piano
Manitoba Centennial Concert Hall,
  Winnipeg, Manitoba

December 13
RECITAL
Wustman, piano
Teatro de la Universidad, San Juan

December 16
RECITAL
Wustman, piano
Bushnell Memorial, Hartford,
  Connecticut

December 19
RECITAL
Wustman, piano
Loew's Theater, Syracuse, New York

January 11
RECITAL
Magiera, piano
Royal Opera House, London

February 3
RECITAL
Magiera, piano
Teatro Comunale, Modena

February 15
RECITAL
Wustman, piano
Hill Auditorium, Ann Arbor, Michigan

March 22
TONIGHT SHOW
Wustman, piano
Stevenson, host
NBC Studios, Burbank, California

April 3
RECITAL
Wustman, piano
Kennedy Center Concert Hall,
  Washington, D.C.

April 6
RECITAL
Wustman, piano
Loew's Theater, New Rochelle,
  New York

April 9
RECITAL
Wustman, piano
Auditorium Theatre, Chicago, Illinois

April 11
CONCERT
Toronto Symphony
Feldbrill
Massey Hall, Toronto, Ontario

April 23
CONCERT
Orchestra Stabile Emilia-Romagna
Savini
Teatro Municipale, Reggio Emilia

April 26
RECITAL
Magiera, piano
Teatro alla Scala, Milan

May 3
RECITAL
Baracchi, piano
Teatro di San Carlo, Naples

May 24
RECITAL
Magiera, piano
Teatro Regio, Parma

May 28
RECITAL
Frazzoni;
Scano, Turtura, Bernardi, Verrini,
  Luperi
Magiera, piano
Teatro Storchi, Modena

June 2
RECITAL
Maruyama, M. Taddei, Scerbinina;
Dvorsky, Raffanti, Palm
Magiera, Pastorino, piano
Teatro Comunale, Modena

July 2
CONCERT
Maruyama
Orchestra Stabile Emilia-Romagna
Patanè
Piazza Verdi, Busseto

July 10
CONCERT
Chorus and Orchestra of the Théâtre
    National
Santi
Salle Garnier, Paris

July 31
RECITAL
Magiera, piano
Grosses Festspielhaus, Salzburg

1976–77

September 26
RECITAL
Wustman, piano
Calderone Concert Hall, Hempstead,
    New York

October 1
MET MARATHON
Amara, Behrens, Blegen, Hunter,
    R. Peters, Scotto, Shane,
    Zylis-Gara, R. Elias, Obraztsova;
Alexander, Cecchele, MacNeil,
    Manuguerra, Quilico, Sarabia,
    Sereni, Stilwell, Díaz, Morris, Tajo
Di Nunzio, Dornemann, Foster,
    Woitach, piano
Metropolitan Opera House, New York

October 3
RECITAL
Wustman, piano
Veterans Memorial Auditorium,
    Providence, Rhode Island

October 18
RECITAL
Wustman, piano
Gilliard Municipal Auditorium,
    Charleston, South Carolina

October 24
RECITAL
Wustman, piano
Symphony Hall, Boston, Massachusetts

October 31
TUCKER MEMORIAL GALA
Arroyo, Cruz-Romo, Moffo, Scotto,
    Obraztsova;
Carpenter, Di Stefano, Sereni, Giaiotti,
    Morris
Silberstein, cello
Levine, Queler, Woitach, piano
A. King, host
Carnegie Hall, New York

November 2
RECITAL
Wustman, piano
Municipal Auditorium, Charleston,
    West Virginia

November 16
MESSA DA REQUIEM (Verdi)
Freni, Cossotto;
Van Dam
Singverein der Gesellschaft der
    Musikfreunde, Vienna
Berlin Philharmonic Orchestra
Karajan
Carnegie Hall, New York

December 3
RECITAL
Wustman, piano
Carnegie Music Hall, Pittsburgh,
    Pennsylvania

December 19
RECITAL
Wustman, piano
Rebecca Cohn Auditorium, Halifax,
    Nova Scotia

January 9
RECITAL
Magiera, piano
Teatro de la Zarzuela, Madrid

February 2
RECITAL
Wustman, piano
Civic Theatre, San Diego, California

February 4
TONIGHT SHOW
Wustman, piano
Carson, host
NBC Studios, Burbank, California

February 6
RECITAL
Wustman, piano
War Memorial Opera House,
    San Francisco, California

February 13
RECITAL
Wustman, piano
Bailey Hall, Ithaca, New York

February 20
RECITAL
Wustman, piano
Orchestra Hall, Minneapolis,
    Minnesota

At La Scala preparing recital with Leone Magiera, a colleague since his debut; going onstage; and during Tosti's "Non t'amo più"

February 26
RECITAL
Wustman, piano
Massey Hall, Toronto, Ontario

March 6
RECITAL
Wustman, piano
Avery Fisher Hall, New York

July 10
CONCERT
Cahill, Freni, Lorengar,
    Te Kanawa, Troyanos;
Tear, Wixell, Howell
Civil, horn
Orchestra of the Royal Opera
Downes, Solti
Royal Opera House, London

1977–78

September 1
RECITAL
Wustman, piano
Teatro de la Universidad, San Juan

September 4
RECITAL
Wustman, piano
Blossom Music Center, Cleveland,
    Ohio

September 6
RECITAL
Wustman, piano
Salle Wilfrid Pelletier, Montréal,
    Québec

September 11
RECITAL
Wustman, piano
Great Hall, Urbana, Illinois

November 6
RECITAL
Wustman, piano
Ambassador Auditorium, Pasadena,
    California

November 7
TONIGHT SHOW
Wustman, piano
Newhart, host
NBC Studios, Burbank, California

November 14
FOL DE ROL
Caballé, L. Mitchell, Ricciarelli, Sills,
    South, Troyanos;
Carreras, Frank, Duesing, Mazurok,
    Wixell, Zancanero, Giaiotti, Tozzi
San Francisco Opera Orchestra and
    Ballet
Simmons
Civic Auditorium, San Francisco,
    California

November 26
RECITAL
Billard, Pellegrineschi;
Agostini, De Bortoli
Magiera, piano
Teatro Carani, Sassuolo

November 30
RECITAL
Wustman, piano
Ewah Woman's University Concert
    Hall, Seoul

December 3
RECITAL
Wustman, piano
Kanagwa Kenritsu Ongakudo,
    Yokohama

December 6
CONCERT
Japan Philharmonic Symphony
    Orchestra
Rucci
Koseinenkin Kaikan, Tokyo

December 9, 12
RECITAL
Wustman, piano
Bunka Kaikan, Tokyo (2)

January 1, 6
MESSA DA REQUIEM (Verdi)
Freni, Obraztsova;
Ghiaurov
Chorus and Orchestra of La Scala
Abbado
Chiesa di San Marco, Milan (2)

January 23, 24
TELEVISION RECITAL
Wustman
Norddeutscher Rundfunk, Hamburg

February 2
RECITAL
Wustman, piano
Jorgensen Auditorium, Storrs,
    Connecticut

Waltzing with Beverly Sills during San Francisco Opera Fol de Rol; autographing for admirer Carol Burnett; rehearsing with Kurt Herbert Adler at Berkeley's Greek Theatre; with composer-arranger Henry Mancini

February 5
RECITAL
Wustman, piano
Symphony Hall, Boston, Massachusetts

February 12
RECITAL
Wustman, piano
Metropolitan Opera House, New York

February 27
RECITAL
Wustman, piano
Music Hall, Cincinnati, Ohio

March 4
RECITAL
Wustman, piano
Fox Theatre, Atlanta, Georgia

April 1
CONCERT
Freni
Orquestra Sinfonica de Puerto Rico
K. H. Adler
Teatro de la Universidad, San Juan

April 22
RECITAL
Wustman, piano
Fine Arts Auditorium, Victoria, Texas

April 25
RECITAL
Wustman, piano
Uihlein Hall, Milwaukee, Wisconsin

April 27
RECITAL
Wustman, piano
Bushnell Memorial, Hartford,
    Connecticut

April 30
RECITAL
Wustman, piano
Academy of Music, Philadelphia,
    Pennsylvania

May 2
RECITAL
Wustman, piano
Municipal Auditorium, New Orleans,
    Louisiana

May 4
RECITAL
Wustman, piano
Carnegie Music Hall, Pittsburgh,
    Pennsylvania

May 5
DINNER RECITAL
Wustman, piano
Civic Opera House, Chicago, Illinois

May 7
RECITAL
Wustman, piano
National Arts Centre, Ottawa, Ontario

May 13
RECITAL
Magiera, piano
Teatro Novelli, Rimini

May 16
RECITAL
Watanabe, Kissel;
Marusin, Padovan, Alaimo
Magiera, Pastorino, piano
Sala Tropical, Rovereto sul Secchia

May ?
RECITAL
Magiera, piano
Faenza Lirica, Faenza
[The exact date of this recital could not be
established with the theater in Faenza.]

June 4
RECITAL
Wustman, piano
Royal Opera House, London

July 31
CONCERT
Del Grande, Kabaivanska,
    Mauti-Nunziata, Molnar-Talajic,
    Ricciarelli, Cortez, Mattiucci;
Giacomini, Lima, Luchetti,
    Boyagian, Bruson, Nucci,
    Zancanaro, Giaiotti, Zardo
Orchestra of the Arena di Verona
Ahronovitch, M. Arena, Gavazzeni
Arena di Verona

August 21
RECITAL
Magiera, piano
Grosses Festspielhaus, Salzburg

1978–79

September 22
CONCERT
Les Petits Chanteurs du Mont-Royal
Les Disciples de Massenet
Orchestra
Decker
Basilique Notre-Dame, Montreal,
    Quebec

September 24
RECITAL
Wustman, piano
Manitoba Centennial Concert Hall,
    Winnipeg, Manitoba

September 27
RECITAL
Wustman, piano
Queen Elizabeth Theater, Vancouver,
    British Columbia

October 3
RECITAL
Wustman, piano
Royal Theatre, Victoria,
    British Columbia

October 6
TONIGHT SHOW
Wustman, piano
Carson, host
NBC Studios, Burbank, California

October 7
RECITAL
Wustman, piano
Ambassador Auditorium, Pasadena,
    California

October 8
CONCERT
San Francisco Opera Orchestra
K. H. Adler
Hearst Greek Theatre, Berkeley,
    California

November 1
RECITAL
Wustman, piano
John Gano Memorial Hall, Liberty,
    Missouri

November 4
RECITAL
Wustman, piano
Music Club, Birmingham, Alabama

November 7
RECITAL
Wustman, piano
Theatre of the Performing Arts,
    Miami Beach, Florida

November 10
RECITAL
Wustman, piano
Van Wezel Performing Arts Hall,
    Sarasota, Florida

November 12
RECITAL
Wustman, piano
Kennedy Center Concert Hall,
  Washington, D.C.

December 3
RECITAL
Wustman, piano
Civic Opera House, Chicago, Illinois

January 7
TUCKER MEMORIAL GALA
Crespin, L. Mitchell, Shane, I. Jones;
Blake, Domingo, Merrill, Milnes,
  Giaiotti, Plishka
Chapin, host
Fulton, piano
Levine
Carnegie Hall, New York

January 11, 15
MASTER CLASSES
Del George, Kalisky, Mann, Marquez,
  Radman, Renée, DeVaughn, Gal,
  Mentzer, Partamian;
Chung, Di Paola, Holt, Schexnayder,
  Briggs
Wustman, piano
Juilliard School, New York (2)

January 22
CONCERT
Sutherland, Renée
Orchestra
Bonynge
Avery Fisher Hall, New York

February 15
CONCERT
Freni
Orchestra Stabile Emilia-Romagna
Magiera
Teatro Comunale, Modena

February 22
REQUIEM (Donizetti)
Cortez;
Bruson, Washington
Chorus and Orchestra of the Arena di
  Verona
Fackler
Filarmonico, Verona

April 4
CONCERT
Ricciarelli
Radio-Symphony Orchestra of Berlin
López-Cobos
Hall of Congress, Berlin

April 20
RECITAL
Wustman, piano
Medinah Temple, Chicago, Illinois

April 22
RECITAL
Wustman, piano
Warner Theater, Erie, Pennsylvania

April 29
CONCERT
Florida Philharmonic Orchestra
Buckley
Theatre of the Performing Arts,
  Miami Beach, Florida

May 13
RECITAL
Wustman, piano
Boettcher Concert Hall, Denver,
  Colorado

May 19
RECITAL
Wustman, piano
Teatro Municipal, Rio de Janeiro

May 21
RECITAL
Wustman, piano
Palácio das Convencões do Anhembi,
  São Paulo

May 26
CONCERT
Toronto Symphony
Davis
Massey Hall, Toronto, Ontario

May 31, June 2
MESSA DA REQUIEM (Verdi)
M. Price, Cossotto;
Ghiaurov
Chorus and Orchestra of La Scala
Abbado
Théâtre des Champs-Élysées, Paris (2)

June 6
RECITAL
Wustman, piano
Nationaltheater, Munich

July 3
CONCERT
Israel Philharmonic
Mehta
Binyenei Ha'oomah, Jerusalem

July 7
CONCERT
Israel Philharmonic
Mehta
Fredric R. Mann Auditorium, Tel Aviv

August 4
RECITAL
Magiera, piano
Palazzo Ducale, Martina Franca

August 22
RECITAL
Wustman, piano
Frederic R. Mann Music Center,
  Philadelphia, Pennsylvania

1979–80

September 9
CONCERT
Toczyska
San Francisco Opera Orchestra
K. H. Adler
Golden Gate Park, San Francisco,
  California

September 14
TONIGHT SHOW
Wustman, piano
Carson, host
NBC Studios, Burbank, California

September 19
RECITAL
Wustman, piano
Opera House, Seattle, Washington

September 23
RECITAL
Wustman, piano
Strawberry Hill, Hillsborough,
  California

September 27
CONCERT
Los Angeles Chamber Orchestra
Bartoletti
Civic Auditorium, Pasadena, California

October 4
In honor of His Holiness
  Pope John Paul II
RECITAL
Little
Haycraft, organ
Holy Name Cathedral, Chicago,
  Illinois

October 14
Twenty-fifth Anniversary of
   Lyric Opera of Chicago
CONCERT
Blegen, Freni, Monastero, L. Price,
   M. Price, E. Shade, Kuhlmann;
Cossutta, A. Kraus, Little, Vickers,
   Evans, Manuguerra, McConnell,
   Milnes, W. Mitchell, Stilwell,
   Stone, D. Carter, Ghiaurov;
Gobbi, Wanamaker, hosts
Chorus, Orchestra and Ballet of
Lyric Opera
Bartoletti, Chailly, Penderecki, Prêtre,
   Pritchard, Rescigno
Civic Opera House, Chicago, Illinois

October 31
RECITAL
Wustman, piano
Jones Hall for the Performing Arts,
   Houston, Texas

November 4
RECITAL
Wustman, piano
Royal Opera House, London

November 15
RECITAL
Magiera, piano
Supercinema 70, Carpi

November 25
RECITAL
Wustman, piano
Salle Garnier, Paris

December 18, 20
RECITAL
Renée (20 only)
Wustman, piano
Gaiety Theatre, Dublin (2)

December 31
RECITAL
Wustman, piano
Avery Fisher Hall, New York

January 14
CONCERT
Fairweather, Perlman
New York Philharmonic
Mehta
Avery Fisher Hall, New York

January 20
RECITAL
Renée
Wustman, piano
Kennedy Center Concert Hall,
   Washington, D.C.

January 26
CONCERT
Leonie Rysanek
Philadelphia Orchestra
W. Smith
Academy of Music, Philadelphia,
   Pennsylvania

February 10
RECITAL
Renée
Wustman, piano
Symphony Hall, Boston, Massachusetts

February 17
TUCKER MEMORIAL GALA
Battle, Cotrubas, Ricciarelli, Soviero,
   Quivar;
Bergonzi, Milnes, Plishka, Van Dam
F. Robinson, host
Fulton, Levine, piano
Carnegie Hall, New York

February 24
GALA OF STARS
L. Price, Scotto, Sills, Soviero,
   M. Horne, Troyanos, Ashley,
   Makarova;
Domingo, Ramey, Van Dam,
   Godunov, Lavery
Elster, harp
Stern, violin
West Side Story Company
Metropolitan Opera Orchestra
Levine
Metropolitan Opera House, New York

February 27
RECITAL
Wustman, piano
Whitman Hall, Brooklyn, New York

February 28
OMNIBUS
Lynn
Wustman, piano
CBS Studio, New York

March 25
RECITAL
Magiera, piano
Teatro alla Scala, Milan

April 4
MESSA DA REQUIEM (Verdi)
Freni, Obraztsova;
Raimondi
Chorus and Orchestra of La Scala
Abbado
Duomo, Parma

*Before a Richard Tucker Gala with Mrs. Tucker; Roberta Peters, a perfect colleague in opera and concert;
during Juilliard School Master Class with pupil Madelyn Renée; studying a score with Mirella Freni*

195

April 6
CONCERT
Orchestra of the Rossini Music
  Conservatory
Magiera
Teatro Rossini, Pesaro

April 26
RECITAL
Renée
Wustman, piano
Dade County Auditorium, Miami,
  Florida

May 17
RECITAL
Wustman, piano
Civic Opera House, Chicago, Illinois

May 30
TONIGHT SHOW
Wustman, piano
Carson, host
NBC Studios, Burbank, California

June 17
RIGOLETTO
Eda-Pierre, Grillo;
MacNeil, Hines;
Metropolitan Opera Chorus and
  Orchestra
Levine
Central Park, New York

June 20
CONCERT
Sinfóniuhljómseit Islands
K. H. Adler
Laugardalshöll, Reykjavik

1980–81

September 7
RECITAL
Wustman, piano
Colden Center for the Performing
  Arts, Flushing, New York

September 11
RECITAL
Wustman, piano
Garden State Arts Center, Holmdel,
  New Jersey

September 14
RECITAL
Wustman, piano
Symphony Hall, Newark, New Jersey

September 23
RECITAL
Renée
Wustman, piano
Opera House, Boston, Massachusetts

September 28
RECITAL
Wustman, piano
Kleinhaus Music Hall, Buffalo,
  New York

October 2
RECITAL
Renée
Wustman, piano
Chrysler Hall, Norfolk, Virginia

October 6
RECITAL
Wustman, piano
McCarter Theatre, Princeton,
  New Jersey

October 9
RECITAL
Wustman, piano
Academy of Music, Philadelphia,
  Pennsylvania

October 12
TUCKER MEMORIAL GALA
L. Mitchell, L. Price, Vaness, Zeani,
  M. Horne;
Malamood, McCauley, Milnes, Quilico,
  Plishka
Fulton, piano
New York City Center, New York

October 15
RECITAL
Wustman, piano
Civic Opera House, Chicago, Illinois

October 19
RECITAL
Renée
Wustman, piano
Great Hall, Urbana, Illinois

November 6
RECITAL
Magiera, piano
Teatro Comunale, Modena

November 10, 12
CONCERT
Zagreb Philharmonic
Franci
Ponedjeljak, Zagreb (1)
Brucknerhaus Grosser Saal, Linz (1)

Concert of the Century: with Marilyn Horne; banner heralding event; Richard Bonynge; Dame Joan Sutherland bestowing kiss

December 7
Italian Earthquake Benefit
CONCERT
Battle, Buchanan, Hayashi, Neblett,
  Scotto, Tomowa-Sintow, Howells,
  Payne, Troyanos;
W. Mitchell, Winkler, Nucci, Stilwell,
  Bogart, Dean, Macurdy, Voketaitis
Chorus and Orchestra of Lyric Opera
Favario, Pritchard, Schaenen
Civic Opera House, Chicago, Illinois

December 15
RECITAL
Renée
Wustman, piano
Van Wezel Performing Arts Hall,
  Sarasota, Florida

December 18
CONCERT
Fort Lauderdale Symphony Orchestra
Buckley
Dade County Auditorium, Miami,
  Florida

January 4
RECITAL
Fernando Pavarotti
Wustman, piano
Metropolitan Opera House, New York

February 8
RECITAL
Wustman, piano
Grand Théâtre, Geneva

February 19
RECITAL
Wustman, piano
Teatro Regio, Turin

February 22
RECITAL
Wustman, piano
Concertgebouw, Amsterdam

March 8
RECITAL
Renée
Wustman, piano
Forum, Harrisburg, Pennsylvania

March 11
RECITAL
Wustman, piano
St. Patrick's Cathedral, New York

March 20, 23
CONCERT
Sutherland, M. Horne;
Gardner
New York City Opera Orchestra
Bonynge
Avery Fisher Hall, New York (2)

March 21
A FESTIVAL AT FORD'S
L. Carter, L. Horne, Lynn, Makarova,
  Principal, Prowse;
Bennett, Benson, Cash, Copperfield,
  Cross, Dangerfield, DeLuise,
  Gennaro, Gibb, Klugman,
  A. Williams
Twyla Tharp Dance
Perlman, violin
Wustman, piano
Ford's Theatre, Washington, D.C.

March 27
CONCERT
Sutherland
Pittsburgh Symphony Orchestra
Bonynge
Heinz Hall, Pittsburgh, Pennsylvania

March 30
ACADEMY AWARDS
Arnaz, Cannon, Cara, Danner,
  Dickinson, Down, Field, Gish,
  Kidder, Kinski, Moore, Parton,
  B. Peters, Seymour, Shields, Spacek,
  Tomlin, Warwick, Weaver;
Arkin, Carson, Chamberlain, Cukor,
  Hoffman, Martin, Nelson, Nicholas
  Brothers, O'Toole, Pryor, Redford,
  Schifrin, Ustinov, Valenti, Vidor,
  B. D. Williams, Zeffirelli
Orchestra
Mancini
Dorothy Chandler Pavilion,
  Los Angeles, California

April 2
CONCERT
Fort Lauderdale Symphony Orchestra
Buckley
War Memorial Auditorium,
  Fort Lauderdale, Florida

April 9
DINNER RECITAL
Lear, Neblett, Zylis-Gara, R. Elias;
Titus, Wixell, Siepi
Wustman, piano
Eden Roc Hotel, Miami Beach, Florida

April 16
RECITAL
Wustman, piano
Constitution Hall, Washington, D.C.

April 27
RECITAL
Wustman, piano
Opernhaus, Zürich

May 2
CONCERT
Orchestra
Rescigno
Opernhaus, Zürich

May 16
RECITAL
Wustman, piano
Pauley Pavilion, Los Angeles,
  California

May 26
RECITAL
Renée
Wustman, piano
Chapman Music Hall, Tulsa, Oklahoma

May 31
RECITAL
Wustman, piano
Garden State Arts Center, Holmdel,
  New Jersey

June 13
Italian Earthquake Benefit
CONCERT
San Francisco Opera Orchestra
K. H. Adler
Civic Auditorium, San Francisco,
  California

June 27
CONCERT
Orchestra
Buckley
Edward A. Hatch Memorial Shell,
  Boston, Massachusetts

1981–82

October 26
RECITAL
Wustman, piano
Palace Theatre, Manchester

November 19
TONIGHT SHOW
Wustman, piano
Carson, host
NBC Studios, Burbank, California

January 17
RECITAL
Renée
Wustman, piano
Massey Hall, Toronto, Ontario

January 17 (midnight)
RECITAL
Renée
Wustman, piano
Four Seasons, Toronto, Ontario

January 24
RECITAL
Sinatra
George Shearing Quintet
Wustman, piano
Radio City Music Hall, New York

February 26
RECITAL
Wustman, piano
Centre de Congrès Auditorium,
    Monte Carlo

March 5
RECITAL
Renée
Magiera, piano
Chiesa di San Carlo, Modena

March 27
CONCERT
Renée, Scherler, P. Johnson, Toczyska;
Kollo, Rundgren, Salminen
Barenboim, piano
Berliner Kinderchor, Knaben des
    Staats-und Domchores, Schöneberger
    Sängerknaben
Chorus and Orchestra of the Deutsche
    Oper Berlin
Barenboim
Deutsche Oper Berlin

April 4, 8
RECITAL
Wustman, piano
Salle Garnier, Paris (2)

April 13
CONCERT
Royal Philharmonic Orchestra
K. H. Adler
Royal Albert Hall, London

April 17
RECITAL
Renée
Wustman, piano
Ballroom, Four Seasons Hotel,
    Houston, Texas

May 30 (afternoon)
CONCERT
Magiera, piano
Orchestra Sinfonica dell'Emilia-
    Romagna Arturo Toscanini
Soudant
Teatro Municipale, Piacenza

May 30
RECITAL
Aliberti; Giordano
Magiera, piano
Supercinema 70, Carpi

1982–83

September 1
TONIGHT SHOW
Carson, host
NBC Studios, Burbank, California

September 5
CONCERT
Los Angeles Philharmonic
K. H. Adler
Hollywood Bowl, Hollywood,
    California

September 26
CONCERT
Orchestra
Buckley
Metropolitan Center, Boston,
    Massachusetts

November 3
LUNCHEON RECITAL
Wustman, piano
Waldorf-Astoria Hotel, New York

November 7
RECITAL
Wustman, piano
Beverly Hilton, Beverly Hills,
    California

November 10
CONCERT
Fort Lauderdale Symphony Orchestra
K. H. Adler
James L. Knight Center, Miami,
    Florida

November 13
CONCERT
Fort Lauderdale Symphony Orchestra
K. H. Adler
Auditorium, West Palm Beach, Florida

November 16
CONCERT
Orchestra
Buckley
Metropolitan Center, Boston,
    Massachusetts

November 19
CONCERT
Montréal Symphony Orchestra
Buckley
Forum, Montréal, Québec

November 21
RECITAL
Wustman, piano
Gaillard Auditorium, Charleston,
    South Carolina

January 7
RECITAL
Wustman, piano
Civic Center Music Hall,
    Oklahoma City, Oklahoma

January 17
RECITAL
Wustman, piano
Neal S. Blaisdell Center Concert Hall,
    Honolulu, Hawaii

January 23
CONCERT
Sutherland
Elizabethan Sydney Orchestra
Bonynge
Opera House, Sydney

February 5
RECITAL
Renée
Wustman, piano
Concert Hall, Melbourne

March 7
RECITAL
Magiera, piano
Teatro alla Scala, Milan

March 27
RECITAL
Campogalliani, piano
G. Verdi Conservatory Auditorium,
    Milan

April 4
CONCERT
Morris
New York Choral Artists Men's Chorus
New York Philharmonic
Mehta
Avery Fisher Hall, New York

April 14
DINNER RECITAL
Cummings, Rolandi, Zschau,
Zylis-Gara;
Boyagian, Hines
Wustman, piano
Pavillon Hotel, Miami, Florida

April 22
CONCERT
Orchestra of Houston Grand Opera
Buckley
Summit Sports Arena, Houston, Texas

April 25
RECITAL
Wustman, piano
Civic Auditorium, San Francisco,
    California

May 15
RECITAL
Wustman, piano
Deutsche Oper Berlin

August 12
RECITAL
Wustman, piano
Tent, Lido di Camaiore, Viareggio

August 31
CONCERT
Garden State Symphony Orchestra
Buckley
Garden State Arts Center, Holmdel,
    New Jersey

1983–84

September 3
CONCERT
Orchestra of Lyric Opera
Bartoletti
Ravinia Pavilion, Chicago, Illinois

September 6
RECITAL
Wustman, piano
Music Hall, Kansas City, Missouri

October 22
METROPOLITAN OPERA
    CENTENNIAL GALA
Amara, Arroyo, Bumbry, Caballé,
    Cotrubas, Daniels, Devia, Meier,
    Merritt, L. Mitchell, Moffo, Moser,
    Neblett, Nilsson, L. Price,
    Ricciarelli, Berini, Dubinbaum,
    M. Dunn, R. Elias, M. Horne,
    Kesling, Kraft, Resnik;
Alexander, Carreras, Ciannella,

Giacomini, Jenkins, W. Lewis, Mauro,
    Rendall, Shicoff, Velis, Winbergh,
    Bruson, Darrenkamp, Duesing, Ellis,
    Elvira, Estes, MacNeil, Merrill,
    Berberian, Cheek, Ghiaurov, Hines,
    Macurdy, Plishka, Tajo
Metropolitan Opera Chorus, Orchestra,
    and Ballet
Bernstein, Fulton, Levine, Pritchard
Metropolitan Opera House, New York

October 29
CONCERT
Yushikawa, piano
New Jersey Symphony Orchestra
Buckley
Tent, Resorts International Hotel,
    Atlantic City, New Jersey

November 7
THE STARS SHINE FOR LIBERTY
Borne, Farrell, Gregory, Homek,
    Jahan, Lee, Tcherkassky;
Bergerac, Coles, Hope, Horiuchi,
    Martins, Radojevic
Dance Theatre of Harlem
New York City Ballet
West Point Glee Club
Wustman, piano
Orchestra
Irving, Kern, Larson
New York State Theater, New York

January 7, 8
MESSA DA REQUIEM (Verdi)
Varady, Denize;
Lloyd
Chorus and Orchestra of Paris
Barenboim
Salle Pleyel, Paris (1)
Palais des Congrès, Paris (1)

January 14
RECITAL
Wustman, piano
Victoria Hall, Geneva

February 14
RECITAL
Magiera, piano
Teatro Petruzzelli, Bari

February 24
RECITAL
Magiera, piano
Palazzo dello Sport, Bologna

March 4
RECITAL
Wustman, piano
Superstar Theater, Resorts
    International Hotel, Atlantic City,
    New Jersey

March 7
CONCERT
Griminelli, flute
Oklahoma Symphony Orchestra
Buckley
Civic Center Music Hall,
    Oklahoma City, Oklahoma

March 10
CONCERT
Griminelli, flute
Fort Lauderdale Symphony Orchestra
Buckley
James L. Knight Center, Miami,
    Florida

March 14
CONCERT
Griminelli, flute
Orchestra
Buckley
Wang Center for the Performing Arts,
    Boston, Massachusetts

March 18
CONCERT
Caballé, D. Ross;
Sinatra
New York Philharmonic
J. Williams
Radio City Music Hall, New York

March 21
CONCERT
Griminelli, flute
Orchestra
Buckley
Constitution Hall, Washington, D.C.

March 24
CONCERT
Griminelli, flute
Las Vegas Symphony Orchestra
Buckley
Riviera Hotel, Las Vegas, Nevada

March 27
RECITAL
Renée
Magiera, piano
Teatro Buenos Aires, Bilbao

May 20
CONCERT
Griminelli, flute
Orchestra of the Royal Opera House
Navarro
Royal Opera House, London

August 13
CONCERT
Griminelli, flute
Orchestra of Lyric Opera
Buckley
Poplar Creek Music Theatre, Chicago,
    Illinois

August 16
CONCERT
Griminelli, flute
New Jersey Symphony Orchestra
Buckley
Madison Square Garden, New York

August 19
CONCERT
Griminelli, flute
Dallas Symphony Orchestra
Buckley
Reunion Arena, Dallas, Texas

August 22
CONCERT
Griminelli, flute
San Francisco Opera Orchestra
Buckley
Civic Auditorium, San Francisco,
    California

August 26
CONCERT
Griminelli, flute
Los Angeles Philharmonic
Buckley
Hollywood Bowl, Hollywood,
    California

1984–85

October 3
RECITAL
Renée
Wustman, piano
Ballroom, Paradise Towers Hotel,
    Nassau, Bahamas

November 16
CONCERT
Griminelli, flute
American Symphony Orchestra
Buckley
Madison Square Garden, New York

February 3
RECITAL
Wustman, piano
Alte Oper, Frankfurt

February 25
RECITAL
Magiera, piano
Teatro Comunale, Florence

March 1
CONCERT
Griminelli, flute
Reno Philharmonic
Buckley
Lawlur Center, Reno, Nevada

March 3
CONCERT
Griminelli, flute
Las Vegas Symphony Orchestra
Buckley
Thomas & Mack Center, Las Vegas,
    Nevada

March 10
CONCERT
Frèni
Metropolitan Opera Orchestra
Levine
Metropolitan Opera House, New York

March 14
CONCERT
Griminelli, flute
Orchestra of the Opera Company of
    Philadelphia
Buckley
Spectrum, Philadelphia, Pennsylvania

March 17
CONCERT
Griminelli, flute
Toronto Symphony
Buckley
Maple Leaf Gardens, Toronto, Ontario

March 21
CONCERT
Griminelli, flute
St. Louis Symphony Orchestra
Buckley
Arena, St. Louis, Missouri

March 24
CONCERT
Griminelli, flute
Oklahoma Symphony Orchestra
Buckley
Lloyd Noble Center, Norman,
    Oklahoma

With Philadelphia competition's Antonio Tonini, Jane Nemeth; "Pavarotti Plus" star, Mary Jane Johnson, Jerry Hadley, Carol Vaness; greeting public at sports arena concert; Lorin Maazel, conductor for Philadelphia Messa da Requiem, *April 1986*

March 27
CONCERT
Sutherland
Phoenix Symphony Orchestra
Bonynge
State University Arena, Phoenix,
    Arizona

March 30
CONCERT
Sutherland
New Jersey Symphony Orchestra
Bonynge
Convention Center, Atlantic City,
    New Jersey

June 7
RECITAL
Wustman, piano
Deutsche Oper Berlin

June 14
RECITAL
Wustman, piano
Staatsoper, Hamburg

June 17
RECITAL
Wustman, piano
Staatsoper, Munich

June 21
CONCERT
Griminelli, flute
Orchestra della Provincia di Bari
Buckley
Piazza Basilica di S. Nicola, Bari

June 25
TONIGHT SHOW
Carson, host
NBC Studios, Burbank, California

June 27
CONCERT
Griminelli, flute
Orange County Pacific Symphony
Buckley
Sports Arena, San Diego, California

June 30
CONCERT
Griminelli, flute
Seattle Symphony Orchestra
Buckley
Coliseum, Seattle, Washington

August 7
RECITAL
Wustman, piano
Grosses Festspielhaus, Salzburg

August 14
CONCERT
Griminelli, flute
Orchestra Sinfonica dell'Emilia-
    Romagna Arturo Toscanini
Buckley
Piazza Grande, Modena

August 23
CONCERT
Plowright;
Cappuccilli, Burchuladze
Chorus and Orchestra of the
    Arena di Verona
Buckley
Arena di Verona

1985–86

September 8
CONCERT
Griminelli, flute
Columbus Symphony Orchestra
Buckley
Coliseum, Richfield, Ohio

September 17
CONCERT
Griminelli, flute
Orchestra
Buckley
Wang Center for the Performing Arts,
    Boston, Massachusetts

October 18
RECITAL
Magiera, piano
Teatro Metropolitan, Catania

November 8
RECITAL
Magiera, piano
Teatro Municipale, Reggio Emilia

November 23
RECITAL
Magiera, piano
Teatro Comunale, Modena

December 31
CONCERT
Griminelli, flute
Central Massachusetts Symphony
    Orchestra
Buckley
Centrum, Worcester, Massachusetts

January 6
PAVAROTTI PLUS!
S. Dunn, M. J. Johnson, Parrish,
    Vaness, Ziegler;
Hadley, Titus, Morris
New York City Opera Orchestra
Buckley
Avery Fisher Hall, New York

January 12
TUCKER MEMORIAL GALA
    MESSA DA REQUIEM (Verdi)
S. Dunn, I. Jones;
Plishka
New York Choral Artists
Members of the Metropolitan Opera
    Orchestra
Patanè
Carnegie Hall, New York

January 28
CONCERT
Griminelli, flute
Indianapolis Symphony Orchestra
Guadagno
Market Square Arena, Indianapolis,
    Indiana

January 30
CONCERT
Griminelli, flute
Louisville Philharmonic
Guadagno
Freedom Hall, Louisville, Kentucky

February 8
RECITAL
Cassello, Ducati, Focile, Izzo d'Amico,
    Pacetti, Palade, Tabiadon, Temesi,
    Komlosi;
Canonici, Costanzo, Mattsey, Picconi,
    Servile, DuPont, Scaltriti
Magiera, piano
Teatro Comunale, Modena

March 9
CONCERT
Griminelli, flute
Delaware Symphony Orchestra
Buckley
Civic Center, Baltimore, Maryland

April 5
MESSA DA REQUIEM (Verdi)
S. Dunn, Komlosi;
Burchuladze
Chorus and Orchestra of the
    Opera Company of Philadelphia
Maazel
Spectrum, Philadelphia, Pennsylvania

Posters proclaim a personal appearance by Pavarotti for a marathon autographing session at Tower Records in Los Angeles

Recorded Repertory

This survey contains the titles for all of Luciano Pavarotti's commercially approved recordings. Most were made under carefully controlled studio conditions; still others derive from "live" performances with audience present. No private issues—so-called "pirate" records —are included.

There are two sections to consider. The first, alphabetically arranged, gives complete works and excerpts expressly recorded as excerpts. The second details the many collections and anthologies on the market, showing how material on the first list is available to the consumer.

The tenor's recordings are released in an increasingly bewildering array of formats—conventional long-playing discs, 45 RPMs, compact discs, videodiscs, video cassettes, audio cassettes, reel-to-reel tape —and this has made impossible the logging of all catalogue numbers. Those given are for LPs and 45s, videodiscs and video cassettes. With this information, consumers should be able to trace the corresponding numbers of other formats with ease.

Please note that catalogue numbers of recordings are sometimes changed even though the contents remain unchanged. In addition, many pieces recorded by Pavarotti are regularly reissued in new packaging, coupled with different selections—a phenomenon common to both domestic and imported labels. What is more, in such reshuffling of content, an aria may be shorn of—or even regain—its recitative or cabaletta.

Dust jacket information, liner notes, and record labels are often in error, contradicting what music is actually contained on a given record. Each selection on this list has been checked against the recording and presents an accurate indication of what the collector can expect to purchase. If a recitative or cabaletta is sung, it is listed. If a piece recorded in a long form has been abbreviated, the shortened version is given.

Record stores in major cities now stock an international inventory of pressings—from the United States, England, Italy, West Germany, France, Japan, the Iron Curtain countries, and elsewhere. With a little effort, most of Pavarotti's recorded repertory can be located, and that is where the pleasure starts!

PART I

Addio, sogni di gloria (Innocenzi, arr. Mancini)
Orchestra, Mancini
London and Decca 411 959-1

Adeste fideles (Wade, arr. Gamley)
Wandsworth Boys Choir; London Voices
National Philharmonic Orchestra, K. H. Adler
London OS 26473; Decca SXL 6781

Adriana Lecouvreur: La dolcissima effigie (Cilèa)
National Philharmonic Orchestra, De Fabritiis
London LDR 10020; Decca SXDL 7504

Adriana Lecouvreur: L'anima ho stanca (Cilèa)
National Philharmonic Orchestra, De Fabritiis
London LDR 10020; Decca SXDL 7504

L'Africana: Mi batte il cor; O paradiso (Meyerbeer)
National Philharmonic Orchestra, De Fabritiis
London LDR 10020; Decca SXDL 7504

L'Africana: Mi batte il cor; O paradiso (Meyerbeer)
Orchestra dell'Ater, Magiera
London JL 41009; Decca SDD 578; Cime SDD 578

Agnus Dei (Bizet, arr. Guiraud and Gamley)
National Philharmonic Orchestra, K. H. Adler
London OS 26473; Decca SXL 6781

Aïda (Verdi)
Chiara, Dimitrova, Renée;
Nucci, Burchuladze, Roni, Gavazzi
Chorus and Orchestra of La Scala, Maazel
London and Decca (for future release)

Aïda (Verdi)
Chiara, Dimitrova, Garbi;
Pons, Ghiaurov, Burchuladze, Gavazzi;
Chorus and Orchestra of La Scala, Maazel
NVC Arts International Video (for future release)

Aïda: Se quel guerrier io fossi; Celeste Aïda (Verdi)
Vienna Volksoper Orchestra, Magiera
London OS 26384; Decca SXL 6649

Aïda: La fatal pietra; O terra addio (Verdi)
Sutherland, Connell
London Opera Chorus
National Philharmonic Orchestra, Bonynge
London OS 26449; Decca SXL 6828

L'alba separa dalla luce l'ombra (Tosti, arr. Faris)
Philharmonia Orchestra, Gamba
London OS 26669; Decca SXL 6850; SXL 7013

Alma del core (Caldara, arr. Faris)
Philharmonia Orchestra, Gamba
London OS 26669; Decca SXL 6850; SXL 7013

Alma del core (Caldara)
Magiera, piano
Mizar PM 1/2

L'Amico Fritz (Mascagni)
Freni, Gambardella, Major;
Sardinero, Di Bella, Pontiggia
Royal Opera Chorus and Orchestra of London, Gavazzeni
Angel SBL 3737; HMV SAN 242-3; SLS 938-2; SLS 5107

L'Amico Fritz: Suzel, buon dì; Han della porpora vivo
  il colore; Tutto tace (Mascagni)
Freni
Orchestra dell'Ater, Magiera
London JL 41009; Decca SDD 578; Cime SDD 578

Andrea Chénier (Giordano)
Caballé, Kuhlmann, Varnay, Ludwig;
Nucci, Cuenod, Andreolli, De Palma, Krause, Tadeo,
  Howlett, Hamer, Morresi
Welsh National Opera Chorus
National Philharmonic Orchestra, Chailly
London and Decca 410 117-1

Andrea Chénier: Colpito qui m'avete; Un dì all'azzurro
  spazio (Giordano)
National Philharmonic Orchestra, Chailly
London LDR 10020; Decca SXDL 7504

Andrea Chénier: Sì, fui soldato (Giordano)
National Philharmonic Orchestra, Chailly
London LDR 10020; Decca SXDL 7504

Andrea Chénier: Come un bel dì di maggio (Giordano)
National Philharmonic Orchestra, Chailly
London LDR 10020; Decca SXDL 7504

Aprile (Tosti, arr. Faris)
Philharmonia Orchestra, Gamba
London OS 26577; Decca SXL 6850

Aprile (Tosti, arr. Faris)
National Philharmonic Orchestra, Tonini
London OS 26669; Decca SXL 7013

L'Arlesiana: È la solita storia del pastore (Cilèa)
Vienna Opera Orchestra, Rescigno
London OS 26192; Decca SXL 6498

L'Arlesiana: È la solita storia del pastore (Cilèa)
Royal Philharmonic Orchestra, K. H. Adler
London LDR 71082; Decca SXDL 7582;
  Pioneer Artists LaserDisc PA-83-043

Atalanta: Care selve (Handel, arr. Gamley)
Teatro Comunale Orchestra of Bologna, Bonynge
London OS 26391; Decca SXL 6650

Attila: Oh dolore (Verdi)
La Scala Orchestra, Abbado
CBS Masterworks M 37228; 74037/40;
  Fonit Cetra LIC 9001

Ave Maria (Bach-Gounod, arr. Gamley)
Wandsworth Boys Choir
National Philharmonic Orchestra, K. H. Adler
London OS 26473; Decca SXL 6781

Ave Maria (Schubert, arr. Gamley)
National Philharmonic Orchestra, K. H. Adler
London OS 26473; Decca SXL 6781

Ave Maria (Schubert)
Beck, organ
London PDV 9001; Decca YG 1

'A vucchella (Tosti, arr. Chiaramello)
Teatro Comunale Orchestra of Bologna, Guadagno
London OS 26560; OS 26577; Decca SXL 6870

'A vucchella (Tosti)
Magiera, piano
Mizar PM 1/2

Un Ballo in Maschera (Verdi)
Tebaldi, Donath, Resnik;
Milnes, Monreale, Christou, Van Dam, Poli, Alessandrini
Santa Cecilia Accademia Chorus and Orchestra, Bartoletti
London OSA 1398; Decca SET 484;
    Highlights: London OS 26278; Decca SET 538;
    Time-Life STL-OP 11/CSL 2042

Un Ballo in Maschera (Verdi)
Ricciarelli, Blegen, Berini;
Quilico, Wildermann, Robbins, Darrenkamp, Anthony,
    Franke
Metropolitan Opera Chorus and Orchestra, Patanè
Pioneer Artists LazerDisc PA-84-089;
    Paramount Home Video 2362

Un Ballo in Maschera (Verdi)
M. Price, Battle, Ludwig;
Bruson, Lloyd, King, Weber, Oliver, Hall
London Opera Chorus; Royal College of Music Junior
    Department Chorus
National Philharmonic Orchestra, Solti
London and Decca 410 210-1

Un Ballo in Maschera: Teco io sto; Non sai tu; Oh, qual
    soave brivido (Verdi)
L. Price
Metropolitan Opera Orchestra, Levine
Pioneer Artists LaserDisc PA-84-095;
    Paramount Home Video 2364

Un Ballo in Maschera: Forse la soglia attinse; Ma se m'è
    forza perderti (Verdi)
Vienna Opera Orchestra, Downes
London OS 26087; Decca SXL 6377

Un Ballo in Maschera: Forse la soglia attinse; Ma se m'è
    forza perderti (Verdi)
Las Vegas Symphony Orchestra, Buckley
U.S.A. Home Video

Il Barcaiuolo (Donizetti, arr. Faris)
Philharmonia Orchestra, Gamba
London OS 26669; Decca SXL 6850; SXL 7013

Beatrice di Tenda (Bellini)
Sutherland, Veasey;
Opthof, Ward
Ambrosian Opera Chorus
London Symphony Orchestra, Bonynge
London OSA 1384; Decca SET 320;
    Highlights: London OS 26140

Beatrice di Tenda: Angiol di pace (Bellini)
Sutherland, Horne
New York City Opera Orchestra, Bonynge
London LDR 71102; LDR 72009; Decca D255D2

Bella Nice, che d'amore (Bellini, arr. Gamley)
Teatro Comunale Orchestra of Bologna, Bonynge
London OS 26391; Decca SXL 6650

Bella Nice, che d'amore (Bellini)
Magiera, piano
Mizar PM 1/2

La Bohème (Puccini)
Freni, Harwood;
Panerai, Maffeo, Ghiaurov, Sénéchal, Pietsch
Deutsche Oper Berlin Chorus
Berlin Philharmonic Orchestra, Karajan
London OSA 1299; Decca SET 565;
    Highlights: London OS 26399; Decca SET 579

La Bohème (Puccini)
Pellegrini, Bellesia;
Mattioli, De Ambrosis, Nabokov, Pasella, Pavaro
Teatro Municipale Chorus and Orchestra of Reggio Emilia,
    Molinari-Pradelli
Mizar/Gall. 30012

La Bohème: Che gelida manina (Puccini)
Royal Opera Orchestra of London, Downes
Decca CEP/SEC 5532

La Bohème: Che gelida manina (Puccini)
New Philharmonia Orchestra, Magiera
London OS 26192; Decca SXL 6498

La Bohème: Che gelida manina (Puccini)
New York City Opera Orchestra, Bonynge
London LDR 71101; LDR 72009; Decca D255D2

La Bohème: Che gelida manina (Puccini)
Las Vegas Symphony Orchestra, Buckley
U.S.A. Home Video

La Bohème: Che gelida manina (Puccini)
Symphony Orchestra of Emilia-Romagna Arturo Toscanini,
    Buckley
Mizar 50055

La campana di San Giusto (Arona, arr. Mancini)
Chorus and orchestra, Mancini
London and Decca 411 959-1

Carmen: La fleur que tu m'avais jetée (Bizet)
Vienna Volksoper Orchestra, Magiera
London OS 26384; Decca SXL 6649

Caro mio ben (Giordani, arr. Faris)
Philharmonia Orchestra, Gamba
London OS 26669; Decca SXL 6850; SXL 7013

Cavalleria Rusticana (Mascagni)
Varady, Gonzales, Bormida;
Cappuccilli
London Voices
National Philharmonic Orchestra, Gavazzeni
London OSA 13125; Decca D83D3;
   Highlights: Decca SXL 6986

Chanson de l'adieu (Tosti, arr. Faris)
Philharmonia Orchestra, Gamba
Decca SXL 6850

Chanson de l'adieu (Tosti, arr. Faris)
National Philharmonic Orchestra, Tonini
London OS 26669; Decca SXL 7013

Chiove (Nardella, arr. Chiaramello)
Teatro Comunale Orchestra of Bologna, Chiaramello
London and Decca 417 117-1

Chitarra romana (Di Lazzaro, arr. Mancini)
Orchestra, Mancini
London and Decca 411 959-1

Chitarra romana (Di Lazzaro, arr. Mancini)
Symphony Orchestra of Emilia-Romagna Arturo Toscanini,
   Buckley
Mizar 50055

Core 'ngrato (Cardillo, arr. Chiaramello)
Teatro Comunale Orchestra of Bologna, Chiaramello
London and Decca 417 117-1

La danza (Rossini, arr. Gamley)
Teatro Comunale Orchestra of Bologna, Bonynge
London OS 26391; Decca SXL 6650

Danza, danza, fanciulla (Durante, arr. Faris)
National Philharmonic Orchestra, Tonini
London OS 26669; Decca SXL 6850; SXL 7013

Danza, danza, fanciulla (Durante)
Magiera, piano
Mizar PM 1/2

Dicitencello vuie (Falvo, arr. Chiaramello)
Teatro Comunale Orchestra of Bologna, Chiaramello
London and Decca 417 117-1

Dolente immagine di Fille mia (Bellini, arr. Gamley)
Teatro Comunale Orchestra of Bologna, Bonynge
London OS 26391; Decca SXL 6650

Dolente immagine di Fille mia (Bellini)
Magiera, piano
Mizar PM 1/2

Don Pasquale: Com'è gentil (Donizetti)
New Philharmonia Chorus and Orchestra, Magiera
London OS 26192; Decca SXL 6498

Don Sebastiano: Deserto in terra (Donizetti)
Vienna Opera Orchestra, Downes
London OS 26087; Decca SXL 6377

Il Duca d'Alba: Inosservato penetrava; Angelo casto e bel
   (Donizetti)
Vienna Opera Orchestra, Downes
London OS 26087; Decca SXL 6377

I Due Foscari: Ah sì, ch'io sento ancora; Dal più remoto
   esilio (Verdi)
Vienna Opera Orchestra, Downes
London OS 26087; Decca SXL 6377

I Due Foscari: Qui ti rimani alquanto; Ah sì, ch'io sento
   ancora; Dal più remoto esilio; Sì lo sento, Iddio mi
   chiama (Verdi)
Savastano
La Scala Orchestra, Abbado
CBS Masterworks M 37228; 74037/40;
   Fonit Cetra LIC 9001

L'Elisir d'Amore (Donizetti)
Sutherland, Casula;
Cossa, Malas
Ambrosian Opera Chorus
English Chamber Orchestra, Bonynge
London OSA 13101; Decca SET 503;
   Highlights: London OS 26343; Decca SET 564

L'Elisir d'Amore (Donizetti)
Blegen, Wohlafka;
Ellis, Bruscantini
Metropolitan Opera Chorus and Orchestra, Rescigno
Pioneer Artists LazerDisc and Paramount Home Video
   (for future release)

L'Elisir d'Amore: Una parola, Adina; Chiedi all' aura
   lusinghiera; Per guarir di tal pazzia (Donizetti)
Freni
Orchestra dell'Ater Magiera
London JL 41009; Decca SDD 578; Cime SDD 578

L'Elisir d'Amore: Una furtiva lagrima (Donizetti)
MGM Studio Orchestra, Buckley
London PDV 9001; Decca YG 1

L'Elisir d'Amore: Una furtiva lagrima (Donizetti)
Royal Philharmonic Orchestra, K. H. Adler
Pioneer Artists LazerDisc PA-83-043

L'Elisir d'Amore: Una furtiva lagrima (Donizetti)
Verona Arena Theater Orchestra, Gatto
Cime ANC 25004

L'Elisir d'Amore: Una furtiva lagrima (Donizetti)
Las Vegas Symphony Orchestra, Buckley
U.S.A. Home Video

L'Elisir d'Amore: Una furtiva lagrima (Donizetti)
Magiera, piano
Mizar PM 1/2

Era de maggio (Costa, arr. Chiaramello)
Teatro Comunale Orchestra of Bologna, Chiaramello
London and Decca 417 117-1

Ernani (Verdi)
Mitchell, Kraft;
Milnes, Raimondi, Vernon, Anthony
Metropolitan Opera Chorus and Orchestra, Levine
Pioneer Artists LazerDisc and Paramount Home Video
   (for future release)

Ernani: D'Ernani i fidi chiedono; Odi il voto (Verdi)
Morresi, Giacomotti
La Scala Orchestra, Abbado
CBS Masterworks M 37228; 74037/40;
   Fonit Cetra LIC 9001

Ernani: Solingo, errante e misero (Verdi)
Sutherland, Horne
New York City Opera Orchestra, Bonynge
London LDR 71101; LDR 72009; Decca D255D2

La Fanciulla del West: Ch'ella mi creda libero e lontano
   (Puccini)
National Philharmonic Orchestra, De Fabritiis
London LDR 10020; Decca SXDL 7504

Faust: Quel trouble inconnu me pénètre; Salut! demeure
   chaste et pure (Gounod)
Vienna Volksoper Orchestra, Magiera
London OS 26384; Decca SXL 6649

La Favorita (Donizetti)
Cossotto, Cotrubas;
Bacquier, Ghiaurov, De Palma, De Franceschi
Teatro Comunale Chorus and Orchestra of Bologna,
   Bonynge
London OSA 13113; Decca D96D3;
   Highlights: Time-Life STL-OP 04/CSL 2015

La Favorita: Favorita del re; Spirto gentil (Donizetti)
Vienna Opera Orchestra, Downes
London OS 26087; Decca SXL 6377

Fedora: Amor ti vieta di non amar (Giordano)
National Philharmonic Orchestra, De Fabritiis
London LDR 10020; Decca SXDL 7504

Fedora: Amor ti vieta di non amar (Giordano)
Symphony Orchestra of Emilia-Romagna Arturo Toscanini,
   Buckley
Mizar 50055

Fenesta che lucive e mò non luce (Bellini,
   arr. Chiaramello)
Teatro Comunale Orchestra of Bologna, Chiaramello
London and Decca 417 117-1

Fenesta vascia (anon., arr. Chiaramello)
Teatro Comunale Orchestra of Bologna, Guadagno
London OS 26560; Decca SXL 6870

La Fille du Régiment (Donizetti)
Sutherland, Sinclair, Coates;
Malas, Bruyère, Garrett, Jones, Godknow
Royal Opera Chorus and Orchestra of London, Bonynge
London OSA 1273; Decca SET 372;
   Highlights: London OSA 26204; Decca SET 491;
   Time-Life STL-OP 04/CSL 2014

Firenze sogna (Cesarini, arr. Mancini)
Griminelli, flute
Chorus and orchestra, Mancini
London and Decca 411 959-1

Funiculì, funiculà (Denza, arr. Chiaramello)
Teatro Comunale Orchestra of Bologna, with chorus,
   Guadagno
London OS 26560; Decca SXL 6870

Gesù Bambino (Yon)
Wandsworth Boys Choir
National Philharmonic Orchestra, K. H. Adler
London OS 26473

La Ghirlandeina (anon., arr. Mancini)
Chorus and Orchestra, Mancini
London and Decca 411 959-1; Mizar 50055

La Gioconda (Ponchielli)
Caballé, Baltsa, Hodgson;
Milnes, Ghiaurov, Del Carlo, Romani, Macann, Varcoe,
   Jenkins, Shaw
London Opera Chorus
National Philharmonic Orchestra, Bartoletti
London LDR 73005; Decca D232D3

La Gioconda: Cielo e mar (Ponchielli)
New Philharmonia Orchestra, Magiera
London OS 26192; Decca SXL 6498

La Gioconda: Cielo e mar (Ponchielli)
MGM Studio Orchestra, Buckley
London PDV 9001; Decca YG 1

La Gioconda: Cielo e mar (Ponchielli)
Orchestra dell'Ater, Magiera
London JL 41009; Decca SDD 578; Cime SDD 578

La Gioconda: Cielo e mar (Ponchielli)
Las Vegas Symphony Orchestra, Buckley
U.S.A. Home Video

La Gioconda: Deh! non turbare (Ponchielli)
Horne
New York City Opera Orchestra, Bonynge
London LDR 71101; LDR 72009; Decca D255D2

La Gioconda: Ecco la barca! Addio (Ponchielli)
Sutherland, Horne
New York City Opera Orchestra, Bonynge
London LDR 71101; LDR 72009; Decca D255D2

Grande Messe des Morts: Sanctus (Berlioz)
Wandsworth Boys Choir; London Voices
National Philharmonic Orchestra, K. H. Adler
London OS 26473; Decca SXL 6781

Griselda: Per la gloria d'adoravi (Bononcini, arr. Gamley)
Teatro Comunale Orchestra of Bologna, Bonynge
London OS 26391; Decca SXL 6650

Griselda: Per la gloria d'adoravi (Bononcini)
Wustman, piano
Homevideo Exclusives 501B

Guglielmo Tell (Rossini)
Freni, Connell, Jones;
Milnes, Ghiaurov, Tomlinson, Mazzoli, De Palma,
 Van Allan, Suárez, Noble
Ambrosian Opera Chorus
National Philharmonic Orchestra, Chailly
London OSA 1446; Decca D219D4

Guglielmo Tell: Non mi lasciare; O muto asil del pianto;
 Corriam! Voliam (Rossini)
Vienna Opera Chorus and Orchestra, Rescigno
London OS 26192; Decca SXL 6498

L'Honestà Neglia Amori: Già il sole dal Gange (Scarlatti,
 arr. Gamley)
Mantovani, trumpet
Teatro Comunale Orchestra of Bologna, Bonynge
London OS 26391; Decca SXL 6650

Idomeneo (Mozart)
Cotrubas, Behrens, Von Stade, Di Franco, Godfrey;
Alexander, Jenkins, Clark, Anthony, Courtney
Metropolitan Opera Chorus and Orchestra, Levine
Pioneer Artists LazerDisc PA-85-134;
 Paramount Home Video 2372

Idomeneo (Mozart)
Popp, Gruberova, Baltsa, Fontana, Hintermeier;
Jenkins, Nucci, Storojew, Yamaji, Hillebrand
Vienna State Opera Chorus
Vienna Philharmonic, Pritchard
London and Decca 411 805-1

If We Were in Love (Williams)
MGM Studio Orchestra, Williams
London PDV 9001; LON45 20103; Decca YG 1

I Left My Heart in San Francisco (Cory)
MGM Studio Orchestra, Buckley
London PDV 9001; Decca YG 1

In questa tomba oscura (Beethoven, arr. Faris)
Philharmonia Orchestra, Gamba
London OS 26577; OS 26669; Decca SXL 6850;
 SXL 7013

In un palco della Scala (Mancini, Kramer, Garinei,
 Giovannini)
Orchestra, Mancini
London and Decca 411 959-1

Io la vidi (Verdi)
Savastano
La Scala Orchestra, Abbado
CBS Masterworks M 37228; 74037/40;
 Fonit Cetra LIC 9001

Iris: Apri la tua finestra (Mascagni)
National Philharmonic Orchestra, De Fabritiis
London LDR 10020; Decca SXDL 7504

I' te vurria vasà (Di Capua, arr. Chiaramello)
Teatro Comunale Orchestra of Bologna, Chiaramello
London and Decca 417 117-1

Linda di Chamounix: Linda! Linda! Ah, Carlo; Da quel dì
 che t'incontrai (Donizetti)
Sutherland
National Philharmonic Orchestra, Bonynge
London OS 26449; Decca SXL 6828

Lolita (Buzzi-Peccia, arr. Mancini)
Griminelli, flute
Orchestra, Mancini
London and Decca 411 959-1

Lolita (Buzzi-Peccia, arr. Mancini)
Griminelli, flute
Symphony Orchestra of Emilia-Romagna Arturo Toscanini,
 Buckley
Mizar 50055

I Lombardi alla Prima Crociata: La mia letizia infondere
 (Verdi)
Teatro Regio Orchestra of Parma, Patanè
London JL 41030; Decca SDD 569; Cime ANC 25001

I Lombardi alla Prima Crociata: Mortal di me più lieto;
 La mia letizia infondere (Verdi)
Royal Philharmonic Orchestra, K. H. Adler
London LDR 71082; Decca SXDL 7582;
 Pioneer Artists LaserDisc PA-83-043

I Lombardi alla Prima Crociata: Mortal di me più lieto;
  La mia letizia infondere; Come poteva un angelo (Verdi)
Magiera, piano
Mizar PM 1/2; PF 3

Lucia di Lammermoor (Donizetti)
Sutherland, Tourangeau;
Milnes, Ghiaurov, Poli, Davies
Royal Opera Chorus and Orchestra of London, Bonynge
London OSA 13103; Decca SET 528;
  Highlights: London OSA 26332; Decca SET 559

Lucia di Lammermoor: Tombe degli avi miei; Fra poco a me
  ricovero (Donizetti)
Vienna Opera Orchestra, Downes
London OS 26087; Decca SXL 6377

Lucia di Lammermoor: Tombe degli avi miei; Fra poco a me
  ricovero (Donizetti)
Royal Philharmonic Orchestra, K. H. Adler
London LDR 71082; Decca SXDL 7582;
  Pioneer Artists LaserDisc PA-83-043

Lucia di Lammermoor: Tombe degli avi miei; Fra poco a me
  ricovero (Donizetti)
Symphony Orchestra of Emilia-Romagna Arturo Toscanini,
  Buckley
Mizar 50055

Luisa Miller (Verdi)
Caballé, Reynolds, Celine;
Milnes, Giaiotti, Van Allan, Fernando Pavarotti
London Opera Chorus
National Philharmonic Orchestra, Maag
London OSA 13114; Decca SET 606

Luisa Miller: Oh! fede negar potessi; Quando le sere al
  placido (Verdi)
Vienna Opera Orchestra, Downes
London OS 26087; Decca SLX 6377

Luisa Miller: Oh! fede negar potessi; Quando le sere al
  placido (Verdi)
Royal Philharmonic Orchestra, K. H. Adler
London LDR 71082; Decca SXDL 7582;
  Pioneer Artists LaserDisc PA-83-043

Luisa Miller: Oh! fede negar potessi; Quando le sere al
  placido (Verdi)
Symphony Orchestra of Emilia-Romagna Arturo Toscanini,
  Buckley
Mizar 50055

Luisa Miller: Oh! fede negar potessi; Quando le sere al
  placido; L'ara, o l'avello apprestami (Verdi)
Magiera, piano
Mizar PM 1/2

Luna d'estate (Tosti, arr. Gamley)
Teatro Comunale Orchestra of Bologna, Bonynge
London OS 26391; Decca SXL 6650

Macbeth (Verdi)
Souliotis, Lawrence;
Fischer-Dieskau, Ghiaurov, Cassinelli, Noble, Fyson,
  Dance, Marsland, Myers
Ambrosian Opera Chorus
London Philharmonic Orchestra, Gardelli
London OSA 13102; Decca SET 510;
  Highlights: Decca SET 539

Macbeth: O figli, o figli miei; Ah, la paterna mano (Verdi)
Vienna Opera Orchestra, Downes
London OS 26087; Decca SXL 6377

Macbeth: O figli, o figli miei; Ah, la paterna mano (Verdi)
Teatro Regio Orchestra of Parma, Patanè
London JL 41030; Decca SDD 569; Cime ANC 25001

Macbeth: O figli, o figli miei; Ah, la paterna mano (Verdi)
Royal Philharmonic Orchestra, K. H. Adler
London LDR 71082; Decca SXDL 7582;
  Pioneer Artists LaserDisc PA-83-043

Madama Butterfly (Puccini)
Freni, Ludwig, Schary, Hurdes, Muhlberger, Heigl;
Kerns, Sénéchal, Stendoro, Rintzler, Helm, Schieder, Frese
Vienna State Opera Chorus
Vienna Philharmonic Orchestra, Karajan
London OSA 13110; Decca SET 584;
  Highlights: London OS 26455; Decca SET 605

Malia (Tosti, arr. Gamley)
Teatro Comunale Orchestra of Bologna, Bonynge
London OS 26391; Decca SXL 6650

Malia (Tosti)
Magiera, piano
Mizar PM 1/2

Malinconia, ninfa gentile (Bellini, arr. Gamley)
Teatro Comunale Orchestra of Bologna, Bonynge
London OS 26391; Decca SXL 6650

Malinconia, ninfa gentile (Bellini)
Magiera, piano
Mizar PM 1/2

Mamma (Bixio, arr. Mancini)
Orchestra, Mancini
London and Decca 411 959-1

Mamma (Bixio, arr. Mancini)
Symphony Orchestra of Emilia-Romagna Arturo Toscanini,
  Buckley
Mizar 50055

Manon Lescaut: Ma se vi talenta; Tra voi, belle (Puccini)
National Philharmonic Orchestra, De Fabritiis
London LDR 10020; Decca SXDL 7504

Manon Lescaut: Donna non vidi mai (Puccini)
National Philharmonic Orchestra, De Fabritiis
London LDR 10020; Decca SXDL 7504

Manon Lescaut: Donna non vidi mai (Puccini)
MGM Studio Orchestra, Buckley
London PDV 9001; Decca YG 1

Manon Lescaut: Ah! non v'avvicinate; Guardate, pazzo son
  (Puccini)
Howlett
National Philharmonic Orchestra, De Fabritiis
London LDR 10020; Decca SXDL 7504

Marechiare (Tosti, arr. Chiaramello)
National Philharmonic Orchestra, Chiaramello
London OS 26560; Decca SXL 6870

Ma rendi pur contento (Bellini, arr. Gamley)
Teatro Comunale Orchestra of Bologna, Bonynge
London OS 26391; Decca SXL 6650

Ma rendi pur contento (Bellini)
Magiera, piano
Mizar PM 1/2

Maria Mari' (Di Capua, arr. Chiaramello)
Teatro Comunale Orchestra of Bologna, Guadagno
London OS 26560; Decca SXL 6870

Maria Stuarda (Donizetti)
Sutherland, Tourangeau, Elkins;
Soyer, Morris
Teatro Comunale Chorus and Orchestra of Bologna,
  Bonynge
London OSA 13117; Decca D2D3;
  Highlights: Decca SET 624

Maristella: Io conosco un giardino (Pietri)
New Philharmonia Orchestra, Magiera
London OS 26192; Decca SXL 6498

Martha: M'apparì (Flotow)
New Philharmonia Orchestra, Bonynge
London OS 26384; Decca SXL 6649

Mattinata (Leoncavallo, arr. Faris)
Philharmonia Orchestra, Gamba
London OS 26577; OS 26669; Decca SXL 6850;
  SXL 7013

Mattinata (Leoncavallo, arr. Luck)
MGM Studio Orchestra, Buckley
London PDV 9001; Decc YG 1

Mefistofele (Boito)
Freni, Caballé, Condò, Jones;
Ghiaurov, De Palma, Leggate
London Opera Chorus; Trinity Boys Choir
National Philharmonic Orchestra, De Fabritiis
London LDR 73010; Decca D270D3

Mefistofele: Dai campi, dai prati (Boito)
National Philharmonic Orchestra, De Fabritiis
London LDR 10020; Decca SXDL 7504

Mefistofele: Ogni mortal mister gustai; Giunto sul passo
  estremo (Boito)
New Philharmonia Orchestra, Magiera
London OS 26192; Decca SXL 6498

Mefistofele: Ogni mortal mister gustai; Giunto sul passo
  estremo (Boito)
National Philharmonic Orchestra, De Fabritiis
London LDR 10020; Decca SXDL 7504

Messa da Requiem (Verdi)
Sutherland, Horne;
Talvela
Vienna State Opera Chorus
Vienna Philharmonic Orchestra, Solti
London OSA 1275; Decca SET 374

Messa da Requiem: Ingemisco (Verdi)
Las Vegas Symphony Orchestra, Buckley
U.S.A. Home Video

Me voglio fa'na casa (Donizetti)
Teatro Comunale Orchestra of Bologna, Guadagno
London OS 26577

La mia canzone al vento (Bixio, arr. Mancini)
Orchestra, Mancini
London and Decca 411 959-1

La mia canzone al vento (Bixio, arr. Mancini)
Symphony Orchestra of Emilia-Romagna Arturo Toscanini,
  Buckley
Mizar 50055

Mille cherubini in coro (Schubert, arr. Melichar and
  Gamley)
National Philharmonic Orchestra, K. H. Adler
London OS 26473

Minuit Chrétien: O Holy Night/Cantique de Noël
  (Adam, arr. Gamley)
National Philharmonic Orchestra, K. H. Adler
London OS 26473; Decca SXL 6781

Musica proibita (Gastaldon, arr. Mancini)
Orchestra, Mancini
London and Decca 411 959-1

Nebbie (Respighi)
Teatro Comunale Orchestra of Bologna, Bonynge
London OS 26391; Decca SXL 6650

Nebbie (Respighi)
Magiera, piano
Mizar PM 1/2

Nevicata (Respighi, arr. Gamley)
Teatro Comunale Orchestra of Bologna, Bonynge
London OS 26391; Decca SXL 6650

Nevicata (Respighi)
Magiera, piano
Mizar PM 1/2

Non t'amo più (Tosti, arr. Gamley)
Teatro Comunale Orchestra of Bologna, Bonynge
London OS 26391; Decca SXL 6650

Non t'amo più (Tosti)
Magiera, piano
Mizar PM 1/2; PF 3

Non ti scordar di me (De Curtis, arr. Mancini)
Chorus and orchestra, Mancini
London and Decca 411 959-1

Non ti scordar di me (De Curtis, arr. Mancini)
Symphony Orchestra of Emilia-Romagna Arturo Toscanini,
    Buckley
Mizar 50055

Norma (Bellini)
Sutherland, Caballé, Montague;
Ramey, Begley
Chorus and Orchestra of the Welsh National Opera,
    Bonynge
London and Decca 414 476-1

Norma: Adalgisa! Alma, costanza; Ma di', l'amato giovane
    (Bellini)
Sutherland, Horne
New York City Opera Orchestra, Bonynge
London LDR 71101; LDR 72009; Decca D255D2

'O marenariello (Gambardella, arr. Chiaramello)
Teatro Comunale Orchestra of Bologna, with chorus,
    Guadagno
London OS 26560; Decca SXL 6870

'O paese d' 'o sole (D'Annibale, arr. Chiaramello)
Teatro Comunale Orchestra of Bologna, Guadagno
London OS 26560; Decca SXL 6870

Orfeo ed Euridice: Che farò senza Euridice (Gluck)
Philharmonia Orchestra, Gamba
London OS 26577; OS 26669; Decca SXL 6850;
    SXL 7013

'O sole mio (Di Capua, arr. Chiaramello)
National Philharmonic Orchestra, Chiaramello
London OS 26560; Decca SXL 6870

'O sole mio (Di Capua)
MGM Studio Orchestra, Buckley
London PDV 9001; Decca YG 1

'O sole mio (Di Capua, arr. Chiaramello)
Las Vegas Symphony Orchestra, Buckley
U.S.A. Home Video

'O sole mio (Di Capua, arr. Chiaramello)
Symphony Orchestra of Emilia-Romagna Arturo Toscanini,
    Buckley
Mizar 50055

'O surdato 'nnammurato (Cannio, arr. Chiaramello)
Teatro Comunale Orchestra of Bologna, with chorus,
    Guadagno
London OS 26560; Decca SXL 6870

Otello: Già nella notte densa (Verdi)
Ricciarelli
Teatro Regio Orchestra of Parma, Patanè
London JL 41030; Decca SDD 569; Cime ANC 25001

Otello: Già nella notte densa (Verdi)
Sutherland
National Philharmonic Orchestra, Bonynge
London OS 26449; Decca SXL 6828

Otello: Già nella notte densa (Verdi)
Sutherland
New York City Opera Orchestra, Bonynge
London LDR 71102; LDR 72009; Decca D255D2

Pagliacci (Leoncavallo)
Freni:
Wixell, Saccomani, Bello, Panocia, Fernando Pavarotti
London Voices
National Philharmonic Orchestra, Patanè
London OSA 13125; Decca D83D3;
    Highlights: Decca SXL 6986

Pagliacci: Recitar! mentre preso dal delirio; Vesti la giubba
    (Leoncavallo)
Vienna Volksoper Orchestra, Magiera
London OS 26384; Decca SXL 6649

Pagliacci: Recitar! mentre preso dal delirio; Vesti la giubba
    (Leoncavallo)
Symphony Orchestra of Emilia-Romagna Arturo Toscanini,
    Buckley
Mizar 50055

La palummella (anon., trans. De Meglio, arr. Chiaramello)
Teatro Comunale Orchestra of Bologna, Chiaramello
London and Decca 417 117-1

Panis angelicus (Franck, arr. Gamley)
Wandsworth Boys Choir
National Philharmonic Orchestra, K. H. Adler
London OS 26473; Decca SXL 6781

Parlami d'amore, Mariù (Bixio, arr. Mancini)
Griminelli, flute
Orchestra, Mancini
London and Decca 411 959-1

Passione (Tagliaferri/Valente, arr. Chiaramello)
Teatro Comunale Orchestra of Bologna, Chiaramello
London and Decca 417 117-1

Pecchè (Pennino, arr. Chiaramello)
Teatro Comunale Orchestra of Bologna, Guadagno
London OS 26560; Decca SXL 6870

Les Pêcheurs de Perles: C'est toi, toi qu'enfin je revois;
   Au fond du temple saint (Bizet)
Ghiaurov
National Philharmonic Orchestra, Stapleton
London OSA 26554; Decca SXL 6858; F 13716

Petite Messe Solennelle (Rossini)
Freni, Valentini Terrani;
Raimondi
Magiera, piano; Rosetta, harmonium
La Scala Polyphonic Chorus, Gandolfi
Decca SDD 567; Cime C3S/134

Pietà, Signore (Neidermeyer, attributed to Stradella,
   arr. Gamley)
National Philharmonic Orchestra, K. H. Adler
London OS 26473; Decca SXL 6781

Pioggia (Respighi)
Teatro Comunale Orchestra of Bologna, Bonynge
London OS 26391; Decca SXL 6650

Pioggia (Respighi)
Magiera, piano
Mizar PM 1/2

Piscatore 'e Pusilleco (Tagliaferri, arr. Chiaramello)
Teatro Comunale Orchestra of Bologna, Guadagno
London OS 26560; Decca SXL 6870

La promessa (Rossini, arr. Faris)
Philharmonia Orchestra, Gamba
London OS 26669; Decca SXL 6850; SLX 7013

I Puritani (Bellini)
Sutherland, Caminada;
Cappuccilli, Ghiaurov, Cazzaniga, Luccardi
Royal Opera Chorus of London
London Symphony Orchestra, Bonynge
London OSA 13111; Decca SET 587;
   Highlights: Decca SET 619

I Puritani: A te, o cara (Bellini)
Auger;
Bunger, Lackner
Vienna Opera Chorus and Orchestra, Rescigno
London OS 26192; Decca SXL 6498

Requiem (Donizetti)
Cortez;
Bruson, Washington
Verona Arena Theater Chorus and Orchestra, Fackler
Decca SDD 566; Decca-Cime SDD 566; Cime ED 25010

Rigoletto (Verdi)
Sutherland, Tourangeau, Te Kanawa, Knight, Clément;
Milnes, Talvela, Grant, Cassinelli, Du Plessis, Gibbs
Ambrosian Opera Chorus
London Symphony Orchestra, Bonynge
London OSA 13105; Decca SET 542;
   Highlights: London OS 26401; Decca SET 580;
   Time-Life STL-OP 01/CSL 2002

Rigoletto: Questa o quella (Verdi)
Royal Opera Orchestra of London, Downes
Decca CEP/SEC 5532

Rigoletto: Questa o quella (Verdi)
Symphony Orchestra of Emilia-Romagna Arturo Toscanini,
   Buckley
Mizar 50055

Rigoletto: Parmi veder le lagrime (Verdi)
Royal Opera Orchestra of London, Downes
Decca CEP/SEC 5532

Rigoletto: La donna è mobile (Verdi)
Royal Opera Orchestra of London, Downes
Decca CEP/SEC 5532

Rigoletto: La donna è mobile (Verdi)
MGM Studio Orchestra, Buckley
London PDV 9001; Decca YG 1

Rigoletto: La donna è mobile (Verdi)
Symphony Orchestra of Emilia-Romagna Arturo Toscanini,
   Buckley
Mizar 50055

Rondine al nido (De Crescenzo, arr. Mancini)
Griminelli, flute
Orchestra, Mancini
London and Decca 411 959-1

Rondine al nido (De Crescenzo, arr. Mancini)
Griminelli, flute
Symphony Orchestra of Emilia-Romagna Arturo Toscanini,
   Buckley
Mizar 50055

Der Rosenkavalier (Strauss)
Minton, Crespin, Donath, Howells, Loose, Schwaiger,
   Auger, Yachmi, Mayr;
Jungwirth, Wiener, Dickie, Lackner, Prikopa, Equiluz,
   Dermota, Jerger, Terkal, Pipal, Tomaschek, Maly,
   Heppe, Setzer, Strack, Simkowsky, Reautschnigg
Vienna State Opera Chorus
Vienna Philharmonic Orchestra, Solti
London OSA 1435; Decca SET 418;
   Highlights: London OS 26200; Decca SET 487

Santa Lucia (Cottrau, arr. Courage)
Romano
MGM Studio Orchestra, Buckley
London PDV 9001; Decca YG 1

Santa Lucia luntana (Mario, arr. Chiaramello)
Teatro Comunale Orchestra of Bologna, Chiaramello
London and Decca 417 117-1

La serenata (Tosti, arr. Gamley)
Teatro Comunale Orchestra of Bologna, Bonynge
London OS 26391; Decca SXL 6650

La serenata (Tosti)
Magiera, piano
Mizar PM 1/2

Le Sette Ultime Parole di Nostro Signore Sulla Croce:
  Parola Quinta: Qual giglio candido (Mercadante,
    arr. Gamley)
National Philharmonic Orchestra, K. H. Adler
London OS 26473; Decca SXL 6781

Silenzio cantatore (Lama, arr. Chiaramello)
Teatro Comunale Orchestra of Bologna, Chiaramello
London and Decca 417 117-1

La Sonnambula (Bellini)
Sutherland, Buchanan, Jones;
Ghiaurov, Tomlinson, De Palma
London Opera Chorus
National Philharmonic Orchestra, Bonynge
London LDR 73004; Decca D230D3

La Sonnambula: Perdona, o mia diletta; Prendi: l'anel
  ti dono; Oh, vorrei trovar parola (Bellini)
Sutherland
National Philharmonic Orchestra, Bonynge
London OS 26449; Decca SXL 6828

Stabat Mater (Rossini)
Lorengar, Minton;
Sotin
London Symphony Chorus and Orchestra, Kertész
London OS 26250; Decca SXL 6534

Te voglio bene assaje (anon., arr. Chiaramello)
Teatro Comunale Orchestra of Bologna, Chiaramello
London and Decca 417 117-1

Torna a Surriento (De Curtis, arr. Chiaramello)
National Philharmonic Orchestra, Chiaramello
London OS 26560; Decca SXL 6870

Torna a Surriento (De Curtis, arr. Chiaramello)
Royal Philharmonic Orchestra, K. H. Adler
London LDR 71082; Decca SXDL 7582;
  Pioneer Artists LaserDisc PA-83-043

Torna a Surriento (De Curtis, arr. Chiaramello)
Las Vegas Symphony Orchestra, Buckley
U.S.A. Home Video

Torna a Surriento (De Curtis, arr. Chiaramello)
Symphony Orchestra of Emilia-Romagna Arturo Toscanini,
  Buckley
Mizar 50055

Tosca (Puccini)
Freni;
Milnes, Tajo, Van Allan, Sénéchal, Hudson, Tomlinson,
  Baratti
Wandsworth Boys Choir; London Opera Chorus
National Philharmonic Orchestra, Rescigno
London OSA 12113; Decca D134D2;
  Highlights: London OS 26666; Decca SXL 6984

Tosca: Recondita armonia (Puccini)
Royal Philharmonic Orchestra, K. H. Adler
London LDR 71082; Decca SXDL 7582;
  Pioneer Artists LaserDisc PA-83-043

Tosca: E lucevan le stelle (Puccini)
Royal Opera Orchestra of London, Downes
Decca CEP/SEC 5532

Tosca: E lucevan le stelle (Puccini)
Royal Philharmonic Orchestra, Magiera
London OS 26384; Decca SXL 6649

Tosca: E lucevan le stelle (Puccini)
Royal Philharmonic Orchestra, K. H. Adler
London LDR 71082; Decca SXDL 7582;
  Pioneer Artists LaserDisc PA-83-043

La Traviata (Verdi)
Sutherland, Jones, Lambriks;
Manuguerra, Oliver, Summers, Tomlinson, Tadeo,
  Gardini, Elvin, Wilson-Johnson
London Opera Chorus
National Philharmonic Orchestra, Bonynge
London LDR 73002; Decca D212D3;
  Highlights: London LDR 71062; Decca SXDL 7562

La Traviata: Libiamo ne' lieti calici (Verdi)
Sutherland
London Opera Chorus
National Philharmonic Orchestra, Bonynge
London OS 26449; Decca SXL 6828

La Traviata: Libiamo ne' lieti calici (Verdi)
Freni
Orchestra dell'Ater, Magiera
London JL 41009; Decca SDD 578; Cime SDD 578

La Traviata: Un dì, felice (Verdi)
Sutherland
National Philharmonic Orchestra, Bonynge
London OS 26449; Decca SXL 6828

La Traviata: Lungi da lei; De' miei bollenti spiriti (Verdi)
Teatro Regio Orchestra of Parma, Patanè
London JL 41030; Decca SDD 569; Cime ANC 25001

La Traviata: Lungi da lei; De' miei bollenti spiriti (Verdi)
Las Vegas Symphony Orchestra, Buckley
U.S.A. Home Video

La Traviata: Signora! Che t'accadde; Parigi, o cara (Verdi)
Sutherland, Fugelle
National Philharmonic Orchestra, Bonynge
London OS 26449; Decca SXL 6828

La Traviata: Parigi, o cara (Verdi)
Freni
Orchestra dell'Ater, Magiera
London JL 41009; Decca SDD 578; Cime SDD 578

Tre giorni son che Nina (Ciampi, attributed to Pergolesi,
  arr. Faris)
Philharmonia Orchestra, Gamba
London OS 26669; Decca SXL 6850; SXL 7013

Tre giorni son che Nina (Ciampi, attributed to Pergolesi)
Magiera, piano
Mizar PM 1/2

Il Trovatore (Verdi)
Sutherland, Horne, Burrowes;
Wixell, Ghiaurov, Clark, Evans, Knapp
London Opera Chorus
National Philharmonic Orchestra, Bonynge
London OSA 13124; Decca D82D3;
  Highlights: Decca SET 631

Il Trovatore: Di qual tetra luce; Ah sì, ben mio; L'onda de'
  suoni mistici; Di quella pira (Verdi)
Flossmann;
Baillie
Vienna Opera Chorus and Orchestra, Rescigno
London OS 26192; Decca SXL 6498

Il Trovatore: Madre? non dormi; Ai nostri monti; Che! non
  m'inganno; Prima che d'altri vivere (Verdi)
Sutherland, Horne;
Gardner
New York City Opera Orchestra, Bonynge
London LDR 71102; LDR 72009; Decca D255D2

Tu, ca nun chiagne (De Curtis, arr. Chiaramello)
Teatro Comunale Orchestra of Bologna, Guadagno
London OS 26560; Decca SXL 6870

Turandot (Puccini)
Sutherland, Caballé;
Ghiaurov, Poli, De Palma, Krause, Pears, Markov
Wandsworth Boys Choir; John Alldis Choir
London Philharmonic Orchestra, Mehta
London OSA 13108; Decca SET 561;
  Highlights: London OS 26377; Decca SET 573

Turandot: Muoia! sì, muoia; Mai nessun m'avrà;
  Nessun dorma (Puccini)
Mitchell
MGM Studio Chorus and Orchestra, Buckley
London PDV 9001; Decca YG 1

Turandot: Nessun dorma (Puccini)
Royal Philharmonic Orchestra, K. H. Adler
London LDR 71082; Decca SXDL 7582;
  Pioneer Artists LaserDisc PA-83-043

Turandot: Nessun dorma (Puccini)
Verona Arena Theater Orchestra, Gatto
Cime ÁNC 25004

Turandot: Nessun dorma (Puccini)
Las Vegas Symphony Orchestra, Buckley
U.S.A. Home Video

Turandot: Nessun dorma (Puccini)
Symphony Orchestra of Emilia-Romagna Arturo Toscanini,
  Buckley
Mizar 50055

L'ultima canzone (Tosti, arr. Faris)
Philharmonia Orchestra, Gamba
London OS 26669; Decca SXL 6850; SXL 7013

L'ultima canzone (Tosti)
Magiera, piano
Mizar PM 1/2

Vaga luna, che inargenti (Bellini, arr. Faris)
Philharmonia Orchestra, Gamba
London OS 26577; OS 26669; Decca SXL 6850;
  SXL 7013

Vanne, o rosa fortunata (Bellini, arr. Gamley)
Teatro Comunale Orchestra of Bologna, Bonynge
London OS 26391; Decca SXL 6650

Vanne, o rosa fortunata (Bellini)
Magiera, piano
Mizar PM 1/2

Les Vêpres Siciliennes: A toi que j'ai chérie (Verdi)
La Scala Orchestra, Abbado
CBS Masterworks M 37228; 74037/40;
  Fonit Cetra LIC 9001

Vieni sul mar (Califano, arr. Mancini)
Chorus and Orchestra, Mancini
London and Decca 411 959-1

Vivere (Bixio, arr. Mancini)
Orchestra, Mancini
London and Decca 411 959-1

Voce 'e notte (De Curtis, arr. Chiaramello)
Teatro Comunale Orchestra of Bologna, Chiaramello
London and Decca 417 117-1

Voglio vivere così (D'Anzi, arr. Mancini)
Orchestra, Mancini
London and Decca 411 959-1

Werther: Pourquoi me réveiller (Massenet)
National Philharmonic Orchestra, De Fabritiis
London LDR 10020; Decca SXDL 7504

Werther: Pourquoi me réveiller (Massenet)
Orchestra dell'Ater, Magiera
London JL 41009; Decca SDD 578; Cime SDD 578

Werther: Pourquoi me réveiller (Massenet)
Las Vegas Symphony Orchestra, Buckley
U.S.A. Home Video

Richard Rollefson and John Harper of London Records with the tenor and his first platinum recording, O Holy Night

PART II

"Alla Mia Città, Luciano"
La Bohème: Che gelida manina
Chitarra romana
Fedora: Amor ti vieta di non amar
La Ghirlandeina*
Lolita (with Griminelli)
Lucia di Lammermoor: Tombe degli avi miei; Fra poco a me
    ricovero
Luisa Miller: Oh! fede negar potessi; Quando le sere al
    placido
Mamma
La mia canzone al vento
Non ti scordar di me
'O sole mio
Pagliacci: Recitar! mentre preso dal delirio; Vesti la giubba
Rigoletto: Questa o quella
    La donna è mobile
Rondine al nido (with Griminelli)
Torna a Surriento
Turandot: Nessun Dorma
Selections played by Griminelli:
    Orfeo ed Euridice: Dance of the Blessed Spirits
    Suite for Flute and Orchestra: Waltz
    The Tale of Tsar Sultan: Flight of the Bumble Bee
Orchestral selections:
    La Gazza Ladra: Overture
    Nabucco: Overture
Andrea Griminelli, flute
Symphony Orchestra of Emilia-Romagna Arturo Toscanini,
    Emerson Buckley
* Chorus and Orchestra, Henry Mancini (courtesy
    London/Decca Records)
Mizar 50055

Arias of Verdi and Donizetti
Un Ballo in Maschera: Forse la soglia attinse; Ma se m'è
    forza perderti
Don Sebastiano: Deserto in terra
Il Duca d'Alba: Inosservato penetrava; Angelo casto e bel
I Due Foscari: Ah sì, ch'io sento ancora; Dal più remoto
    esilio
La Favorita: Favorita del re; Spirto gentil
Lucia di Lammermoor: Tombe degli avi miei; Fra poco a me
    ricovero
Luisa Miller: Oh! fede negar potessi; Quando le sere al
    placido
Macbeth: O figli, o figli miei; Ah, la paterna mano
Vienna Opera Orchestra, Edward Downes
London OS 26087; Decca SXL 6377

Benvenuto Luciano!
Mamma (Mancini)
La mia canzone al vento (Mancini)
Parlami d'amore, Mariù (Mancini, with Griminelli)
Rondine al nido (Mancini, with Griminelli)
Teldec 6.20431

The Best of Pavarotti
Aïda: Se quel guerrier io fossi; Celeste Aïda (Magiera)
L'Arlesiana: È la solita storia del pastore (Rescigno)
Un Ballo in Maschera: Di' tu se fedele (complete Bartoletti,
    with Donath, Monreale, Christou)
    Forse la soglia attinse; Ma se m'è forza perderti
    (Downes)
La Bohème: Che gelida manina (complete Karajan)
Carmen: La fleur que tu m'avais jetée (Magiera)
Don Pasquale: Com'è gentil (Magiera)
Don Sebastiano: Deserto in terra (Downes)
Il Duca d'Alba: Inosservato penetrava; Angelo casto e bel
    (Downes)
I Due Foscari: Ah sì, ch'io sento ancora; Dal più remoto
    esilio (Downes)
L'Elisir d'Amore: Quanto è bella (complete Bonynge)
    Una furtiva lagrima (complete Bonynge)
Faust: Quel trouble inconnu me pénètre; Salut! demeure
    chaste et pure (Magiera)
La Favorita: Favorita del re; Spirto gentil (complete
    Bonynge)
La Fille du Régiment: Ah! mes amis, quel jour de fête;
    Que dire, que faire; Pour mon âme quel destin
    (complete Bonynge, with Garrett)
    Écoutez-moi, de grâce! Pour me rapprocher de Marie
    (complete Bonynge)
La Gioconda: Cielo e mar (Magiera)
Guglielmo Tell: Non mi lasciare; O muto asil del pianto;
    Corriam! Voliam (complete Chailly)
Lucia di Lammermoor: Tombe degli avi miei; Fra poco a me
    ricovero (complete Bonynge)
Luisa Miller: Oh! fede negar potessi; Quando le sere al
    placido (complete Maag)
Macbeth: O figli, o figli miei; Ah, la paterna mano
    (complete Gardelli)
Maria Stuarda: Ah, rimiro il bel sembiante (complete
    Bonynge, with Soyer)
Maristella: Io conosco un giardino (Magiera)
Martha: M'apparì (Bonynge)
Mefistofele: Ogni mortal mister gustai; Giunto sul passo
    estremo (Magiera)
Messa da Requiem: Ingemisco (complete Solti)
Pagliacci: Recitar! mentre preso dal delirio; Vesti la giubba
    (Magiera)
I Puritani: A te, o cara (complete Bonynge, with
    Sutherland, Ghiaurov, Luccardi)
Rigoletto: Questa o quella (complete Bonynge)
    Ella mi fu rapita; Parmi veder le lagrime (complete
    Bonynge)
    La donna è mobile (complete Bonynge)
Der Rosenkavalier: Di rigori armato in seno (complete Solti)
Stabat Mater: Cujus animam (complete Kertész)
Tosca: Recondita armonia (complete Rescigno, with Tajo)
    E lucevan le stelle (complete Rescigno)
Il Trovatore: Di qual tetra luce; Ah sì, ben mio; L'onda de'
    suoni mistici; Di quella pira (Rescigno, with Flossmann,
    Baillie)
Turandot: Non piangere, Liù (complete Mehta, with
    Caballé, Ghiaurov)
    Nessun dorma (complete Mehta)
London PAV 2009

The Bing Years II: 1961–72
Lucia di Lammermoor: Fra poco a me ricovero (Downes)
Other selections sung by:
  Grace Bumbry, Montserrat Caballé, Régine Crespin,
    Mirella Freni, Evelyn Lear, Pilar Lorengar, Anna
    Moffo, Birgit Nilsson, Roberta Peters, Leontyne Price,
    Leonie Rysanek, Renata Scotto, Teresa Stratas, Joan
    Sutherland, Renata Tebaldi, Marilyn Horne, Christa
    Ludwig, Regina Resnik, Sieglinde Wagner;
  Carlo Bergonzi, Franco Corelli, Placido Domingo,
    Nicolai Gedda, Alfredo Kraus, James McCracken, Jon
    Vickers, Gabriel Bacquier, Walter Berry, Cornell
    MacNeil, Sherrill Milnes, Rolando Panerai, Hermann
    Prey, Mario Sereni, Thomas Stewart, Nicolai
    Ghiaurov, Alfredo Mariotti, Giorgio Tozzi
Met 406

Bravo Pavarotti!
Un Ballo in Maschera: Leggere vi piace; La rivedrà
  nell'estasi (complete Bartoletti, with Donath,
  Monreale, Christou)
    È scherzo od è follia (complete Bartoletti, with Donath,
    Resnik, Montreale, Christou)
La Bohème: In un coupé; O Mimì, tu più non torni
  (complete Karajan, with Panerai)
L'Elisir d'Amore: Chiedi all'aura lusinghiere; Per guarir di
  tal pazzia (complete Bonynge, with Sutherland)
La Favorita: Favorita del re; Spirto gentil (complete
  Bonynge)
La Fille du Régiment: Ah! mes amis, quel jour de fête;
  Que dire, que faire; Pour mon âme quel destin
  (complete Bonynge, with Garrett)
    Écoutez-moi, de grâce! Pour me rapprocher de Marie
    (complete Bonynge)
Lucia di Lammermoor: Chi mi frena in tal momento
  (complete Bonynge, with Sutherland, Tourangeau,
  Milnes, Ghiaurov, Davies)
    Tu che a Dio spiegasti l'ali (complete Bonynge, with
    Ghiaurov)
Luisa Miller: Oh! fede negar potessi; Quando le sere al
  placido (complete Maag)
Messa da Requiem: Ingemisco (complete Solti)
I Puritani: A te, o cara (complete Bonynge, with
  Sutherland, Ghiaurov, Luccardi)
Rigoletto: Ella mi fu rapita; Parmi veder le lagrime
  (complete Bonynge)
    La donna è mobile; È là vostr'uomo; Un dì, se ben
    rammentomi; Bella figlia dell'amore (complete
    Bonynge, with Sutherland, Tourangeau, Milnes,
    Ghiaurov)
Der Rosenkavalier: Di rigori armato in seno (complete Solti)
Tosca: E lucevan le stelle (Magiera)
La Traviata: Libiamo ne' lieti calici (Bonynge, with
  Sutherland)
    Un dì, felice (Bonynge, with Sutherland)
Il Trovatore: Se m'ami ancor; Ai nostri monti (complete
  Bonynge, with Horne)
Turandot: Non piangere, Liù (complete Mehta, with
  Caballé, Ghiaurov)
London PAV 2001; Decca D129D2

Favourite Italian Arias
La Bohème: Che gelida manina
Rigoletto: Questa o quella
  Parmi veder le lagrime
  La donna è mobile
Tosca: E lucevan le stelle
Royal Opera Orchestra of London, Edward Downes
Decca CEP/SEC 5532

Gala Concert at the Royal Albert Hall
L'Arlesiana: È la solita storia del pastore
L'Elisir d'Amore: Una furtiva lagrima (not in London or
  Decca collections)
I Lombardi alla Prima Crociata: Mortal di me più lieto;
  La mia letizia infondere
Lucia di Lammermoor: Tombe degli avi miei; Fra poco a me
  ricovero
Luisa Miller: Oh! fede negar potessi; Quando le sere al
  placido
Macbeth: O figli, o figli miei; Ah, la paterna mano
Torna a Surriento
Tosca: Recondita armonia
  E lucevan le stelle
Turandot: Nessun dorma
Orchestral selections:
  La Forza del Destino: Overture (not in London or Decca
    collections)
  Un Giorno di Regno: Overture (not in Pioneer Artists
    collection)
  Les Troyens: Royal Hunt and Storm (not in Pioneer
    Artists collection)
Royal Philharmonic Orchestra, Kurt Herbert Adler
London LDR 71082; Decca SXDL 7582;
  Pioneer Artists LaserDisc PA-83-043

Le Grandi Voci dell'Arena di Verona, Vol. 2
L'Elisir d'Amore: Una furtiva lagrima (Gatto)
Turandot: Nessun dorma (Gatto)
Selections sung by Cappuccilli:
  Andrea Chénier: Son sessant'anni (Gatto)
    Nemico della patria (Gatto)
  Faust: O santa medaglia (Gatto)
Selections sung by Kabaivanska:
  Adriana Lecouvreur: Io sono l'umile ancella (Martinotti)
  Otello: Ave Maria (Martinotti)
Selections sung by Raimondi:
  Faust: Le veau d'or (Gatto)
    Vous qui faites l'endormie (Gatto)
Selections sung by Ricciarelli:
  Un Ballo in Maschera: Morrò, ma prima in grazia
    (Martinotti)
  Turandot: Signore ascolta (Martinotti)
Raina Kabaivanska, Katia Ricciarelli; Piero Cappuccilli,
  Ruggero Raimondi
Verona Arena Theater Orchestra, Armando Gatto; Bruno
  Martinotti
Decca SDD 571; Cime ANC 25004

Great Artists at the Met
Un Ballo in Maschera: Ma se m'è forza perderti (complete Bartoletti)
La Bohème: Che gelida manina (Magiera)
L'Elisir d'Amore: Una furtiva lagrima (complete Bonynge)
La Favorita: Favorita del re; Spirto gentil (Downes)
La Fille du Régiment: Ah! mes amis, quel jour de fête; Que dire, que faire; Pour mon âme quel destin (complete Bonynge, with Garrett)
   Écoutez-moi, de grâce! Pour me rapprocher de Marie (complete Bonynge)
Lucia di Lammermoor: Fra poco a me ricovero; Tu che a Dio spiegasti l'ali (complete Bonynge, with Ghiaurov)
I Puritani: A te, o cara (complete Bonynge, with Sutherland, Ghiaurov, Luccardi)
Rigoletto: La donna è mobile (complete Bonynge)
Il Trovatore: Ah sì, ben mio; Di quella pira (Rescigno, with Flossmann)
MET 106

The Great Pavarotti/The Art of Pavarotti
Un Ballo in Maschera: La rivedrà nell'estasi (complete Bartoletti, with Donath, Monreale, Christou)
   Di' tu se fedele (complete Bartoletti, with Donath, Monreale, Christou)
L'Elisir d'Amore: Quanto è bella (complete Bonynge)
   Una furtiva lagrima (complete Bonynge)
La Fille du Régiment: Écoutez-moi, de grâce! Pour me rapprocher de Marie (complete Bonynge)
Lucia di Lammermoor: Tu che a Dio spiegasti l'ali (complete Bonynge, with Ghiaurov)
Macbeth: O figli, o figli miei; Ah, la paterna mano (complete Gardelli)
Maria Stuarda: Ah, rimiro il bel sembiante (complete Bonynge, with Soyer)
Messa da Requiem: Ingemisco (complete Solti)
Rigoletto: Questa o quella (complete Bonynge)
   Ella mi fu rapita; Parmi veder le lagrime (complete Bonynge)
Stabat Mater: Cujus animam (complete Kertész)
Turandot: Non piangere, Liù (complete Mehta, with Caballé, Ghiaurov)
London OS 26510; Decca SXL 6839

Great Performers: Luciano Pavarotti
Aïda: Se quel guerrier io fossi; Celeste Aïda (Magiera)
L'Amico Fritz: Suzel, buon dì; Han della porpora vivo il colore; Tutto tace (complete Gavazzeni, with Freni)
L'Arlesiana: È la solita storia del pastore (Rescigno)
La Bohème: Che gelida manina (complete Karajan)
   O soave fanciulla (complete Karajan, with Freni, Panerai)
Cavalleria Rusticana: Mamma! Mamma, quel vino è generoso (complete Gavazzeni, with Varady, Bormida)
La danza (Bonynge)
L'Elisir d'Amore: Quanto è bella (complete Bonynge)
   Una furtiva lagrima (complete Bonynge)
Funiculì, funiculà (Guadagno)
La Gioconda: Cielo e mar (Magiera)
Guglielmo Tell: Non mi lasciare; O muto asil del pianto; Corriam! Voliam (Rescigno)

Lucia di Lammermoor: Sulla tomba che rinserra; Qui di sposa eterna fede; Ah! verranno a te sull'aure (complete Bonynge, with Sutherland)
   Tombe degli avi miei; Fra poco a me ricovero (complete Bonynge)
Luna d'estate (Bonynge)
Madama Butterfly: Dovunque al mondo; Amore o grillo, dir non saprei (complete Karajan, with Kerns, Sénéchal)
Marechiare (Chiaramello)
'O sole mio (Chiaramello)
'O surdato 'nnammurato (Guadagno)
Pagliacci: Recitar! mentre preso dal delirio; Vesti la giubba (Magiera)
I Puritani: A te, o cara (Rescigno, with Auger, Bunge., Lackner)
   Vieni, vieni fra queste braccia (complete Bonynge, with Sutherland)
Rigoletto: Questa o quella (complete Bonynge)
   Parmi veder le lagrime (complete Bonynge)
   La donna è mobile (complete Bonynge)
La serenata (Bonynge)
Stabat Mater: Cujus animam (complete Kertész)
Torna a Surriento (Chiaramello)
Tosca: Recondita armonia (complete Rescigno, with Tajo)
   E lucevan le stelle (complete Rescigno)
Il Trovatore: Di qual tetra luce; Ah sì, ben mio; L'onda de' suoni mistici; Di quella pira (complete Bonynge, with Sutherland, Clark)
Turandot: Nessun dorma (complete Mehta)
Time-Life STL-PO3

Great Tenors of Today
L'Amico Fritz: Ed anche Beppe amò; O amore, o bella luce del core (complete Gavazzeni)
Selections sung by other tenors:
   Bergonzi/*La Forza del Destino:* Oh, tu che in seno agli angeli
     Tosca: Dammi i colori; Recondita armonia (with Taddeo)
   Corelli/*Aïda:* Se quel guerrier io fossi; Celeste Aïda
     Andrea Chénier: Come un bel dì di maggio
   Domingo/*Manon Lescaut:* Donna non vidi mai
   Gedda/*Carmen:* La fleur que tu m'avais jetée
     Faust: Salut! demeure chaste e pure
   King/*Die Meistersinger:* Am stillen Herd
   McCracken/*Otello:* Niun mi tema (with De Palma, Giacomotti, Monreale)
   Vickers/*Samson et Dalila:* Arrêtez, ô mes frères
Carlo Bergonzi, Franco Corelli, Piero De Palma, Placido Domingo, Nicolai Gedda, James King, James McCracken, Jon Vickers, Alfredo Giacomotti, Leonard Monreale, Giorgio Taddeo
Angel S-36947

Hits from Lincoln Center
Aprile (Gamba)
'A vucchella (Guadagno)
La danza (Bonynge)
L'Elisir d'Amore: Una furtiva lagrima (complete Bonynge)
In questa tomba oscura (Gamba)
Lucia di Lammermoor: Tombe degli avi miei; Fra poco a me ricovero (complete Bonynge)

Luisa Miller: Oh! fede negar potessi; Quando le sere al
placido; L'ara, o l'avello apprestami (complete Maag,
with Giaiotti)
Mattinata (Gamba)
Me voglio fa'na casa (Guadagno)
Orfeo ed Euridice: Che farò senza Euridice (Gamba)
Tosca: E lucevan le stelle (Magiera)
Turandot: Nessun dorma (complete Mehta)
Vaga luna, che inargenti (Gamba)
Vanne, o rosa fortunata (Bonynge)
London OS 26577

Joan Sutherland & Luciano Pavarotti Duets
L'Elisir d'Amore: Chiedi all'aura lusinghiera; Per guarir di
tal pazzia
La Fille du Régiment: Oh ciel! Me v'là, mamzelle;
Depuis l'instant; De cet aveu si tendre
Lucia di Lammermoor: Sulla tomba; Qui di sposa eterna
fede; Ah! verranno a te sull'aure
I Puritani: Finì, me lassa; Nel mirarti un solo istante;
Da quel dì che ti mirai; Vieni, vieni fra queste braccia
Rigoletto: È il sol dell'anima; Addio, addio, speranza ed
anima
Drawn from complete Bonynge recordings
London OS 26437; Decca SXL 6991

King of the High C's
La Bohème: Che gelida manina (complete Karajan)
La Favorita: Favorita del re; Spirto gentil (Downes)
La Fille du Régiment: Ah! mes amis, quel jour de fête;
Que dire, que faire; Pour mon âme quel destin
(complete Bonynge, with Garrett)
Guglielmo Tell: Non mi lasciare; O muto asil del pianto;
Corriam! Voliam (Rescigno)
I Puritani: A te, o cara (Rescigno, with Auger, Bunger,
Lackner)
Der Rosenkavalier: Di rigori armato in seno (complete Solti)
Il Trovatore: Di qual tetra luce; Ah sì, ben mio; L'onda de'
suoni mistici; Di quella pira (Rescigno, with Flossmann,
Baillie)
London OS 26373; Decca SXL 6658

Live from Lincoln Center
Beatrice di Tenda: Angiol di pace (with Sutherland,
Horne)**
La Bohème: Che gelida manina*
Ernani: Solingo, errante e misero (with Sutherland,
Horne)*
La Gioconda: Deh! non turbare (with Horne)*
Ecco la barca! Addio (with Sutherland, Horne)*
Norma: Adalgisa! Alma, costanza; Ma di', l'amato giovane
(with Sutherland, Horne)*
Otello: Già nella notte densa (with Sutherland)**
Il Trovatore: Madre? non dormi; Ai nostri monti;
Che! non m'inganno; Prima che d'altri vivere
(with Sutherland, Horne, Gardner)**
Selection sung by Horne:
La Donna del Lago: Mura felice**
Selection sung by Sutherland:
I Masnadieri: Dall'infame banchetto; Tu del mio Carlo*
Joan Sutherland, Marilyn Horne; Jake Gardner
New York City Opera Orchestra, Richard Bonynge
London LDR 72009; *LDR 71101; **LDR 71102;
Decca D255D2

Luciano
Aïda: Se quel guerrier io fossi; Celeste Aïda (Magiera)
Aprile (Gamba)
'A vucchella (Guadagno)
La Bohème: Che gelida manina (complete Karajan)
La Fille du Régiment: Ah! mes amis, quel jour de fête;
Que dire, que faire; Pour mon âme quel destin
(complete Bonynge, with Garrett)
Luna d'estate (Bonynge)
Marechiare (Chiaramello)
Maria Mari' (Guadagno)
Pagliacci: Recitar! mentre preso dal delirio; Vesti la giubba
(complete Patanè)
Panis angelicus (Adler)
Torna a Surriento (Chiaramello)
Tosca: E lucevan le stelle (complete Rescigno)
Il Trovatore: Di quella pira (Rescigno, with Flossmann)
Vanne, o rosa fortunata (Bonynge)
London PAV 2013

Luciano Pavarotti a Modena
Alma del core
'A vucchella
Bella Nice, che d'amore
Danza, danza, fanciulla
Dolente immagine di Fille mia
L'Elisir d'Amore: Una furtiva lagrima
I Lombardi alla Prima Crociata: Mortal di me più lieto;
La mia letizia infondere; Come poteva un angelo
Luisa Miller: Oh! fede negar potessi; Quando le sere al
placido; L'ara, o l'avello apprestami
Malia
Malinconia, ninfa gentile
Ma rendi pur contento
Nebbie
Nevicata
Non t'amo più
Pioggia
La serenata
Tre giorni son che Nina
L'ultima canzone
Vanne, o rosa fortunata
Leone Magiera, piano
Mizar PM 1/2

Luciano Pavarotti Sings Duets
Un Ballo in Maschera: Teco io sto; Non sai tu; Oh, qual
soave brivido (complete Bartoletti, with Tebaldi)
La Bohème: O soave fanciulla (complete Karajan, with
Freni, Panerai)
In un coupé; O Mimì, tu più non torni (complete
Karajan, with Panerai)
La Fille du Régiment: Marie, je vous aime; Depuis l'instant;
De cet aveu si tendre (complete Bonynge, with
Sutherland)
Luisa Miller: Ah, piangi; il tuo dolore (complete Maag,
with Caballé)
Madama Butterfly: Viene la sera; Bimba dagli occhi pieni di
malìa; Dolce notte! Quante stelle (complete Karajan,
with Freni)
Les Pêcheurs de Perles: C'est toi, toi qu'enfin je revois;
Au fond du temple saint (with Ghiaurov)
I Puritani: Dunque m'ami, mio Arturo? Sì; Vieni, vieni fra
queste braccia (complete Bonynge, with Sutherland)
London OS 26554; Decca SXL 6858

Mamma (Popular Italian Songs)
Addio, sogni di gloria
La campana di San Giusto
Chitarra romana
Firenze sogna
La Ghirlandeina
In un palco della Scala
Lolita
Mamma
La mia canzone al vento
Musica proibita
Non ti scordar di me
Parlami d'amore, Mariù
Rondine al nido
Vieni sul mar
Vivere
Voglio vivere così
Andrea Griminelli, flute
Chorus and Orchestra, Henry Mancini
London and Decca 411 959-1

Mattinata/Pavarotti in Concert, Vol. 2
L'alba separa dalla luce l'ombra
Alma del core
Aprile*
Il barcaiolo
Caro mio ben
Chanson de l'adieu*
Danza, danza, fanciulla*
In questa tomba oscura
Mattinata
Orfeo ed Euridice: Che farò senza Euridice
La promessa
Tre giorni son che Nina
L'ultima canzone
Vaga luna
Philharmonia Orchestra, Piero Gamba
*National Philharmonic Orchestra, Antonio Tonini
London OS 26669; Decca SXL 6850; SXL 7013

Metropolitan Opera Centennial Gala
Un Ballo in Maschera: Teco io sto; Non sai tu; Oh, qual
 soave brivido (with L. Price)
Other selections sung by:
 Kathleen Battle, Judith Blegen, Grace Bumbry,
  Montserrat Caballé, Ileana Cotrubas, Loretta
  Di Franco, Mirella Freni, Catherine Malfitano, Eva
  Marton, Leona Mitchell, Edda Moser, Birgit Nilsson,
  Roberta Peters, Katia Ricciarelli, Elisabeth
  Söderström, Joan Sutherland, Kiri Te Kanawa,
  Anna Tomowa-Sintow, Gail Dubinbaum,
  Marilyn Horne, Diane Kesling, Frederica von Stade;
 José Carreras, Giuliano Ciannella, Placido Domingo,
  Nicolai Gedda, Alfredo Kraus, William Lewis,
  James McCracken, Robert Nagy, Dano Raffanti,
  David Rendall, Renato Bruson, John Darrenkamp,
  Brian Schexnayder, Ara Berberian, Sesto Bruscantini,
  Nicolai Ghiaurov, Ruggero Raimondi, Julien Robbins
Leonard Bernstein, Richard Bonynge, Thomas Fulton,
 James Levine, Sir John Pritchard, David Stivender,
 Jeffrey Tate
Pioneer Artists LaserDisc PA-84-095;
 Paramount Home Video 2364

Met Stars at Christmas
Adeste fideles (Adler, with Wandsworth Boys Choir,
 London Voices)
Gesù Bambino (Adler, with Wandsworth Boys Choir)
Minuet Chrétien: O Holy Night/Cantique de Noël (Adler)
Panis angelicus (Adler, with Wandsworth Boys Choir)
Selections sung by Price:
 Ave Maria [Schubert]
 God Rest Ye Merry, Gentlemen
 Silent Night
 We Three Kings of Orient Are
Selections sung by Sutherland:
 Hark the Herald Angels Sing
 Joy to the World
 The Twelve Days of Christmas
 What Child Is This
Selections sung by Tebaldi:
 Ave Maria [Bach-Gounod]
 Mille cherubini in coro
 O Divine Redeemer
 Tu scendi dalle stelle
Leontyne Price; Singverein der Gesellschaft der
 Musikfreunde, Vienna Grosstadtkinderchor,
 Vienna Philharmonic Orchestra, Herbert von Karajan
Joan Sutherland; Ambrosian Singers, New Philharmonia
 Orchestra, Richard Bonynge
Renata Tebaldi; Ambrosian Singers, New Philharmonia
 Orchestra, Anton Guadagno
MET 203

My Own Story
Agnus Dei (Adler)
L'Arlesiana: È la solita storia del pastore (Rescigno)
'A vucchella (Guadagno)
La Bohème: Che gelida manina (complete Karajan)
 O soave fanciulla (complete Karajan, with Freni,
  Panerai)
Il Duca d'Alba: Inosservato penetrava; Angelo casto e bel
 (Downes)
L'Elisir d'Amore: Quanto è bella (complete Bonynge)
La Fille du Régiment: Écoutez-moi, de grâce! Pour me
 rapprocher de Marie (complete Bonynge)
Guglielmo Tell: Non mi lasciare; O muto asil del pianto;
 Corriam! Voliam (complete Chailly)
Luna d'estate (Bonynge)
Malia (Bonynge)
Marechiare (Chiaramello)
Maria Mari' (Guadagno)
Martha: M'apparì (Bonynge)
Mefistofele: Ogni mortal mister gustai; Giunto sul passo
 estremo (Magiera)
Me voglio fa'na casa (Guadagno)
Non t'amo più (Bonynge)
'O sole mio (Chiaramello)
Rigoletto: Ella mi fu rapita; Parmi veder le lagrime
 (complete Bonynge)
 La donna è mobile (complete Bonynge)
La serenata (Bonynge)
La Sonnambula: Perdona, o mia diletta; Prendi: l'anel ti
 dono; Oh, vorrei trovar parola (Bonynge, with
 Sutherland)
Stabat Mater: Cujus animam (complete Kertész)
London PAV 2007; Decca D253D2

220

O Holy Night
Adeste fideles
Agnus Dei
Ave Maria [Bach-Gounod]
Ave Maria [Schubert]
Gesù Bambino (not in Decca collection)
Grande Messe des Mortes: Sanctus
Mille cherubini in coro (not in Decca collection)
Minuit Chrétien: O Holy Night/Cantique de Noël
Panis angelicus
Pietà, Signore
Le Sette Ultime Parole di Nostro Signore Sulla Croce:
    Quinta Parola—Qual giglio candido
Wandsworth Boys Choir; London Voices
National Philharmonic Orchestra, Kurt Herbert Adler
London OS 26473; Decca SXL 6781

Opera's Great Love Duets
L'Amico Fritz: Il padrone tra poco sarà desto; Suzel, buon
    dì; Han della porpora vivo il colore (complete
    Gavazzeni, with Freni)
Selections sung by other artists:
    Arroyo-Cova-Bergonzi/*La Forza del Destino:* M'aiuti,
        signorina; Oh, per sempre; Pronti i destrieri
    Callas-Tagliavini/*Lucia di Lammermoor:* Sulla tomba;
        Qui di sposa eterna fede; Ah! verranno a te sull'aure
    Jones-McCracken/*Otello:* Già nella notte densa
    Nilsson-Corelli/*Aïda:* Fuggiam gli ardori inospiti
    Scotto-Bergonzi/*Madama Butterfly:* Vogliatemi bene;
        Dolce notte! Quante stelle
    Sills-Gedda/*La Traviata:* Un dì felice
Martina Arroyo, Maria Callas, Mila Cova, Mirella Freni,
    Gwyneth Jones, Birgit Nilsson, Renata Scotto,
    Beverly Sills;
Carlo Bergonzi, Franco Corelli, Nicolai Gedda,
    James McCracken, Ferruccio Tagliavini
Angel S-36935, AV 34057

Operatic Arias and Duets
L'Africana: Mi batte il cor; O paradiso (Magiera)
L'Elisir d'Amore: Una parola, Adina; Chiedi all'aura
    lusinghiera; Per guarir di tal pazzia (Magiera, with Freni)
La Gioconda: Cielo e mar (Magiera)
I Lombardi alla Prima Crociata: La mia letizia infondere
    (Patanè)
Macbeth: O figli, o figli miei; Ah, la paterna mano (Patanè)
Otello: Già nella notte densa (Patanè, with Ricciarelli)
Petite Messe Solennelle: Domine Deus (Gandolfi, Magiera,
    Rosetta)
Requiem: Ingemisco (Fackler)
La Traviata: Libiamo ne' lieti calici (Magiera, with Freni)
    Lungi da lei; De' miei bollenti spiriti (Patanè)
    Parigi, o cara (Magiera, with Freni)
Turandot: Nessun dorma (Gatto)
Werther: Pourquoi me réveiller (Magiera)
Decca-Cime 410 166-I

Operatic Concert with Mirella Freni
L'Africana: Mi batte il cor; O paradiso
L'Amico Fritz: Suzel, buon dì; Han della porpora vivo il
    colore; Tutto tace (with Freni)
L'Elisir d'Amore: Una parola, Adina; Chiedi all'aura
    lusinghiera; Per guarir di tal pazzia (with Freni)

La Gioconda: Cielo e mar
La Traviata: Libiamo ne' lieti calici (with Freni)
    Parigi, o cara (with Freni)
Werther: Pourquoi me réveiller
Selections sung by Freni:
    La Figlia del Reggimento: Convien partir
    Mefistofele: L'altra notte in fondo al mare
    I Vespri Siciliana: Mercè, dilette amici
Mirella Freni
Orchestra dell'Ater, Leone Magiera
London JL 41009; Decca SDD 578; Cime SDD 578

Operatic Duets with Joan Sutherland
Aïda: La fatal pietra; O terra addio (with Connell)
Linda di Chamounix: Linda! Linda! Ah, Carlo; Da quel dì
    che t'incontrai
Otello: Già nella notte densa
La Sonnambula: Perdona, o mia diletta; Prendi: l'anel ti
    dono; Oh, vorrei trovar parola
La Traviata: Libiamo ne' lieti calici
    Un dì, felice
    Signora! Che t'accadde; Parigi, o cara (with Fugelle)
Joan Sutherland, Elizabeth Connell, Jacquelyn Fugelle
National Philharmonic Orchestra, Richard Bonynge
London OS 26449; Decca SXL 6828

O Sole Mio (Favorite Neapolitan Songs)
'A vucchella
Fenesta vascia
Funiculì, funiculà
Marechiare*
Maria Mari'
'O marenariello
'O paese d' 'o sole
'O sole mio*
'O surdato 'nnammurato
Pecchè
Piscatore 'e Pusilleco
Torna a Surriento*
Tu, ca nun chiagne
Teatro Comunale Orchestra of Bologna, with chorus,
    Anton Guadagno
* National Philharmonic Orchestra,
    Giancarlo Chiaramello
London OS 26560; Decca SXL 6870

Passione (Favorite Neapolitan Love Songs)
Chiove
Core 'ngrato
Dicitencello vuie
Era de maggio
Fenesta che lucive e mò non luce
I' te vurria vasà
La palummella
Passione
Santa Lucia luntana
Silenzio cantatore
Te voglio bene assaje
Voce 'e notte
Teatro Comunale Orchestra of Bologna,
    Giancarlo Chiaramello
London and Decca 417 117-1

Pavarotti

Un Ballo in Maschera: Forse la soglia attinse;
  Ma se m'è forza perderti
La Bohème: Che gelida manina
L'Elisir d'Amore: Una furtiva lagrima
La Gioconda: Cielo e mar
Messa da Requiem: Ingemisco
'O sole mio
Torna a Surriento
La Traviata: Lungi da lei; De' miei bollenti spiriti
Turandot: Nessun dorma
Werther: Pourquoi me réveiller
Selections played by Griminelli:
  Concertino for Flute and Orchestra in D Major
  The Tale of Tsar Sultan: Flight of the Bumble Bee
Orchestral selections:
  Guglielmo Tell: Overture
  Semiramide: Finale of Overture
Andrea Griminelli, flute
Las Vegas Symphony Orchestra, Emerson Buckley
U.S.A. Home Video

Pavarotti at Juilliard

Griselda: Per la gloria d'adoravi
Selections sung by students:
  Le Nozze di Figaro: Non so più (Mentzer)
  Rigoletto: Questa o quella (di Paolo)
  Tosca: E lucevan le stelle (Chung)
Susan Mentzer; Kwang Chung, Tonio di Paolo
John Wustman, piano
Homevideo Exclusives 501B

Pavarotti in Concert

Atalanta: Care selve
Bella Nice, che d'amore
La danza
Dolente immagine di Fille mia
Griselda: Per la gloria d'adoravi
L'Honestà Neglia Amori: Già il sole dal Gange
Luna d'estate
Malia
Malinconia, ninfa gentile
Ma rendi pur contento
Nebbie
Nevicata
Non t'amo più
Pioggia
La serenata
Vanne, o rosa fortunata
Teatro Comunale Orchestra of Bologna, Richard Bonynge
London OS 26391; Decca SXL 6650

Pavarotti Premieres Verdi/Arie Inedite di Verdi

Attila: Oh dolore
I Due Foscari: Qui ti rimani alquanto; Ah sì, ch'io sento
  ancora; Dal più remoto esilio; Sì lo sento, Iddio mi
  chiama (with Savastano)
Ernani: D'Ernani i fidi chiedono; Odi il voto (with
  Morresi, Giacomotti)
Io la vidi (with Savastano)
Les Vêpres Siciliennes: A toi que j'ai chérie

Orchestral selections:
  Aïda: Overture
  Simon Boccanegra: Prelude
Antonio Savastano, Giuseppe Morresi, Alfredo Giacomotti
La Scala Theater Orchestra, Claudio Abbado
CBS Masterworks M 37228; 74037/40;
  Fonit Cetra LIC 9001

Pavarotti's Greatest Hits

Aïda: Se quel guerrier io fossi; Celeste Aïda (Magiera)
Ave Maria [Schubert] (Adler)
La Bohème: Che gelida manina (complete Karajan)
Carmen: La fleur que m'avais jetée (Magiera)
La danza (Bonynge)
L'Elisir d'Amore: Una furtiva lagrima (complete Bonynge)
Faust: Quel trouble inconnu me pénètre; Salut! demeure
  chaste et pure (Magiera)
La Favorita: Favorita del re; Spirto gentil (complete Bonynge)
La Fille du Régiment: Ah! mes amis, quel jour de fête;
  Que dire, que faire; Pour mon âme quel destin
  (complete Bonynge, with Garrett)
Funiculì, funiculà (Guadagno)
La Gioconda: Cielo e mar (Magiera)
Mattinata (Gamba)
Messa da Requiem: Ingemisco (complete Solti)
Pagliacci: Recitar! mentre preso dal delirio; Vesti la giubba
  (complete Patanè)
Panis angelicus (Adler)
I Puritani: A te, o cara (complete Bonynge, with
  Sutherland, Ghiaurov, Luccardi)
Rigoletto: Questa o quella (complete Bonynge)
  La donna è mobile (complete Bonynge)
Der Rosenkavalier: Di rigori armato in seno (complete Solti)
Torna a Surriento (Chiaramello)
Tosca: Recondita armonia (complete Rescigno, with Tajo)
  E lucevan le stelle (complete Rescigno)
Il Trovatore: Di qual tetra luce; Ah sì, ben mio (complete
  Bonynge, with Sutherland)
  Di quella pira (complete Bonynge, with Sutherland)
Turandot: Nessun dorma (complete Mehta)
Vanne, o rosa fortunata (Bonynge)
London PAV 2003; Decca D236D2

Primo Tenore/Tenor Arias from Italian Opera

L'Arlesiana: È la solita storia del pastore (Rescigno)
La Bohème: Che gelida manina (Magiera)
Don Pasquale: Com'è gentil (Magiera)
La Gioconda: Cielo e mar (Magiera)
Guglielmo Tell: Non mi lasciare; O muto asil del pianto;
  Corriam! Voliam (Rescigno)
Maristella: Io conosco un giardino (Magiera)
Mefistofele: Ogni mortal mister gustai; Giunto sul passo
  estremo (Magiera)
I Puritani: A te, o cara (Rescigno, with Auger, Bunger,
  Lackner)
Il Trovatore: Di qual tetra luce; Ah sì, ben mio; L'onda de'
  suoni mistici; Di quella pira (Rescigno, with Flossmann,
  Baillie)
Arleen Auger, Gildis Flossmann; Peter Baillie, Reid
  Bunger, Herbert Lackner
Vienna Opera Chorus and Orchestra, Nicola Rescigno
New Philharmonia Chorus and Orchestra, Leone Magiera
London OS 26192; Decca SXL 6498

Scuola di Canto
L'Elisir d'Amore: Una furtiva lagrima
I Lombardi alla Prima Crociata: Mortal di me più lieto;
    La mia letizia infondere; Come poteva un angelo
Non t'amo più
Selections sung by Freni:
    Gianni Schicchi: O mio babbino caro
    Turandot: Tu che di gel sei cinta
Master Class on singing conducted by Pavarotti and Freni
    with the participation of these young artists: Lidia La
    Marca, Luana Pellegrineschi, Maria-Angela Rosolen;
    Giuliano Bernardi, Bruno Bulgarelli, Giuliano Cavaterra,
    Emilio Cuoghi, Giuseppe Novi, Raoul Ostorero
Mirella Freni
Leone Magiera, piano
Mizar PF 3

Ten Famous Tenors, Ten Famous Arias
Rigoletto: La donna è mobile (complete Bonynge)
Selections sung by other tenors:
    Bergonzi/*La Bohème:* Che gelida manina
    Björling/*Cavalleria Rusticana:* Mamma! Mamma, quel
        vino è generoso
    Corelli/*Tosca:* E lucevan le stelle
    Del Monaco/*Pagliacci:* Recitar! mentre preso dal delirio;
        Vesti la giubba
    Di Stefano/*Carmen:* La fleur que tu m'avais jetée*
    Di Stefano/*L'Elisir d'Amore:* Una furtiva lagrima†
    Domingo/*Aïda:* Se quel guerrier io fossi; Celeste Aïda*
    Domingo/*Carmen:* La fleur que tu m'avais jetée†
    King: *Lohengrin:* Mein lieber Schwann
    McCracken: *Turandot:* Nessun dorma
    Prevedi: *La Fanciulla del West:* Ch'ella mi creda libero e
        lontano
Carlo Bergonzi, Jussi Björling, Franco Corelli, Mario
    Del Monaco, Giuseppe di Stefano, Placido Domingo,
    James King, James McCracken, Bruno Prevedi
London OS 26207*, 414 356-1†

Verdi Concert with Katia Ricciarelli
I Lombardi alla Prima Crociata: La mia letizia infondere
Macbeth: O figli, o figli miei; Ah, la paterna mano
Otello: Già nella notte densa (with Ricciarelli)
La Traviata: Lungi da lei; De' miei bollenti spiriti
Selections sung by Ricciarelli:
    Aïda: Qui Radames verrà; O patria mia
    Il Corsaro: Egli non riede ancora; Non so le tetre imagini
    Falstaff: Sul fil d'un soffio etesio
    La Forza del Destino: Pace, pace mio dio
Katia Ricciarelli
Teatro Regio Orchestra of Parma, Giuseppe Patanè
London JL 41030; Decca SDD 569; Cime ANC 25001

Verismo Arias
Adriana Lecouvreur: La dolcissima effigie
    L'anima ho stanca
L'Africana: Mi batte il cor; O paradiso
Andrea Chénier: Colpito qui m'avete; Un dì all'azzurro
    spazio*
    Sì, fui soldato*
    Come un bel dì di maggio*
La Fanciulla del West: Ch'ella mi creda libero e lontano

Fedora: Amor ti vieta di non amar
Iris: Apri la tua finestra
Manon Lescaut: Ma se vi talenta; Tra voi, belle
    Donna non vidi mai
    Ah! non v'avvicinate; Guardate, pazzo son
Mefistofele: Dai campi, dai prati
    Ogni mortal mister gustai; Giunto sul passo estremo
Werther: Pourquoi me réveiller
Neil Howlett
National Philharmonic Orchestra, Oliviero de Fabritiis;
    * Riccardo Chailly
London LDR 10020; Decca SXDL 7504

The World's Favorite Tenor Arias
Aïda: Se quel guerrier io fossi; Celeste Aïda (Magiera)
La Bohème: Che gelida manina (complete Karajan)
Carmen: La fleur que tu m'avais jetée (Magiera)
Faust: Quel trouble inconnu me pénètre; Salut! demeure
    chaste et pure (Magiera)
Martha: M'apparì (Bonynge)
Pagliacci: Recitar! mentre preso dal delirio; Vesti la giubba
    (Magiera)
Rigoletto: La donna è mobile (complete Bonynge)
Tosca: E lucevan le stelle (Magiera)
Turandot: Nessun dorma (complete Mehta)
Il Trovatore: Di quella pira (Rescigno, with Flossmann)
London OS 26384; Decca SXL 6649

Yes, Giorgio
Ave Maria [Schubert] (Beck)
L'Elisir d'Amore: Una furtiva lagrima (Buckley)
La Gioconda: Cielo e mar (Buckley)
If We Were in Love (Williams)*
I Left My Heart in San Francisco (Buckley)
Manon Lescaut: Donna non vidi mai (Buckley)
Mattinata (Buckley)
'O sole mio (Buckley)
Rigoletto: La donna è mobile (Buckley)
Santa Lucia (Buckley, with Romano)
Turandot: Muoia! sì, muoia; Mai nessun m'avrà;
    Nessun dorma (Buckley, with Mitchell)
Orchestral selections:
    Aïda: Ballet Music (Buckley)
    Comme facete Mammeta (Buckley)
    Did I Remember (Lewis)
    End Titles: If We Were in Love (Williams)
    If We Were in Love (Williams)*
    Overture (Lewis)
    This Heart Of Mine (Lewis)
Leona Mitchell, David Romano
MGM Studio Chorus and Orchestra, Emerson Buckley;
    Michael J. Lewis; John Williams
William Beck, organ
London PDV 9001; *LON45 20103; Decca YG 1
Complete film: MGM/UA Home Video 800208;
    Pioneer Artist LazerDisc 100208

Your Hundred Best Tunes: No. 1
La Bohème: In un coupé; O Mimì, tu più non torni
    (complete Karajan, with Panerai)
Les Pêcheurs de Perles: C'est toi, toi qu'enfin je revois;
    Au fond du temple saint (with Ghiaurov)
Decca F 13716

Picture Credits

Warring Abbott/DG: 188 (Giulini)

© *The Age.* Sydney 1986: 68–69

Agostino Arletti: 59

Paul Bailey/NBC-TV: 132–33

© Clive Barda 1986: 39 (Domingo), 188 (Muti, Barenboim)

Baroni/DG: 187 (Abbado)

© Beth Bergman 1986: 32B (color *Ernani* Act II with Mitchell, Raimondi), 32G (color *Idomeneo* Act III "Torna la pace"), 38, 109, 111, 178 (Wixell), 180 (Verrett, Blegen), 182 (Tomowa-Sintow)

Courtesy of Richard Bonynge: 23 (Mario)

Boston Museum of Fine Arts/Bequest of John T. Spaulding: 23 (García)

Holly Bower/Courtesy of WNET: 195 (Renée)

Phil Brodatz: 117

© Robert Cahen 1986: 58, 142–43, 144H (color Griminelli), 184–85

Carafoli: 64

Courtesy of Giovanna Cavaliere: 182 (Tebaldi)

© *Chicago Sun Times*/Fredric Stein 1986: 164, 165

© Trudy Lee Cohen 1986: 160–62

Giovanni Consoli: 173 (Tucci)

Courtesy of Emilio Cuoghi: 56–57

© Erika Davidson 1986: 87, 127, 149, 154–55, 187 (Kohn), 192 (Sills) 195 (Tucker, Peters), 215

© The Decca Record Company Limited 1986: 192 (Mancini), 195 (Freni)

Fernand de Guedre: 30 (Schipa)

Lou de Herr: 171 (Zeani)

© Sergio del Grande/*Epoca* 1986: 26–27, 89 (three daughters)

© Vic De Lucia/*The New York Times* 1980: 128 (Biaggi/Carter/Cuomo/Koch)

DG/Waring Abbott: 188 (Giulini)

DG/Baroni: 187 (Abbado)

© Zoë Dominic 1986: 114–15

Dufor Studios: 177 (Sills)

Agenzia Dufoto, Rome: 32A (color Ponnelle *Rigoletto),* 46–47, 60 (bakery), 95 (poster)

Aimé Dupont: 24 (De Reszke)

Ellinger: 181 *(Der Rosenkavalier),* 188 (Solti)

© Enrico Ferorelli/DOT 1986: 60–61 (father at home), 96A (color Pesaro painting), 96B-C (color Pesaro guests lunching), 96F-G (color daughters at pool, swimming, wife in pool)

David H. Fishman/Lyric Opera of Chicago: 178 (Sutherland)

© Gerald Fitzgerald 1986: 146–47

Frassoldati: 171 (Verrini/Pola)

Branco Gaica: 116 (Renée)

© Guy Gravett 1986: 67

© Grossetti/Mondadori Editori 1986: 6–7, 89 (wife)

© Henry Grossman 1986: 41–43, 76–78, 100–1, 128 (New York crowd at parade), 129, 144A (color in snow by poster), 144F-G (color Metropolitan Opera Centennial Gala with Price), 177 (Resnik)

© William Harris/Education Department, Metropolitan Opera Guild 1986: 32C (color *Ernani* Act IV with Mitchell, Raimondi)

© Bill Hayward 1986: 157

© George Kalinsky/Major League Graphics 1986: 144D-E (color with Buckley, audience at Madison Square Garden)

© Korody/Sygma 1986: 192 (Burnett)

© Kranichphoto 1986: 177 (Lorengar)

© Siegfried Lauterwasser 1986: 8

© Lelli & Masotti/Archivio Fotografico, Teatro alla Scala 1986: 72–73 (La Scala auditorium), 98–99, 168–69, 181 (Kabaivanska), 191 (singing)

© Elisa Leonnelli 1985: 144H (color Modena concert panorama)

Miriam Lewin/Opera Company of Philadelphia: 159

Robert M. Lightfoot III: 188 (Levine)

Lillofoto: 171 (Serafin, *Madama Butterfly)*

© Giorgio Lotti 1986: 80A-C (color Modena home exterior, Pavarotti in window, interior car, Pavarotti at piano with Casarini), 80H (color riding horse)

Lufthansa Archive USA: 172 (Miami arrival)

Courtesy of Spiro Malas: 68–69

Jack Maley/Courtesy of Massachusetts Film Bureau: 134 (airview Boston)

Foto Marco: 32H (color Verona *La Gioconda)*

Courtesy of Massachusetts Film Bureau/Jack Maley: 134 (airview Boston)

Louis Mélançon/Metropolitan Opera Archives: 36 (Björling)

Metropolitan Opera Archives: 36 (Björling), 116 (Kirsten)

Michael 187 (Albanese)

Courtesy of Nancy and Sherrill Milnes: 177 (Hamburg *Ballo)*

Herman Mishkin: 25 (Caruso), 28 (Martinelli), 29 (Gigli), 30 (Lauri-Volpi)

Il Museo Teatrale alla Scala: 22 (Donzelli)

NBC-TV/Paul Bailey: 132–33

© Ira Nowinski 1986: 15–17, 20, 92–93, 112–13, 119–21, 135, 137–40, 181 (Kaye/Caballé), 182 (MacNeil), 191 (Magiera, going onstage)

Courtesy of Fernando Pavarotti: 51, 53 (top and bottom), 54 (top)

© Luis Péres 1986: 196 (Horne, banner, Sutherland)

Erio Piccagliani/Archivio Fotografico, Teatro alla Scala: 37, 72–73 *(Manon, La Figlia del Reggimento, La Bohème, L'Elisir d'Amore),* 82–83, 85, 95 (Molinari-Pradelli), 173 (Rinaldi, Aragall), 174 (Freni), 181 (Kleiber/Cotrubas)

© David Powers 1986: 12–13, 18–19

© Publifoto 1986: 71

© Mirella Ricciardi/Gamma-Liason Agency 1986: 80D-E (color family in Modena orchard), 80F (color Modena fields, poplars), 80G (color father playing bocce), 96B (color girls at piano, Di Nunzio at piano Pesaro), 96D-E (color on horseback near Gradara), 96H (color Pesaro beach)

Houston Rogers: 172 *(La Traviata)*

© Francesco Scavullo 1986: 124–25

© Ron Scherl 1986: 32D-E (color San Francisco *Turandot),* 34, 134, 178 (Tozzi, Thomas)

© Beatriz Schiller 1986: 32C (color Act III *Ernani* with Kraft, Milnes, Mitchell)

Courtesy of Alfred Slesinger: 180 (Domingo/Carreras)

© Vernon L. Smith/Scope Associates, Inc. 1986: 39 (Bergonzi)

© Elisabeth Speidel 1986: 177 (Milnes)

© Frederic Stein/*Chicago Sun-Times* 1986: 164, 165

© Eduard Straub 1986: 104 (sitting with Freni, holding bottle), 105

© Susanne Faulkner Stevens/Lincoln Center for the Performing Arts 1986: 60 (father backstage), 152, 200 ("Pavarotti Plus!")

Courtesy of © Susanne Faulkner Stevens 1986: 200 (waving during arena concert)

Courtesy of the Teatro Comunale, Modena: 64 (opera house)

Robert A. Tuggle Collection: 30 (Pertile)

Underwood & Underwood: 30 (Pertile)

© Jack Vartoogian 1986: 32F (color *Idomeneo* Act I entrance and Act I ensemble), 144B-C (color Mehta rehearsing)

Lino Vignoli: 64–65 *(La Bohème* group), 95 (Carpi *Rigoletto)*

Marié Pierre Vincent: 200 (Tonini/ Nemeth)

© Gert von Bassewitz 1986: 103, 104 (kissing Freni), 106, 180 (Taddei)

© Reg Wilson 1986: 75, 172 (Sutherland)

Courtesy of WNET/Holly Bower: 195 (Renée)

Young's Photography: 202–3

© Axel Zeininger 1986: 182 (Battle)